SUB

SUB

AN ORAL HISTORY OF
U.S. NAVY SUBMARINES

MARK ROBERTS

BERKLEY CALIBER, NEW YORK

THE BERKLEY PUBLISHING GROUP
Published by the Penguin Group
Penguin Group (USA) Inc.
375 Hudson Street, New York, New York 10014, USA
Penguin Group (Canada), 90 Eglinton Avenue East, Suite 700, Toronto, Ontario M4P 2Y3, Canada
(a division of Pearson Penguin Canada Inc.)
Penguin Books Ltd., 80 Strand, London WC2R 0RL, England
Penguin Group Ireland, 25 St. Stephen's Green, Dublin 2, Ireland (a division of Penguin Books Ltd.)
Penguin Group (Australia), 250 Camberwell Road, Camberwell, Victoria 3124, Australia
(a division of Pearson Australia Group Pty. Ltd.)
Penguin Books India Pvt. Ltd., 11 Community Centre, Panchsheel Park, New Delhi—110 017, India
Penguin Group (NZ), 67 Apollo Drive, Mairaingi Bay Auckland 1311, New Zealand
(a division of Pearson New Zealand Ltd.)
Penguin Books (South Africa) (Pty.) Ltd., 24 Sturdee Avenue, Rosebank, Johannesburg 2196,
South Africa

Penguin Books Ltd., Registered Offices: 80 Strand, London WC2R 0RL, England

The publisher does not have any control over and does not assume any responsibility for author or
third-party websites or their content.

This book is an original publication of the Berkley Publishing Group.

Copyright © 2007 by Bill Fawcett & Associates
Book design by Tiffany Estreicher

First edition: April 2007

Library of Congress Cataloging-in-Publication Data

Roberts, Mark K.
    Sub : an oral history of U.S. Navy submarines / By Mark K. Roberts.
        p.   cm.
    ISBN-13: 978-0-425-20812-0 (alk. paper)
    1. United States. Navy—Submarine forces—History.   2. United States. Navy—Submarine forces—
Biography.   3. Oral history.   I. Title.
    V858.R63   2007
    359.9'30973—dc22

                                                                                    2006022013

PRINTED IN THE UNITED STATES OF AMERICA

10   9   8   7   6   5   4   3   2   1

CONTENTS

INTRODUCTION

Since the first drawings by Leonardo da Vinci, men have dreamed of an underwater vessel suitable for transportation and use as a weapon of war. The first truly effective "submersible" saw service in the American Civil War and managed to sink several surface ships. Yet it remained far distant from the ultimate, which we will examine later in the SSN-class boats. By 1940, the submarine was a far more sophisticated craft than in any of da Vinci's wildest dreams.

On the eve of WWII, the United States Navy Submarine Service still used boats from the WWI era for training and as some fleet boats. There were some more modern boats available, built in the 1930s, but they also followed the design plans of the boats built between 1918 and 1920. Cramped and crowded, they smelled horribly after even a short cruise. The torpedoes they fired were hit-and-miss at best, totally ineffective at worst.

Within these pages you will read the remarkable stories of some of the men who served with such valor through World War II, Korea,

An artist's rendition of the USS *Grayback* releasing UDT-carrying SDVs while still underwater. *Courtesy of United States Navy*

the Cold War, Gulf One, and Operation Iraqi Freedom. Life on a submarine is not all adventure and excitement. Frequently it is dull, monotonous routine. There is constant training to keep the edge; there's always equipment and machinery to repair, spaces to be cleaned, and the daily tasks of living to be attended to. However, a huge difference exists between life on shore or on a large vessel like an aircraft carrier, and life in a submarine.

For example, taking a shower—something most people take for granted—is a major undertaking in a sub. In the early boats, they might be taken once or twice during a patrol. It was impossible to wash clothing, and men continued to sweat and produce odors, hence the derogatory name for the sub, "Pig Boat." When the nuclear subs came along, the quantity of fresh water produced daily greatly increased. The advent of washing machines also helped to make

A sailor eating a sandwich beneath the propellers of a torpedo being loaded aboard a U.S. submarine at New London, Connecticut, August 1943.
Courtesy of United States Navy

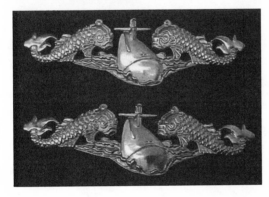

Gold dolphins are worn by officers, silver by enlisted ranks.
Courtesy of United States Navy

the atmosphere more pleasant, as did improved air filtration equipment.

Through it all, though, the men and the boats they served in remained tough and resolute. Meet them now.

1

JOSEPH MCGRIEVY
COMMANDER, USN (RET.)

Joe McGrievy went from seaman recruit in 1943 to retirement as full commander in 1989.

His training consisted mostly of On the Job Training (OJT) aboard diesel subs and classroom work in the crew's quarters. Like his friend Stan Nicholls, by the time Joe McGrievy arrived on station at Midway, very few Japanese cargo and tanker vessels remained to pick on; combat vessels were even harder to find. More adventure awaited McGrievy after the war, when he served in nuclear subs off the coast of Vietnam during that country's conflict.

One day, when I was a kid, I looked out on the sidewalk in St. Louis and saw a big man coming up the way with a sea bag on his shoulder and a very large, flat hat. That was my cousin Harry. He had just completed a tour of duty on the Asiatic Fleet. He gave me his dress blue jumper. I put that on and my grandmother couldn't get it off me. Even to take a bath, she couldn't get it off me. That made a big impression on a kid, because I always wanted to be in the navy. Always.

When I hit eighteen . . . I was eighteen on June 14, 1936. I joined the navy on August 17, 1936. I went to Great Lakes, Illinois, for my boot training. When I completed my boot training, my first ship was the USS *Holland,* a submarine tender, AS-3. I got on board the *Holland* as a seaman second class; I made first class on my second try. There were only 480,000 people in the navy at the time. Whenever I worked overside in my undress blues, I could see these submarines tied up alongside. The crew was sitting up topside in dungarees, having their ten o'clock soup and coffee.

I told myself, "I think I'd like that."

As time went by, I became involved with signal instruction. I worked with the signalmen and quartermasters who worked as signalmen. We worked with the signal lamps—flashing lights—and with semaphore flags. This close association gave me the chance to stand watch on both the tender and the subs, which offered me an opportunity to learn more about the submarine service.

One day, one of the sub guys came up to me and said, "Hey, Joe, how'd you like to come down for lunch?"

I told him yes and went on board the sub, the USS *Pickerel.* We went down below and he took me in and introduced me to the executive officer.

Then he says, "Mr. Executive Officer, here's the guy you've been looking for. He's a seaman first class and a signalman striker." The exec agreed, so I put in my papers for a transfer and joined that sub crew.

We took the *Pickerel* up to Alaska in 1937 and began sounding the bottom. We didn't know why we were doing it, then. It was presented

USS *Pickerel* (SS 177) at sea.
Courtesy of United States Navy

USS *Searaven* (SS 196).
Courtesy of United States Navy

as something that needed to be done for safe underwater navigation in the future; those soundings off Alaska and the Aleutian Islands were part of it. I was permanently attached to the *Pickerel* and served in her on the Asiatic Station until my enlistment ran out. Earlier, when we got the word about new construction, I went to the captain and told him I would extend my enlistment for new construction. I received my term in construction and went back to Portsmouth [NS Portsmouth, Maine] to put the USS *Searaven* (SS 196) in commission.

By then, I had been married for a while. Our daughter was born on August 1, 1941, and on August 27 we left port. We arrived in San Diego, where we were *supposedly* stationed. We stayed a week and shipped out for Pearl Harbor. We stayed there for two weeks, and then we were on our way out to the Asiatic Station. Ironically enough, I tied up right alongside the ship I'd just left: the *Pickerel*. The guys aboard the *Pickerel* got a big laugh out of that. Our sub flotilla tied up in the Philippines. In fact, I was in Manila Bay the day the war started.

At that time, I was a second class signalman. I qualified in submarines and then along came the war.

We left Manila on December 11 and we went out on our first patrol run. We weren't sure what the hell would happen. We had never even fought a war. We hadn't even conditioned ourselves to fight a war. Our skipper would not even let the chow barge come alongside because he was worried that someone might carry a hand grenade or something on board, so we had just what chow we had. We had our torpedoes to put aboard, because we'd just off-loaded [for maintenance] and we were scheduled to relieve the *Sealion* and the *Seadragon* at the navy yard at Cavite with the *Searaven* and the *Seawolf*. So, anyway, we reloaded our torpedoes and took on some chow from the *Kanopus* and got underway.

Our first run lasted forty-eight days and it was a pitiful thing. We ran out of coffee; we ran out of cigarettes. It was terrible because our skipper did not know anything about fighting a war. I thought the war would be over in about three weeks, that we would whip the Japs, but it didn't happen that way. As it was, I ended up making four runs on the *Searaven*. Our skipper was relieved after the second run, and Hiram Cassidy took over. Cassidy was, at the time, executive officer on the *Sailfish*, which was the old *Whalen*. Frank Walker was our exec at the time we made our third patrol run. And that's when we got some shooting done.

We left Fremantle, Australia, and entered our patrol area off the Philippines. When we were under water most of the day, the crew knew little about what went on. It was one of those things that the ship's company didn't know very much about. It was strictly the captain and the exec, although I was in the conning tower on the helm as my battle station. We acquired a target, and judging from the headings I was being given, I was convinced we were lining up a shot. Suddenly,

USS *Sailfish* (SS 192) on patrol in 1943.

Courtesy of United States Navy

I heard, "Fire torpedoes! Fire torpedoes!" We got one hit on the ship and that was it. Right away, we went deep because, once again, we didn't know how to fight a war.

We went back into Fremantle and were told that on our next patrol we would be going to Corregidor. "You're going to take fifty tons of three-inch ammunition up there, which they need to fight airplanes," our exec told us.

So we loaded fifty tons of boxed three-inch fifty-caliber high-explosive shells in the fore and aft torpedo rooms, and off we went. There were no ladders leading up to the wardroom; only the engine room and the after battery had ladders to the topside. We got about one-fourth of the way from Corregidor and we got word that the defenses had surrendered.

At that point, we were told to go out to our usual patrol area. When we reached it and began patrol runs, we were contacted again and told to stop what we were doing and go to the island of Timor to rescue some Australian flyers whose plane had been downed.

Let me give a little background on this patrol assignment:

Somewhere on the island of Timor, a transport had landed and discharged a group of Australian Air Force personnel. These men had been sent to beef up the base maintenance group, which had arrived at Timor earlier in September 1941. They quickly settled into their barracks and enjoyed good solid meals served by Timorese waiters. They were experiencing another culture, drinking in both the island's beauty and beer.

9

About this same time, the submarine *Searaven* (SS 196), with an American crew of about sixty-five men and officers, was operating in and around the seas surrounding the Philippine Islands. Fully aware of the possibility of war, all units of the Asiatic Fleet were on full wartime footing. From the vantage of hindsight, we can look and wonder at the part fate played in the lives of these two groups.

As mentioned above, on December 7, Pearl Harbor Day—actually December 8 in the Western Pacific—*Searaven* was preparing to enter the Cavite Naval Shipyard for a short upkeep and overhaul period. Suddenly, with little or no warning, bombs rained down on the capital city of Manila and the American ships in Manila Bay, and the war was on.

Over the next year, the superior Japanese forces moved rapidly, extending their will and power throughout the entire Southwestern Pacific region, from the Philippines to the Great Barrier Reef just north of Australia. The Philippines, Borneo, Celebes, New Guinea, Java, and Timor were the constant targets of the Japanese Navy men-o'-war and the swift and deadly Zeros of the carrier forces. An invasion of paratroopers and, finally, a landing of army troops during continual bombing and strafing followed. This was the fate that befell Timor as it became a Japanese stronghold.

Before retreating from the oncoming Japanese forces, the Aussie Air Force personnel destroyed the communications towers, the landing strip, ammunition, and fuel oil storage, and left the area in a state of ruin. They then took off into the jungle, seeking a means of escape. We learned that before the Aussie Air Force members destroyed their base, headquarters in Australia had informed the group that rescue from their end was not possible. They promised a corvette and later promised flying boats. All attempts ended days later, when Japanese bombings destroyed Broome and Darwin. By the time fate intervened and we entered the picture, the air guys were on their own in a wild jungle, pursued by the Japanese Army.

Arriving off the shores of Timor, *Searaven* reconnoitered the beach and surrounding jungles by periscope during the day, hoping to find evidence of the survivors or a visual signal from them. Surfacing later in darkness, we approached the vicinity of the rescue position as close to the beach as possible. A fire was seen on the beach, leading the submariners to believe this was the location of the rescue. The exec called for volunteers to go ashore and verify.

Ensign George Cook was assigned as the boat officer and put in charge of the operation. "All right," he asked, "who wants to go ashore?"

"Okay, I'll go," I piped up.

My friend Swede Markeson, quartermaster first class (submarine service) agreed to go with us. In preparation for our trip to Timor, a small, sixteen-foot wherry, carried in the submarine's superstructure, was hoisted over the side to carry us ashore. We were loaded for bear. We had machine guns and hand grenades, food, water, brandy—a little bit of everything.

"Good luck, men." The captain's wishes ghosted to us over the increasing distance between us and the submarine.

With fate already playing a hand, bad luck struck immediately. Although the diesel engine had a pressure cover on it to protect it from water, it had gone for months and months without being used. So the engine failed to start, and no amount of elbow grease, cussing, or repair work could get it to cough to life.

The crew hastily manufactured paddles out of the tops of the ammunition boxes. With three very unwieldy oars in hand, we volunteers headed for the beach. The currents remained swift, the sea rough, and the useless engine remained an obstacle to rowing. Worse yet, sharks as big as torpedoes were observed knifing through the water. The Japanese loomed all around, and no further signals came from the beach. Our first attempt at rescue was a dismal failure.

Cook swam to the beach, heading for a fire we had observed from seaward. Landing on shore, he shouted out, "Hello! I am George Cook, an ensign in the United States Navy. Come out, show yourselves."

His voice came faintly to us two volunteers in the boat. He continued to call out and stride toward the fire area. When he arrived in full sight of the blaze, he saw a group of shadows hustling into the jungle darkness. Unsure, for they could have been the enemy, Cook returned to the small boat and we beat a hasty retreat to the safety of the *Searaven*.

LT Cook reported what had happened to the captain, who thought a second, then said, "Oh, hell, let's get out of here. We'll report to headquarters, then wait for further orders."

With dawn approaching, *Searaven* headed to the open sea, charged batteries, and headed toward Australia. Before submerging, we sent a report to headquarters, covering the events of the night.

They replied, "Stay there. Go back. They'll be there Friday night at nine o'clock." In addition, they gave us the identification signal: *SR-SR*.

Submerged, we went through our routine duties through the rest of the day. Tension became something we could almost touch. Surfacing that night, we were informed that the rescue was still in order.

When *Searaven* reached the rescue area, the small boat was hoisted overside once again. This time without the engine—it had been removed and jettisoned the night before. We three volunteers were outfitted with some first-class paddles the engineers had made. We were soon on our way to the shoreline. Once we reached a spot near the line of breakers, about five hundred yards off the beach, we tossed a makeshift anchor—made from a Fairbanks-Morse diesel cylinder—over the side. The three of us went into the water and headed for the beach. We trailed long lines behind us. These lines were the only connections with the small boat. I thought I was the smart one; I took along a mattress cover to drift along with the tide, going faster as I swam. Then, when I looked over the top of the bag, the island was quite a bit off my starboard hand. So I wound up with a lot of swimming to do.

When we reached the beach, we reacted in horror to the sight of thirty-four or thirty-five Australians in various stages of near-death. Most of them suffered from malaria and malnutrition; many had tropical ulcers under the armpits or between their legs, and three of them were stretcher cases. Those heaving lines, which we brought in with us, were our only communication with the beach.

After a close examination and a brief discussion, a guy named Rolf, who was the warrant officer in charge of the Aussies, said, "Who can swim and who can't swim, and who's healthy and who's not healthy? We're going to take the healthy ones. They can fight again. You other guys, we'll come back and get you later." The wounded and sickly would wait until the second trip. It was a harsh decision for him to have to make, but necessary to their point of view.

We three Americans led the selected group out through the surf. With all the trouble we had with the boat, Cook returned to the wherry in order to be available to hoist the weakened men into the boat. Markeson and I swam alongside the men who were not going hand-over-hand along the line. All sixteen men in the first group made it to the boat, but not without one close shave and two near-casualties.

Two of the men, weakened further by the exertion of hauling themselves along the line, swallowed a lot of salt water. They let go to see if they could get to the boat on their own and found themselves being swept farther away from the small craft. Cook, standing on the stern of the boat, directed Swede Markeson and me to get the Aussies back to the line and on toward the sub. Leonard and I got to the Aussies and wrestled them back toward the boat. Even in their weakened condition, they fought their rescuers. It took almost superhuman strength to get them back to that line and to the sub.

Time was now our major enemy. When the small boat reached the submarine, dawn was not too far away. The passengers were hurriedly lowered belowdecks, given first aid, bowls of hot tomato soup, sandwiches, cigarettes, and clean skivvies. The small boat was hoisted in, as the skipper decided the risk was too great to try another rescue trip at this time. The remainder of the party that stayed on the beach was notified that the submarine would return the next night to pick them up. Knowing that the Japanese Army was but one half-day's march away from their position, these brave men sent a brief but cheery message, "Okay, Yank, good on ya."

Searaven returned to deep water, charging batteries en route. The Australians were hurriedly indoctrinated into life aboard a submarine. Our COB handed out information slips to instruct them as to what to do in case of an emergency, where and when smoking would be permitted, and the all-important "how to blow the head" (how to flush the toilet, quite an operation aboard a submarine). A peaceful day was spent submerged off the island. The Aussies were greatly concerned about the safety of their mates left on the beach. They knew the Japanese were not too far away, for they had received a note from the Japanese stating the group would be treated with kindness if they surrendered. Our submarine crew tried to assure them that the small boat would beat the Japanese to the punch. Plans were formulated as to how we would get the stretcher cases off the island. This time our CO insisted that different volunteers from the previous night take the boat into the beach. We quickly talked him out of that with a counterproposal.

Being that we had been there once and knew how things went, the decision was made to take one additional man, who would remain with the boat and assist in helping the injured into the boat. The three swimmers would secure the wrists of the badly injured with bandage material, loop the bound arms around the neck of a swimmer, and then swim them through the surf to the small wherry. All agreed this was the best solution to the problem.

After dark, *Searaven* surfaced and again headed for a position as close to the breakers as would be considered prudent. When the submarine reached an acceptable position, the small boat was hoisted over the side for a third trip to the beach. Johnny Lintz, a hefty, strong, young chief machinist mate, was the fourth man in the boat. He remained with the small craft while we three swimmers—Swede Markeson, Cook, and I—headed to the beach to effect a rescue of the stretcher cases.

When we reached the beach, we were greeted with a cheer and a "Thanks, Yanks, for coming back for us."

We accepted their gratitude curtly; there was a lot to do.

The Japanese had chased these men around the island for about three months. They didn't have a lot to eat; their bones showed, and all of those left were very weak. I took the first man on my back and entered the water. It took me great effort to instruct a semiconscious man on how he would have to act as we came to the breakers. I tried my best to get through to him as we headed out. When we reached a depth of water where the patient became less of a load, I took hold of the line and began to hand-over-hand the long trip through the surf to the anchored vessel. Forcing our way through the surf was a major undertaking, since we had to make sure the injured passenger did not swallow too much seawater.

When I reached the small boat, Lintz made short work of getting the injured man into the bottom of the wherry. In a few minutes, Markeson arrived with his first passenger, followed close behind Cook, who deposited his man into the boat. We got two boatloads to *Searaven* and went back for another. We quickly loaded them and started out. At this moment, while we sucked in deep draughts of breath, the seas decided to change a very smooth rescue into a tragedy: The wind began to blow and the seas began to mount. Our small boat began to drag anchor and finally turned broadside to the waves.

In a flash, the boat was swept toward the beach. It smashed through the breakers and deposited itself—we four Americans and three injured Aussies—onto the sand of the beach. Fighting time, we got the injured and sick men into the bottom of the boat, and shoved the wherry back toward the breakers. All hands took hold of the boat wherever they could grab. Forcing our way forward in the rising waves became daunting. We struggled and struggled—and lost. Overpowered by the pounding waves, we shot through the surf until we crashed on the beach. No sooner than we regained our breath, we started out again. This time we gained maybe ten yards over our first attempt, only to be defeated again by the Pacific waters.

Our third try resulted in another disastrous failure. Three tries and we blew them! Finally, we gathered our last bit of strength and asked the Almighty for a helping hand and made another try. We put the sickest ones in the bottom of the boat, those a little better we put on the oars, the ones in best shape we put in the water with us. Then we set out. Suddenly, the water that churned around us seemed to change for the better. The Good Lord reached out a hand and picked up the stern and shoved that little boat and its battling crew into calmer waters. From there, the rowers were able to make forward progress. After getting all hands into the boat with considerable struggle, we made our way back to *Searaven*.

Our task of transferring the seven rescued men onto the submarine and getting them belowdecks almost ended in another tragedy. The first man brought aboard was a semicomatose Aussie who drifted in and out of consciousness. Some of our crew shoved him aft on the deck in order to facilitate getting the others aboard. Finally, the small boat was empty and hoisted in, and topside was secured. *Searaven* prepared to head to sea and dive, for dawn was not too far away. When the order was passed down, "Secure the hatches," a sailor came topside to close the afterbattery hatch.

Suddenly, he thought he heard someone moaning and trying to call. He said it sounded like, "Hey, mite, wot abute mei?" Our seaman froze for a second then looked around and spotted the stretcher on the afterdeck area. He shakily alerted the captain on the bridge. *Searaven* was slowed and a bunch of willing hands came topside to lower the injured man, Phil Kean, to the safety of belowdecks. Worse luck was to follow.

En route to Australia, a major fire broke out in the maneuvering room. A small loosened bolt had fallen into the main electrical cubical and [fire] rapidly spread. There is nothing more dangerous than a fire aboard a submarine—whether it's surfaced or submerged. The fire running through the boat flowed so fast the cries came in rapid succession: "Fire in the forward engine room! Fire in the aft engine room! Fire in the control room! Fire in the after torpedo room!" That's the way it went.

I went to the aft torpedo room, because that was where I was stationed at the time. There was a lot of heat and dense smoke, with people all around, coughing and confused. I couldn't find the ladder to the hatch trunk in the center overhead to close the hatch—there's no ladder below the inner combing of the trunk of the hatch. I forgot that there was no ladder. There was this guy, by the name of Neal Nemick. He was chief torpedoman in the after room. He had just finished making sure the door was dogged down and was coming back when he saw me. He reached out and grabbed me and threw me up into the hatch trunk, where I grabbed the ladder, pulled myself up, and closed the hatch. That quickly got rid of the smoke. I went down into the emergency fresh water tank and filled up some rags with fresh water so the guys could breathe a little better. We fought the fire for an hour. Finally, we took all the unused extinguishers left aboard the ship and threw them into the engine rooms. With the hatches closed and the ventilation system secured, the fire snuffed itself out.

After morning came, we surfaced and radioed headquarters for help and the crew turned to. We took stock and found that we had a couple of Lewis machine guns, a couple of fifty-caliber Browning automatics and a three-inch gun. We had no propulsion. The electricians and the machinists had worked all night trying to get something hooked up. They finally got cables hooked up and working. After hours of hard effort, we were able to jury-rig the auxiliary engine to the main electrical system and produce enough power to proceed at about two knots. We kept going, more influenced by the tidal flow than the power of our engine. All at once, our lookout spotted an approaching aircraft. For all we knew, the only planes nearby were Japanese, but no matter, there was nothing we could do about it. We were supposed to get coverage from Australia. So we watched as an old PBY (seaplane) came in close and circled around and says [sic] on the radio, "I'm your coverage." About fifteen minutes later he radioed to let us know he was low on fuel and had to go back to base. The

HMAS *Marlborough*, an Australian corvette, came out and an Aussie submarine, the *Saurie*, came alongside us, hooked onto our anchor cable, and started towing us. Then we got airplanes on the NXP radar, so the *Saurie* cut loose and submerged. We were left alone on the surface. All of a sudden—no aircraft. (The NXP radar wasn't every effective; a good-sized pigeon could set it off.) Anyway, the HMS *Saurie* resurfaced and took us under tow again. She towed us back to Australia at roughly ten knots in rough seas. We felt like a carp on the end of a fishing pole. We got back and had one anchor left, which we dropped in the center of the bay, returning the rescuers and the rescued to the port of Fremantle. The injured were taken from the submarine under highly secretive orders. The Allied governments did not want the Japanese to know that American submarines were being utilized as rescue-and-delivery vessels. The Aussies went to the hospital to recover, and we were towed in the next day and tied up right alongside the pier. We stayed in Fremantle for quite a while, taking on supplies and having repairs done and got all new people [aboard], who had come over from the States. At last, *Searaven* went back on patrol to take up the business of sinking enemy shipping. On our departure we received a very heartfelt, warm, sincere "Thank You" from the Australian Navy, but not much else. No liberty in Perth, no medals. That was the end of our fourth run.

After we got under way on the way out of Fremantle, I was starting up the aft ladder and the skipper was coming down, so I stood aside.

The captain stopped and turned to me and said, "McGrievy, I hate to say this, but I'm transferring you."

I said, "What for? I put the boat into commission. I own [had his signature on] three tiers of rebar."

"They need people back home, because the boats are building so fast they need crews over there."

So I went to the *Skipjack,* which was the 184 Boat [SS 184], and that of Jesse Wiggins Cohen. He had been skipper of the Ness boat when he got the *Skipjack.* While he was with us, he wrote this wonderful letter about toilet paper. It was [a communication] for tending ship, 137s they called them. What you did was write down anything you wanted: stock number, paper, toilet. He sent it back to Mare Island and the Mare Island people reply, "Cannot identify." Then the skipper would write up another requisition form with another stock number and send along a square of toilet paper and wrote this letter, in which he told this supply officer how we're using air sacks and dungaree pant legs and all sorts of things trying to take care of our bodily needs. We couldn't figure out why he could not find any toilet paper; it was hanging from everything in the supply department.

"Cap" Clemmins was exec and we did sink two ships on that run. So, when we get back to Pearl, the pier was stacked with toilet paper, just stacked with it. The band was all wearing toilet paper ties; they had toilet paper stuffed in their instruments so that when they'd go *ump-pa-pa* the toilet paper would go flying out. Admiral Lockwood was down to meet us, along with all his staff.

Our skipper said to Hide, our quartermaster, "Go down and get that pipe with all that toilet paper on it. We've been bitchin' about it, let's go get some."

Anyway, we took the *Skipjack* back to the States and I was assigned to the USS *Skate.* I went aboard and was on the *Skate* for about ten days, when I got a set of orders to report to the *Seahorse* (SS 304). I went to the *Seahorse;* our skipper was Don McGregor and our exec was Slade Cutter. I'd known Slade Cutter since I was a young seaman on the *Pickerel* in San Diego.

One day Slade calls me into his office and says, "McGrievy, I'm making you chief of the boat."

USS *Skate* (SSN 578) was the first sub-marine to surface at the North Pole.
Courtesy of United States Navy

And I said, "Mr. Cutter, you've got two chief petty officers who have twelve, fourteen, sixteen years' service. I'm a boot; I've got only eight."

He replied, "You've got something they haven't got. You've got five war patrols."

So I went on as COB. I took the first routine Navy Yard work, getting the boat ready to go to sea. I was working hard; the crew worked hard right along with the yard personnel, because if we didn't get the boat ready, the crew would be transferred. As it happened, we all worked fast and hard enough to get the boat going. One of my jobs was to take the crew up to the lookout training area and take night-vision training, because regulations declared everyone on the entire ship had to be able to function as lookouts. Therefore, I started taking them up there, some twenty-five the first day. The chief ex-plained what would happen.

"Once you are in the chamber, I'll slowly turn the rheostat up and the light in the background will start coming up. As soon as any of you spots anything, holler 'Mark!' and then you identify it." He paused and said, "Here we go."

And I immediately said, "Mark."

"What's that?" the chief asked.

"I see an oiler, a tanker or something like that. Bearing zero-nine-zero."

He said, "Lucky guess. Let's try it again."

So we started out again and boom! I called out a destroyer.

Finally the chief said, "You don't need this drill, you catch 'em before I get 'em out there."

The upshot was I could see better at night than most people can during the day, although I had to wear glasses to read. I never needed glasses for distance. Finally, we went out on our first run with Don McGregor as skipper. We made contact with the enemy and fired six torpedoes at a tanker making fifteen knots away from us. Firing range was seventy-five hundred yards. Torpedoes don't run that far, even at low speeds. Our torpedoes just ran out and exploded and that was it.

As a result, McGregor was going to put Slade Cutter and Phil Budding out of the navy, or at least out of the submarine force, because he didn't think they were "submarine-type people." We pulled into Midway Island after that miserable patrol and Admiral Lockwood was at Midway to welcome us. First thing, he relieved Don McGregor and sent him back to the Bureau and made Slade Cutter skipper. It wasn't long before I heard the rumor that went around the ship that Slade was a madman and no one wanted to go to sea with him.

I went up to the Wardroom and Slade said, "Mac you've got something on your mind?"

So I said, "Yeah, I have, Captain. There's some of our people don't want to go to sea with you. They think you are a madman."

"Fine," he says. "At quarters tomorrow morning, make a list of those who don't want to go and we'll have them transferred."

I got up before quarters and said, "All right, sailors, if you don't want to go to sea with Slade take one step forward. And when you take that step, know that you will be going elsewhere."

One guy stepped forward, and that was all. So we got rid of him in a hurry and we all went to sea with Slade Cutter. Under Slade Cutter we made four patrol runs on the *Seahorse*, and he sank more ships on those four patrol runs than any other boat in all of their runs. He was the second-biggest ship sinker, who sunk the most ships in the least number of runs. Some skippers made larger kills, but it took them up to seven, eight, nine, or more runs to build up their records.

We were running out [from our base] and we contacted this convoy. We started chasing it. It was moving slowly enough that we end-a-rounded it. When we drew closer, we saw that there were four ships and four escorts. I was on the bridge, handling the lookout job, what with my good eyes. Slade fired two torpedoes at the fourth ship in line, then two at the third ship in line, and two more at the second ship in line and then said, "Right full rudder."

As we started to turn, I caught sight of a destroyer coming around the bow of the first ship in line. If we had continued that right full rudder command, we would have been exposed to that tin can.

I shouted, "Check that!" and we went to left full rudder. By then the ships began blowing up and that was the end of our worry. When we settled down, we chased that convoy for quite a while. We went down five hundred feet and took a break for a while.

During this time I was pretty much our permanent lookout. I always kept a pair of glasses [binoculars] next to my bunk, so I could grab them whenever we surfaced to make an attack run or to recharge batteries at night. I'd go up on the bridge and into the lookout station and, if I saw smoke or a ship on the horizon, I'd notify the captain and we'd dive. Slade Cutter proved to me to be the best skipper I ever served under through these patrols.

I was at my station on the bridge. The exec, Steve "Speed" Curry was OOD (Officer of the Deck). He was giving speed and range to the skipper in the conning tower. We could see the Japs on deck going about their business as we made our way through the convoy and its escorts.

Suddenly, the Japs spotted us. I could see them run to their guns and open fire on us.

The skipper yelled up, "Speed, let me know if they get too close to us and we'll dive."

Speed was a hell of a good exec and a real Southern gentleman. He talked with a slow, Southern drawl and they called him Speed because he did not do anything fast, including speaking. I didn't think he would ever get the word to the captain to dive. I was damned close to shouting, "Dive!" myself, because the first shot was so close. [Remark made off record: "This next part, from Slade Cutter, embarrasses the hell outta me."]

"Chief Quartermaster Joseph McGrievy was the ultimate chief of the boat—the top enlisted man aboard any submarine and right behind the exec in value to the skipper's command. McGrievy was Curry's man and brought things to me regularly on a man-to-man basis, yet was respectful. He was truly a naval professional petty officer and a top submariner.

"McGrievy had the best night vision of anyone on the boat. He was like a cat. I made several night attacks during the war, but we could get in closer and didn't have to worry about escorts. I put McGrievy on the periscope. I couldn't see anything, but he could see those black hulls through the 'scope. The way he did it was to move the 'scope from the black blurb until he could see a star, then he would move back to the hulk and say, 'Fire!' Then he would move the 'scope back the other direction until he saw another star and then swing back and say, 'Fire!' He was inside their bow and inside their stern and that's when he estimated where the middle of the target would be. That's when he was an enlisted man and I made him an officer. He was also my OOD at night during battle stations-surface. When we made a night approach—and mind you, he was only a petty officer—I would be in the conning tower where I had the Torpedo Data Computer (TDC), he was feeding data to me such as the bearing and disposition of the target ship. He was invaluable and absolutely fearless."

[Interviewer: "It's great!"]

Yeah, but I was only about twenty-seven years old then. Now I'd think a little before doing anything like that.

I came back and got in *Sailfish* and we went to Guantanamo Bay Naval Station (Gitmo) and we trained DEs (Destroyer Escort Class) for anti-submarine warfare. They were going to the Pacific, so we weren't there very long. We arrived there in early May and left in August. From there we pulled into the Philadelphia Navy Ship Yard and the war ended for us on August 15. I was assigned to the Nineteenth Fleet, which was deactivating and decommissioning submarines and putting them in storage for future use—what they later called the Mothball Fleet. The next thing I know, I get a set of orders for squadron commander for a group of LSTs (Landing Ship Tanks) in Cold Springs, Florida, on the Saint John's River.

When I got on the ship I talked to—ah—Cleveland, a submarine four-striper and he said, "Yeah, and they're sending me to a carrier, so you might as well throw your medals away." Then he said, "You know Slade Cutter, don't you?"

I said, "Yeah, I know Slade."

"Slade's got a boat up at Portsmouth. Why don't you give him a call?"

So I got back to Philadelphia and called Slade. Meantime my wife was in the hospital, awaiting the arrival of our son. I made my call and said, "Slade I need a favor here. They're trying to transfer me to some surface unit. I need a boat."

And he said, "Pack your bag and come on up."

I replied, "Cap'n, you don't do things like that. This is peacetime."

He repeated, "Pack your bag and come on up. I'll have a set of orders for you before you arrive."

So I thanked him and went on to the hospital where my son was born. Two days later, Monday, I took my wife upstairs [in our home] to bed and I was on my way to Portsmouth. Slade left the boat about three months after I got in the yard, but I just stayed and went on with my naval career.

Slade was the guy who changed my life. I'd told him that before, but now I put it in writing. I still keep in touch with him. He went from Portsmouth to instruct at the Academy. I enjoyed my thirty years in the navy. I loved the navy. Nothing stands out more than that rescue of the Australians. I made a lot of good friends on that operation. When they had their first reunion, I went down to Australia and we had a grand old time.

2

STANLEY J. NICHOLLS
LCDR, USN (RET.)

On October 5, 1945, the chief of naval operations released a final tally of warship losses in World War II. It appeared to be a staggering number: 696 ships of all types. However, call to mind that a good number of these were destroyed at anchor or tied up to piers at Pearl Harbor on December 7, 1941. Included in the total are two battleships, five fleet aircraft carriers, six escort carriers, seven heavy cruisers, three light cruisers, a terrible toll of seventy-one destroyers and *fifty-two submarines*.

On November 16, Fleet Admiral King made the demoralizing statement when he testified before Congress, that the rapid demobilization of the navy was causing a major disintegration of capability. In particular, he remarked on *the massive reduction in submarines*. According to King's testimony, "the navy could not fight a major battle." The next day, Fleet Admiral Nimitz addressed the issue of defense unification by stating, "Unification would hinder the navy and reduce the role of sea power in the nation's defense." Nimitz went on to state that, "A separate air force is no more needed than a special agency to control submarines."

Obviously then, naval history after the war took on an entirely different color. Gone was a cause to fight and destroy an enemy. Peace reigned throughout the world . . . at least for a little while. The submarine service did not sit idle. First they had the development of the snorkel and the refitting of fleet boats with this breathing device. It served for fresh air and engine operation, while keeping the sub underwater. Next, advances in guided missiles, intermediate range missiles, and nuclear-propelled submarines. However, many of the old warriors hung on, adapted to the changes and inventions, and went forward to extraordinary careers.

LCDR Stanley J. Nicholls served with honor and valor from March 17, 1941, until his retirement in 1989. Events he underwent on war patrols in WWII add a flavor of adventure and excitement. His account of his training and description of the submarine school at New London, Connecticut, is typical of all those who entered the Silent Service during WWII and after. Let it serve as a guide and an inspiration to this unique experience.

M y good friend—my best buddy—and I were going to join the navy in 1938, but my mother wouldn't sign the papers. Man, did that ever embarrass me. So he went in, but since I still wanted to go in, I stayed at home until I was old enough to join. I entered the navy on St. Paddy's Day, March 17, 1941. I went to Submarine School at New London, Connecticut. It was big—a big base, with an upper and lower facility. It still is big. I don't know how many acres it has, but it's huge.

We studied about the various operations aboard a submarine: how to start the engines, how to operate all the equipment. We didn't actually have to be able to perform them. This was sort of a safety measure so if anyone was unable to do his duties, someone else in the crew could take over. Then when we finally got aboard a submarine,

Like most submariners in WWII, Stan Nicholls looked forward to leave in Hawaii.

Courtesy of Stan Nicholls

we had hands-on practice at doing all the things we'd learned about in classrooms and mock-ups. One other thing we had to do: We had to train on the one-hundred-foot tower. It was filled with water and you had to make an ascent from different depths, starting at twenty feet and increasing in depth as your technique improved. This is for determining if you can make an unassisted ascent from the escape hatch of a sub if it is unable to surface, and to teach submariners how to escape safely. That can be real scary if someone is claustrophobic— but of course, claustrophobics are weeded out before they can enter sub school.

Here's how it works: Some of the cadre stand on small platforms to supervise. The candidate enters through an air lock and begins to ascend from the shallower depths, after deep breathing to store oxygen. Bubbles surround you as you breathe out continuously until your head clears the surface. That's what the safetymen are for, in the event you don't get to the surface before you run out of air. When you go deeper you have a self-contained breathing apparatus to help you get up. The first few times, you have this cold knot in your stomach. But every submariner in the service has done it and been successful.

Basically, submarine school taught the theory of how and what kind of things are expected of submariners: how to stand watch, how to operate as a lookout, operate the bow and stern planes, all of that. The boats we took out were *really* old. They dated from 1919 to the early twenties. Diesel boats, of course, so everything smelled of diesel fuel. I was glad when I finished that training.

My first duty assignment was in late '43. I went out to Midway and joined my first sub. I caught the USS *Pompon* (SS 267) just before it made its sixth patrol. It was a Manitowoc boat. The Manitowoc Naval Boat Works was famous for the submarines built there. I served on it all through World War II. There were about eighty in the crew, including the torpedo men, electricians, radar and sonar operators, bow and stern planesmen, of course, the yeomen, including me, the officers, and the chief of the boat. All together it was a busy, busy thing. After the war, I served first on the USS *Segundo* (SS 398), then the USS *Greenfish* (SS 351), and the USS *Buffalo* (SSN 681).

As an aside, let me mention that firefighting was critical on all the boats. Let me differentiate firefighting from fire control, which was the duty station from which the torpedoes are fired. That is where the Torpedo Data Computer was located. The TDC took the bearing off the bow, the range, and other data. This information was fed into the torpedoes so they would run straight and hit the target.

But let's get back to something burning aboard a boat. If we were submerged, fire could quickly be fatal to all hands. We were each required to wear a breathing apparatus while fighting a fire. We used the Emergency Breathing System (EBS) for any firefighting situation.

USS *Greenfish* (SS 351) in approximately 1950.

Courtesy of United States Navy

USS *Segundo* (SS 398) in WWII configuration.

Courtesy of United States Navy

The other breathing apparatus aboard was the Momson Lung. In the event we had to escape, we would go to the sign [on the locker] where we kept the Momson Lungs and fit them on. We had lines to go over the side in case of an emergency. But I never had to do it. It was so popular and efficient that the Lung became the only equipment we had for submerged actions—that's being underwater inside the sub, I mean. I qualified as a second class diver while we were in Midway one time.

Now, talking about the effects of a fire aboard, every submariner knows that the most dangerous were battery fires. Those could become deadly almost in an instant. The batteries, in both the forward and aft compartments, were chemical, with sulfuric acid and lead plates for reaction. The fumes alone were deadly. If a fire broke out in the batteries, it could shut down the boat's operation. It could even prevent us from making a controlled surfacing. To fight a battery fire,

Stan Nicholls at his duty station. *(Courtesy of Stan Nicholls)*

we had the [airline-fed] mask that fit over the nose and mouth so we could breathe. Because of the chemicals and the electrical generation, we could not use water to put out a fire in a battery compartment; we had some sort of foam to smother the blaze. As a result of how critical the batteries were, we had to enter the compartments and check them out every day. It was dirty work and, since we were limited to only one shower a week, it could be downright nasty.

To get an idea of life aboard a sub, consider this: We had to take along everything we would wear. For example, if we were going to be out eleven weeks, we'd take along eleven pair of dungarees, eleven pair of skivvies, same for socks and undershirts. There was no way to wash anything and the boats quickly took on a strong aroma. Believe me, it wasn't a pleasant odor in the least. Also, the clock regulated everything. We stood four-hour watches, normally from eight to twelve, twelve to four, and so on. The first meal served was for the ongoing watch, the second setting was for the watch coming off, and the third one for stragglers. We stood our watches, normally four on, and eight off.

I had a wheel watch and a radar or sonar, depending on whether we were surfaced or submerged. This is the standard routine for submarines, and nothing changed after the war. The only variations came along with the advent of the modern classes of nuclear subs. One thing you have to understand is how small the space was inside a World War II submarine. The torpedo rooms were good sized and the mess decks were large enough to serve. But the control room and maneuvering stations were crowded. When Battle Stations sounded, we were always bumping elbows, or moving along the companionways back-to-back—not at all as roomy as the 688 Class subs, like the USS *Buffalo* (SSN 681), off which I retired. When you come to the nuke subs, you have more space to move around, though in some of the compartments there is even less room than in some of the newer diesel boats. They're more crowded, but the torpedo rooms are lots bigger. The mess decks are much larger, and of course the engineering plant is very much bigger. Another good thing is that they have room for a washing machine and a dryer. So the stench is not quite as bad as in the old boats. The biggest difference between the nuke boats and the diesel boats is in the way they operate.

A diesel boat is primarily a surface ship that submerges. A nuclear submarine goes out there past Poppa Hotel—the buoy out there at the end of the channel—and dives. I went out there on one boat and we dove right after the first of the year, in January, and the next time we surfaced was off Mombassa, Kenya, in the Indian Ocean. Unlike the diesel boats, which cruise on the surface and only dive when it is necessary, the only time the nukes surface is to come into port or if they are in trouble. One really big difference between the nukes and the diesel boats is that the nukes smell a lot better. The air is much cleaner. On the diesel boats, everything always stank of diesel fuel, but each boat always possessed its own *distinct* aroma. You could tell if you drove over on the beach and came back after a night of drinking, hitting all the bars in San Diego, or Yokuska [Yokasuka, Japan], or the Philippines, and if you happened to go down the ladder on the wrong boat, you could tell you were not on your boat because it smelled different.

Let me add here that the greatest skipper I ever served under was Captain Steve Gimber. He was my first skipper on the *Pompon*. I credit him for getting us out of a really bad situation.

We were in the Yellow Sea. It was early morning and it was routine for us to dive just before dawn. We would remain submerged until dark. The main reason we cruised on the surface was to charge the batteries. We were close to a large Jap convoy and would run in for an attack after we got trimmed out. But when we dove this time, neither the upper or lower conning tower hatch could be closed. So we started taking on water aft and began to flood down.

Of course, at once the diving officer began shouting, "Surface! Surface!"

So we blew out the tanks and we were able to get partway up. The pharmacist's mate was able to close the lower conning tower hatch, which stopped the water from coming down into the control room. However, before we fully surfaced, we had flooded the pump room, and taken in about a foot and a half of water into the control room. As a result we lost all of the hydraulics and radar—we didn't have any surface coverage. The air search radar was the only electronics we had because it was in the control tower, up above the water. What was really bad was that we couldn't make air to breathe, and had to survive on the air we had in the bottles. Each compartment has a way to open and close the ballast tanks, so we had to do hand dives into the compartments to reach those valves. We were crawling around in the dark compartments, wearing Momson Lungs, with watertight battle lanterns, searching for those petcocks. Everybody was hoping they could hold their breath long enough to open the valves and get back out. That's where our hundred-foot-tower training came in handy. We still had some high-pressure air, enough to get us up—at least to clear the conning tower. Then we finally got the low-pressure air back in commission, in order to get us up to where we should be on the surface. All the while, we were slopping around in seawater and the boat was rolling from side to side. With the pump room shut down, we could not ship the water inside overside and resume normal operation. After everything was stabilized and the control room bailed out, we had to remain submerged all day. Then we surfaced and got out of the straits into the Pacific Ocean, and went up by Bonin Island. Since we had no radio, we had to stay clear of everything.

When we got clear of Bonin, we went on to Midway. Then we had to lay off Midway because we hadn't any radio to communicate. This went on until we spotted another submarine. It turned out to be one of our sister ships, the *Pito*. They radioed in and got a destroyer to come out and escort us into port. All in all, it was a hairy experience. To many of us, it seemed more dangerous than closing with the enemy for a torpedo attack. Through it all, though, Captain Gimber remained cool and issued orders in a calm voice.

Our war patrols lasted an average of fifty to sixty days. I made four war patrols on the *Pompon*. On the *Pompon*'s sixth patrol—my first—we made contact with a large freighter. Sound made the first contact. The TDC estimated the target at seven thousand yards, at an angle on the bow of ten degrees. Our executive officer had the duty, so he ordered a change of course that put us at an angle on the bow of twenty-five degrees. We began to close. There was no escort with it, because the Japs didn't have enough combat vessels to escort every ship, only the main convoys. There weren't many cargo vessels left, for that matter. Captain Gimber was called to the control room. He looked through the 'scope at the target and immediately ordered forward torpedo tubes loaded. Our exec ran the problem though the Torpedo Data Computer and got a solution.

We wanted to get in closer, to make sure the torpedoes would hit the target. Early on, there was a lot of trouble with torpedoes that would hit the target but not detonate. Some even ran out beyond the target and came back at the sub that fired them. We had one circular run. We were aware of it and it sure increased our pucker factor. Everyone knew about them after they got into the subs. We had a couple that would not start running.

(Electrical exploding was also a real problem. I'm not a technician in that area but I know we solved it right there in Pearl Harbor. They ran them up on a rigging deal and dropped them. When the trigger failed to detonate on several of the torpedos, they carefully took them apart. I can imagine those guys stayed plenty nervous. They knew that those torpedoes could go off with the slightest mistake. After a methodical search of the innards they finally found out the real problem and soon corrected it. There's a lot of talk today about how good the homing torpedo was. Believe me, they were not all that good. They caused more circular runs than any other type. Everyone got a little tense during a torpedo run and the new guys were really uptight about it. The ideal situation was to approach the target at an angle on the bow of twenty-five to thirty degrees. That's what we did on the first war patrol I went on after joining the *Pompon*.)

When we reached the desired range, based on the TDC solution, Captain Gimber gave the order. "Fire One! Fire Four!" Sonar told us they were running hot, straight, and normal. The seconds ticked off. Only the officers, the torpedomen, and the sonar operator knew the exact running time. The first thing we heard was the distant thump of an explosion. Then a second, dull *whump* sounded.

"I'm getting sounds of a breakup," the sonar operator announced. "I'd say we cracked her keel."

That was our first sinking on that patrol. Captain Gimber ordered tubes two and three fired and the second freighter was badly damaged. By that time, it was hard to find anything to shoot at. We had cleaned them out pretty good by then. For the rest of the patrol we concentrated on smaller ships, which were about all that they had left.

When we spotted the first of these—it wasn't much bigger than a sampan—we surfaced. We went to battle stations-surface and broke out the five-inch gun. You could see the Japs running around on the deck. They tried to fire at us, only they missed. We damaged them pretty badly with three five-inch shells and finished them off with our twenty-millimeter antiaircraft gun. It took little time to locate more of these small ships—call them "tramp steamers"—and we sank them all with surface fire. I was pointer on the five-inch and the action grew hot and heavy for a while. Imagine something as small as a sub bouncing in the troughs of waves and trying to place rounds aboard a ship that is steaming away at flank speed. About every third round struck home and the captain yelled down from the conning tower for us to do a better job. I gritted my teeth and told the gunner to wait until I said to fire; then we started getting better hits. The twenty-millimeters were doing a good job, too, being up higher than us. The Japs were putting tracers across our deck, and small splashes in the

Stan Nicholls manning a range finder.
Courtesy of Stan Nicholls

water told where they struck. Our strikes began to take a big toll while we slowly continued to close on the Japanese ships. Three of them were burning now. At last, we sank them all with surface fire. This action pretty much finished that war patrol.

On our next patrol we encountered a huge enemy convoy. They had plenty of escort vessels: destroyers and fast pursuit craft. That's when we had our problem with the hatches and flooding. We were lucky: they never made contact and even in our crippled condition we managed to draw clear of their locating devices after we submerged. The only drawback was we didn't sink anything on that patrol. After that, we did a couple of Life Guard runs picking up downed aircrews.

We were off of Truk on one of those, with an assignment to locate and pick up pilots who had been shot down. Usually the fliers managed to get out of a crippled aircraft and land safely. They would inflate their raft and paddle away from the site of the crash; that was so the enemy would have a hard time finding them. As I recall, we rescued several pilots on the two patrols.

Our most exciting patrols, of course, were when we sank ships. The others were more or less boring. That changed several times when the Japanese airplanes depth-charged us. Their ash cans and bombs weren't very effective; we were able to dive under their detonation depth and escape any damage. Depth-charging by their surface ships was a lot more effective and certainly worse to endure than what their aircraft attacks could do. They shook me up fairly good more than once, even though each time we were in for refit between patrols, we'd go out and make a trim dive and a destroyer would drop a depth charge some distance away. We never knew how close they were, but we could sure feel it because the water pressure would build up quite a lot. Unless you were close enough to hear the *click-click* of the detonator just before the depth-charge went off, they were far enough away to do no harm, even if the pressure affected your ears and equilibrium.

When we were subjected to a careful depth-charging plan, with zigzagging of two or more destroyers, *then* we had a really hard time. Unlike Hollywood's version, only the sonar operator could hear the decreasing lapses between the *ping* of the sonar signal being sent and the *pong* of the echo he received. When we faced some smart skippers, it was almost always the same. We'd hear the destroyer screws turning faster revs. They would swiftly come closer, until we could hear the swish of their propellers. Before that, though, we could hear the splashes as the ash cans got dropped over the side. Then came what seemed a long wait, while the depth-charges sank to their preset detonation level. Like everyone, I got sweaty palms while the enemy kept dropping more. When they came in closer we could hear the *chunk-chunk* of the catapults on their cruisers as they fired even more ash cans. All of a sudden we'd hear that *click-click* real quick and close, and then sharp explosions. If they were close enough, we'd be knocked around in the sub and some of the cork lining would get broken loose. A couple of times some of the guys got several bruises. If there were ever a time when you wanted to wet your pants, that was it. But everybody contained their nervousness.

I never experienced any incidents when one or more crew members went off the deep end. We later heard about such things happening: guys screaming and hitting things until they broke skin on their knuckles, other guys who blubbered like babies. But that was the rare exception, nowhere close to the norm. Not that we were supermen, just that the psychological exams we had to take weeded out the unstable and the weaklings. Taken all together, the crew stood tall. We prayed a lot, quite often; it seemed to help. Maybe that's why we never received any major damage. We had a few stanchion lines snapped, some dents, and such. We lost some lightweight chain that served the same purpose of the gunwale railing on a surface ship. And, of course, that time we nearly sank ourselves. That resulted in more costly damage than any enemy action. But unless a sub took a couple of direct hits from depth charges, it's only in Hollywood movies that the lightbulbs break and chunks of the hull lining go flying or the air fills with powdered rust. What we received was enough to satisfy anyone's sense of adventure.

Yet, even on patrol there were quiet times when we had nothing pressing to do. So we played a lot of poker and Acey-Deucey. And we had movies. We'd show them in the forward torpedo room. We didn't have too many of Hollywood's version of war. Particularly, we didn't receive any submarine movies. The "girlie" movies were the most popular, like the ones done by Mitzie Gaynor, Jane Russell, Rita

Hayworth, and Betty Grable—they were on our "want" list. I don't remember the men that much. I suppose Tyrone Power, Bogart, Clark Gable, the star from *Gone With the Wind*, guys like that.

Also, when I was not standing watch, I normally had paperwork to do. We yeomen had to keep up certain reports, the log, records, and other documents. We had to type the log from the quartermaster book. As a yeoman, every division officer or chief would come to me with their paperwork to be recorded and/or filed.

Along the line of outstanding duties, our cooks were great. They were mostly black guys and, later, Filipinos and, *man*, could they turn out the chow. They especially shined when they fixed stuff for the fourth setting—for the midwatch, those going on watch at midnight. The cooks would do up sandwiches, real thick ones, with ham and cheese or roast beef, so long as the fresh meat lasted, then we got frozen . . . bologna and such. For as long as it lasted, we had fresh beef, chicken, and hams. The food for all settings was made in the after battery, served and consumed right there. The officers usually ate the same food, but in their case it was taken forward to the wardroom. There was also service in the chief's quarters, served up there by stewards. We had good bakers, too; there were always fresh-baked bread, cinnamon rolls, pies, and cakes. One time we got some mutton from Australia, which was a disaster. The smell in the boat was terrible. Our circulation system was not adequate to handle that stink. We didn't have the air-cleaning crystals that are in the nuclear subs today.

By and large, the food was far better than in the surface fleet. That went for all the boats. At the start of a war patrol, we had shrimp and lobster, beef steaks, roasts, and fresh eggs. When the fresh eggs ran out, we had to do with powdered eggs. From then on, we ate a lot of French toast and pancakes for breakfast, instead of fried or soft-boiled eggs. Only when we had to go on to frozen rations did we get the corned beef, the rubber chickens, pork roasts and chops, and somewhat soggy vegetables. We didn't have an ice cream machine, but we had lots of ice cream when we began the patrol. (On today's nukes they have ice cream machines, even for soft ice cream.) We had to provide our own candy bars, but there were sodas and a few bulk candies, including chewing gum. Our smokes came from sea stores ashore. We didn't get that issue in the field of five ration packs with each meal like the marines and the army did. We didn't have C rations.

Now, the hairiest thing we had to undergo—notwithstanding a depth-charge attack—was surface gunnery attacks. I was assigned as pointer of the five-inch gun. We were cruising on the surface one time and came upon a couple of sampans. We closed and the loader shoved in a five-inch [diameter] shell. Slowly the range closed until I had a clear sight picture of the first one. I told the gunner and he fired. Real quick, the loader slid in another round and we fired again. We could hear them howl through the air.

Both rounds struck the closest sampan. It must have had fuel aboard because bulwarks blew outward and it burst into flame. It's very difficult to sink a sampan unless you completely knock it out. They're made of real light wood, and float easily. It seemed that only three of the Japs aboard the enemy ship remained calm enough to return fire. We could see the muzzle flash from one of those seven-millimeter [Type 92, 7.7mm heavy machine gun] Jap naval machine guns. Next thing, we hear these *pings* and *zings* off the pressure hull close to the water line. They did us no harm and, at the captain's order, we shot up that sampan and moved on to the other target. This one we raked with twenty-millimeter gunfire and finished it off with a five-inch shell.

On the same patrol up past Midway we came upon this small vessel. It was showing no running lights and no interior illumination. Until we learned the identity, we went to battle stations-surface and got the five-inch gun ready. When you come upon a strange ship in the dark, it's a gut-twisting experience. It was no different this time. We ran in alongside and discovered it was a boat out of Hawaii. Unbeknownst to the man aboard, he had strayed into one of the combat areas that our subs patrolled on a regular basis. We began breathing easier right then. We learned that he had run out of fuel and was short on rations. We told the guy that we could refuel, reprovision, and see him on the right course back home. He said it was not his boat, so we helped him aboard the *Pompon* and we sunk that boat to keep it from bring a hazard.

After the war, a lot of things changed. During the fighting, we always went into Australia or Midway or back to Pearl to reprovision and take on more torpedoes and ammunition. In the fifties and early sixties, many times we would tie up alongside a sub tender and resupply. That way we could remain out on patrol a lot longer and cover a great deal more ocean. There was normally a nest of submarines tied up around the tender. For instance, in San Diego after the war, we were tied up off the Second Street Pier, with eight or nine submarines tied in the nest. The funniest thing to see was the crew of the last sub tie up and leave their boat. They had to go across a lot of gangways to get off the ship. These tenders were well fitted out. They had dental and sick bays and, of course, they could reprovision the subs. Mostly we refueled from bunker ships rather than tenders, unless we were in a harbor of an island in a patrol area.

If you asked me about policy, I wouldn't have been able to answer with a lot of accuracy, at least until I'd climbed up the ladder to lieutenant commander. Let me say this, though: I never believed—and darned few other guys thought—that our antiaircraft weapons were adequate to the task. The twenty-millimeters were too slow in tracking and in rate of fire to work against the airplanes the Japanese had—even if they weren't all that fast. They were suited only for engaging sampans and other small craft in a surface gunfire encounter. We always sought to avoid an encounter with Japanese aircraft. Such actions always increased the pucker factor. The truth is, we never really relaxed until we came in from patrol.

It goes without saying, you know, that we always had lots of fun when we came in off patrol. We drank a lot of beer and we always saved as much of the alcohol that we carried aboard as we could. It was not denatured and 180 proof, and we had alcohol in every compartment. It was used to clean equipment, to dry it out and make it quickly operative. We'd always drain that on patrol and then on the way back we'd have gillie parties. Bottom line, we all had fun and I can't cite one individual who stood out as a character or any sort of conscious clown, nor did we have any troublemakers. Liberty was important to all of us and, though the crew on the *Pompon* didn't have a particular favorite liberty port, we did have great times in Guam and Midway. We weren't lucky enough to get into Australia, where the best liberty ports—Brisbane and Perth—were located, only to the supply depots. For the most part during the war, we didn't have a dedicated liberty port. We did spend one time on liberty at the *Royal Hawaiian*. It was really classy. They had great food, plenty of beer, and a swimming pool that was *fresh water*—few people who have never served in submarines appreciate how important *that* was. All of this made it a really fun liberty. Then we went back to our war patrols.

My last war patrol was life guard duty off of Truk. Like always, we had not the slightest idea where we would be going until we got

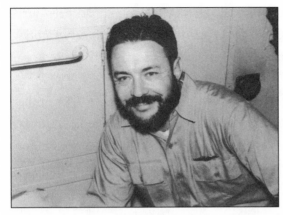

Stan Nicholls (bearded) late in WWII.

Courtesy of Stan Nicholls

well under way. It was all speculation on our part. Of course, everybody *knew* where we were going even before we got under way. And how many were right? I'll guarantee not very many. Anyway, we were sent out to locate downed pilots and aircrews. Often the Japanese would also be able to send search vessels. They weren't very good at it . . . and as time went on, there weren't many of them left to do the job. We were cruising the surface one day on that last patrol when we were steered to a small yellow raft. There was a pilot in there and, not far beyond, a Japanese motor sampan. The Japs kept hauling in closer to the downed pilot. Through the 'scope the captain said he could see them manning a machine gun in the bow to cut down the helpless pilot.

"Blow all ballast! Surface! Surface!" he commanded.

"All hands stand by for battle stations. Surface," the COB announced.

All it took was for the Japanese to spot our periscope surging upward out of the water, and they started to run like hell was after them. We surfaced and manned the five-inch thirty-eight. We sent a few rounds after them and one hit near the bow of the largest sampan. It started to go down quickly by the stern. The motor had been jury-rigged to the stern bulkhead for longer-range operations, weighting down. That was the last engagement in which we participated near the end of World War II.

There was another exciting time—a fun time, really—when they turned to all of us who had not crossed the equator before. It was for the ceremony to make us shellbacks. During the war, they were somewhat restricted in what they did. We had to hold the initiation in the boat while submerged. Like always, we had the Royal Court. We were made to eat something unpleasant. Nothing gross really, but we did have to kiss the hairy belly of the Royal Baby, which is usually the ugliest guy in the crew who was a duly-initiated shellback. We got boffed with a T-shirt stuffed with old socks and other such crazy things, but it was a lot different from some ceremonies I participated in after the war as a full-fledged shellback. Nowadays, King Neptune has his trident, crown and conch shell trumpet, and there's room on a modern sub for a full court to assemble on the subs, as well as surface ships.

Actually, I went from pollywog to shellback and made g*old* shellback on the boat we took from the States to Mombasa [USS *Buffalo*, SSN 681]. That's where you cross the equator right at the International Date Line. They saved the garbage for a few days. Then they made the garbage into this terrible crap you had to drink. It all really stunk to high heaven. In fact, the whole boat stunk. We took garbage bags and hung them in the middle of the operations compartment passageway. That way none of it would seep down into the torpedo room. But even after doing that, the boat still smelled really horrible when we got to Mombasa, which was about two weeks away from the initiation.

Things were better for me during the six years I served on the *Tunny*. I crossed the equator twice while I was on the *Tunny*. That was *really* cool. As a seasoned shellback, I got to hand out the torment instead of receiving it. Like I said, things changed a lot after the war.

First, the navy made the general conversion from straight diesel boats to snorkel-equipped fleet boats. Then the nukes came in. They are magnificent machines. The crews are top-notch young men. After submarine school, they go through a two-year college course in a matter of less than a year; I think it's six months. So they have to be bright. When I was on the staff, I had to ride the various submarines, evaluate performances of the equipment and the men. I found the nuclear subs to be of the most remarkable designs, and the people serving on them, without a doubt, were the greatest. If I were younger, I'd go for serving on one of the SSN boats again, say a boomer, in a flash. At my age now, I'd have a hard time getting up and down the ladders, but if I was young again, I'd love it.

After I left the boats the first time, I did three years' shore duty in Spain, which was really great! They had a lot of good-looking local women around and the weather was terrific. The duty was good, too. Then I came back to San Diego and did shore duty at Naval Air Station, North Island. After that I went back to the submarines and became what they call a "professional boat hopper."

I was a single guy and I would take a boat to WesPac and make a six-month deployment, then come back to San Diego. I'd then go on to the next boat due to deploy and find a torpedoman who was married and didn't want to go on deployment and I'd say, "Do you want to swap? I'll swap with you."

We'd go up to Squadron and tell them we wanted to swap and

they'd say okay. I did this until I was on my third boat and I made chief. Then it got a little harder to do. I made chief on the *Medregal* (SS 480). There were two chief torpedomen on board and we both wanted to go back to WesPac. When we got back to San Diego, I found a chief on the *Medregal*. That got me back to WesPac and into Tokyo. When we came back, I stayed on the *Medregal* until they put her out of commission. In fact, they made me chief of the boat [COB] on there. In August of '70, I became decommissioning chief for the boat. Then I went on to commission another boat and the same thing happened.

I was sent to another boat and we made the shakedown cruise, the boat's first real mission. I stayed for only six months after I put her into commission. I was sent up to staff duty. There, I was put on the team doing the first Mark 48 training certification tests. The navy was just coming out with the Mark 48 torpedo then, in 1972, and it replaced all the other types of torpedoes we had in inventory, except for the nuclear ones. We had to learn how to care for them, how to handle them in preparation to shoot, and how to hook them up to the fire control system. We'd then take them out, fire the torpedoes, certify their run and detonation and, in turn, certify the boat. As I recall, there was only one boat we could not certify. They were pretty bad. Believe me, there's no comparison between the Mark 48 Torpedo and any other torpedo. They were faster, could run truer, and never seemed to cause trouble.

I did that for three years and then I got transferred off the boat. Since then they've made a lot of improvements, even after I left the navy. So far, there has never been a torpedo fired in anger, but every time they take a "sink" exercise and they take out an old ship, usually a destroyer, and take the shot, they always sink it with one torpedo.

The M-48s don't actually strike the ship like in the old days. They go underneath the target and detonate and crack the keel.

I went on the *Drum* and we took her out from Vallejo on her shakedown cruise. Then we came over to Pearl Harbor. The civilian side of our lives got mixed in here in that we were supposed to be making arrangements to move our wives and families down to San Diego, which was to be our home port. The bad part was that there were no navy funds for our transportation and I had to pay my own way back to Vallejo and then back here [to Pearl] again. They paid for my wife, but I had to pay for my own trip out. Anyway, I got back and I've been here ever since. My last seventeen years in the navy I spent in Pearl Harbor and stayed on after.

I can honestly say that while I was on the diesel boats I was never bored. Some of the guys thought transiting was boring. I didn't see it that way. On the diesel boats, one could go up on deck during surface transiting and see the blue sky and the sun and the ocean around you. You could watch sunrises and sunsets and watch the stars come out before submerging. On the nuke boats, where you submerge right out of port and go from point A to point B and it's maybe two thousand miles away, there's nothing to do but stand watches and train and stand watches and train and eat and sleep and train and never get to see the sun or moon or clouds or the water's surface. Now, to me, that sounds like it might get a little boring.

Training always continued even when we were in port. We'd go back over to the hundred-foot tower and do a series of ascents. I never had any trouble with the Momson Lung, but Spankey was a free-ascent-type thing.

"Four-oh-one, go," they'd tell me.

I always got the feeling I was going to run out of air before I got to the top. In the tower, they'd always make you say, "Ho-ho-ho! Ho-ho-ho," so the trainer could make sure you were breathing out all the way up. If they ever told you that you didn't get enough ho-ho-hos out, some guy would come over and punch you in the stomach, and you'd sure know you were not doing it right. All in all, I guess the free ascents were the best. Actually, the EADs came later on.

They're especially good on the nuke boats. When something goes wrong or there's smoke in the boat, it's really easy. You put a mask over your face and plug into the air system. They have manifolds all through the boat and you just hook up. You could wear them for several days—as long as the air held up. Like I said before, on the diesel boats they didn't have that type of emergency air system. In an emergency, you'd have to surface anyway. On the nuke boats they would probably come up enough to put their snorkel mast up and recirculate. And the crew would be in their EADs, so they could breathe while they fought the fire, or whatever affected the air system.

We were lucky in that we were never severely damaged by enemy action, nor did we go aground like a lot of subs did, in shallow water. The only incident along those lines was once when we had tied up to the pier in Yokosuka Bay. We had partly reprovisioned. We were going to get under way, going down to Yankee Station, which was in the gulf off Vietnam [Tonkin Gulf]. We'd go down to Australia and then head for Vietnam. As it happened, the boat outboard of us was getting under way, too. We had our maneuvering watch stationed to check clearances when we cast off. I had the forward torpedo room and I was up there when the captain came through on his way topside.

Just before he went up the ladder, he asked me, "What are all them [sic] eggs doing there between the tubes and the ladder?"

I said, "That's where I was told to stow them."

He said, "Well, you have to keep an open space in there. How do you expect us to be able to operate the interlock?"

"I can't, not without takin' all the eggs out," I told him. What was bothering me most was the idea of having to take all those eggs out, because I had about a dozen cases of eggs stacked up. With thirty dozen to a case, that's a whole lot of eggs. I had no desire to be moving them around, especially while we were maneuvering to leave port.

The captain frowned and said, "Well, somehow, we'll have to change that."

Not feeling too happy about it, I said, "Yes, sir."

Meaning *I'd* have to change it.

He went on up the ladder, and he no sooner got up when he disappeared from my sight, in the forward escape trunk, I guess. Anyway, the next thing I know I'm laying on my *okole* [Hawaiian for ass] on the deck. I suddenly realized that something had hit us. What had happened is that, when you're in Yokuska, there's a little basin where we tied up. To get out of there, we had to back down and make a little turn, then swing around and out. Whatever boat it was—I think it was the *Pickerel*—they backed out and they had a new officer, in fact, he was getting his qualification OOD-type student wrangler, and when he backed out and came around to make the turn, he missed his point and slammed into the *Mandrake*, and the next thing we know we're both in dry dock. Nobody got injured, there was just a lot of material damage. And our boat didn't even take a lot of damage, but we still had to go into dry dock and be inspected. We spent a week there checking things out. We made some minor repairs and the dock crew did the heavy work. It was ruled not our captain's fault, and so there was no reprimand, either, for the only other incident we experienced.

We ran aground on a shoal one time, but I think that's still classified and I can't say much about it. We were hung up for a few hours until we could float free, using our own gear and a rising tide.

Well, I think I'll leave it at that, with a hoist of a foam-capped glass of San Miguel beer to the *yo-yos* of Subic Bay. After thirty-five years in the navy, they still stand out in my mind.

3

WILLIAM YOUNG
RADIOMAN FIRST CLASS, USN (RET.)

Even before the United States entered WWII, naval authorities had expressed much concern about the usefulness and quality of our torpedoes. Many failed to detonate when they struck a target. Others dived deeply and ran far under the keels of the intended targets. Others made circular runs and came back at the boats that had launched them. We all observed how long it took to solve many of these problems in the narrative of LCDR Nicholls. Some of those difficulties did not go away until the advent of the Mark 48 torpedo.

Fortunately, morale was not a problem; these men were highly motivated, eager, and ready to take the fight to the "Sneaky Japs" and the "Goose-Stepping" Nazis. While the German U-boats remained dominant in the North and South Atlantic, efforts were made to curtail this action. Their submarine pens in Southern France, Norway, and in Hamburg, Kiel, and Wilhelmshaven in Germany, were bombed repeatedly while destroyers, DEs, and our submarines lurked outside in the open sea to finish off the deadly

Wolf Packs when they ventured out to escape the bombs. Compared to the wily *unterseeboot* [under sea boat] commanders, the Japanese were rank amateurs when it came to submarine warfare. Their boats were noisy, as opposed to the quiet of the U-boats and our own. That made them easy prey for our surface craft and submarines.

Other problems assailed our Submarine Service. With our naval forces spread over three oceans, the Arctic, Atlantic, and Pacific, better long-range communications became a necessity. Also, there was only one base where basic submarine craft was taught—New London, Connecticut. As more and more submarines slid down the ways at the manufacturing plants, and more crews were lost to accidents or enemy action, the demand grew exponentially for more submarine sailors. To answer these demands, not only mustang officers (those who did not graduate from the Naval Academy at Annapolis), but also mustang enlisted men came into being. They were already "submarine savvy" and many of them made rank quickly, some attending Navy Officer Candidate School or being given deckside commissions.

Hollywood often portrays submariners as bare-chested, grease- and sweat-smeared semiliterates with thick Brooklyn accents. Particularly, torpedomen were selected for such misrepresentation. Take note: It's not so! If

Poseiden missile launch.
Courtesy of United States Navy

anything, the forward and aft torpedo rooms were, are, and always will be meticulously clean, as are the missile silo rooms in modern nuke subs. In the diesel sub days (WWII to 1964) torpedomen frequently gave their deadly, self-propelled weapons alcohol baths to keep them so clean they actually shined. (See LCDR Nicholls's account of how else they employed this alcohol, page 44.) Usually, the only time one could see a dirt- and grease-grimed crewman was when a member of the engineering department cleaned the ballast tanks (done on the surface only), or crewmen cleaned battery rooms, shaft alley, or the grease trap in the galley.

Whenever there was internal damage, however, all bets were off. The men of the Submarine Service worked easily and routinely as a team, and did it quickly. Firefighting was a primary skill taught to those at the Submarine School at New London and drills were frequently held at sea. No one knows

Galley of USS *Tucson*.
Courtesy of United States Navy

for certain what happened on those boats that are on Eternal Patrol, yet it is a good guess that fire broke out due to enemy action or some other stressful cause, disabling them while they were submerged.

As pointed out earlier, every crewmember received instruction in the duties of a lookout. Aircraft and ship identification became primary fields of study and provided some worthwhile, as well as educational, entertainment during off-duty hours. All officers and the signalmen aboard were required to have expert knowledge of how to use signal flags and the Aldus Lamp signaling light. As a hedge against boredom, amateur cooks had a free hand in the galley to invent or duplicate their favorite dishes, sometimes to the crew's regret.

The enlisted men of the submarine force were as capable as the officers were; witness the great number who came "up through the hawse-hole" (mustangs and battlefield promotions) to became officers. Case in point:

USS *Reuben James* (FFG 57) as seen through the periscope of the submarine USS *Tucson* (SSN 770). *Courtesy of United States Navy*

There is not a submarine course at the Naval Academy at Annapolis. One had to *go* to New London and *do* Submarine School to be admitted to the hallowed ranks of the dolphin wearers.

On another front, great advances at such locations as Great Lakes Naval Training Center; Philadelphia Navy Yard; Pearl Harbor, Hawaii; and Portsmouth, Maine; in Puerto Rico, in San Diego, Mare Island, and Vallejo, California, began to develop. Primarily, these centered on improved submerged radio communication, the ultimate fine definition for sonar, accuracy, and increased range of surface radar, and accuracy, failproof propulsion, and detonation of torpedoes.

As stated by LCDR Nicholls, much of this work on torpedoes proceeded at Pearl Harbor. Their success varied with the torpedo type, detonation systems, and speed. Finally, they solved the problem of broaching by placing weights forward, in front of, and behind the warhead. Predetonation and failure to detonate took a bit longer. It required a change in the type and nature of the detonators.

One of those enlisted men, William Young, served with expertise and endurance, took his orders—the good along with the bad—and came out of the war with pride in the accomplishments of the boats he served in and the men he served beside. As a radioman, he was one of the "in-group" who sent and received the messages that often weighed the survival of his submarine in the balance. A radioman in the early days of WWII was required to know Morse code and have a good "fist" on the telegrapher's key that was adapted to send radio messages in dots and dashes of static. Eventually, the method of communication improved until voice radio communication became commonplace in late 1944, and through 1945 and beyond. Later came the keyboard and computer transmissions—similar to civilian e-mail—but that was a long time coming for William Young. His remembrances of those days are compelling and intriguing.

I joined the Navy in June 1941, right out of high school, and served until June 1947, a six-year cruise. Then I was recalled in 1950 for Korea—which was not a submarine war. Naturally, I attended submarine school at New London. The studies were rather complicated. We had to trace LANGs (which are the hydraulic systems), electrical systems, fresh- and seawater systems, and air flow systems—both pressurized and breathable—throughout the whole ship. We had to learn how to let air in and out of the tanks. And then came instruction in diving procedures, torpedo firing, and other gunnery. We didn't have to do it all at once; we had time to absorb what they taught. We'd qualify in one thing and then go on to the next and qualify in that. It took months to do it all. When we had finished and completed a couple of shakedown cruises, we took the boat down through the Canal and over to Hawaii. My home port was Pearl Harbor.

During the war, I served on the *Wahoo,* the *Burrfish,* and the *Seafox.* During Korea, I was on the USS *Char.* During wartime, we had our watch quarters and station bill posted in the mess hall. They told us where we were supposed to be at different times. The COB made that up. Our wartime routine was just that, *routine.* We had certain hours when we could sleep, when we could eat, and when we were standing our watch. We barely had enough fresh water or time to wash our faces, which was about all we ever got [sic] to wash, unless we wanted a saltwater bath in one of the bilges or ballast tanks. Things got hot, though, when we had some action going.

Now, in Korea, we had very little to do. When I got on the *Char,* about a week later, we went up to Anacortes, Washington. Our patrol area was Puget Sound. We stayed a year up there. We spent every morning going out and letting the planes from Sand Island NAS come out and find us. They'd drop sonobouys on us. They called these

The USS *Burrfish* (SS 312) at Pearl Harbor circa 1945. The *Burrfish* is a Balao-class boat with a length of 311 feet 10 inches and displaces 1,526 tons on the surface, 2,424 tons submerged. Her diesel engines would drive her at a top speed of 20.15 knots on the surface while the electric motors would push her at 8.75 knots submerged. With a crew of sixty enlisted and six officers, this class of submarine had a depth limit of 400 feet. *Courtesy of United States Navy*

hunter-killer exercises. As it turned out, it was more for their benefit than for ours. We were just a target. That's the way I spent the Korean War. Not at all like the old days on the *Wahoo*.

Without a doubt, no question at all the greatest skipper I ever served under was Captain Morton. Not only the greatest *I* ever served under, the greatest skipper *anyone* served with, *anywhere*.

Captain Morton would come on board the *Wahoo* every time before we went out and say, "Now, we're going to go in harm's way. Anyone who wants to get off can get off, no questions asked. There will be nothing in your military records to indicate that you didn't want to go or anything like that. You'll just be set to go."

Not one person ever left. If he would have said, "We're all going

SONOBOUY going into a launch bay of a P-3C Orion patrol aircraft.
Courtesy of United States Navy

to go out and we're all gonna get killed," we would have gone [anyway]. That's the kind of a guy he was. I never saw another skipper like him. I did three tours on the *Wahoo* and four on the *Burrfish*. The *Wahoo* was pretty exciting. On the *Burrfish* it wasn't very exhilarating; in 1944 and '45 we didn't have much of anything left to shoot at. We got involved with the line of sub stations [that ran] from Clark Field in Hawaii, north and west from [around] the Philippines. Our navy air and the army air corps (they'd already started calling it the U.S. Air Force by then) began bombing Okinawa, Iwo Jima, and on up. We had a picket line of submarines on the air flight pattern. In the event anyone got shot down, we could pick them up. We never recovered anyone, but some of the submarines picked up quite a few. But it was monotonous duty.

Torpedoed Japanese destroyer photographed through periscope of USS *Wahoo* or USS *Nautilus*, June 1942.
Courtesy of United States Navy

My most exciting patrols were, of course, on the *Wahoo*. Captain Morton was after anyone or anything he could shoot. In addition to the enormous tonnage we sank, we got one Jap destroyer and one submarine. The rest were all tankers, troop ships, and cargo ships of all kinds. Other boats had larger tonnage totals than we did, but at that time [the *Wahoo*'s third war patrol] we had the biggest record, with forty thousand tons of shipping sunk.

Taken from the declassified war patrols of the USS *Wahoo*, their third and my first war patrol went somewhat like this: On December 31, LCDR W. Morton relieved LCDR M. G. Kennedy. The executive officer was LT R. H. O'Kane. As a first class petty officer, I was the number two radioman. After we resupplied, refit, and made minor repairs, we set out from Brisbane, Queensland, Australia, at 0900 (local time) on January 16. Over that day and three of the next four—we conducted a series of dives, maneuvering exercises, and gunnery practice. On January 19, Captain Morton ordered a speed run at "three" engine speed [eighty to ninety turns of the propeller shaft per minute] in order to pass through Vitiaz Straits during daylight, thus gaining time. This would give us an extra day at Wewak and still arrive on station as directed. The captain considered the additional fuel spent in this operation to be well worth it. Our third patrol had begun.

Our operations order routed us through the vicinity of Wewak, a more or less undetermined spot located in whole degrees of latitude and longitude as 400 degrees south and 144 degrees east. Air reconnaissance had reported considerable shipping there, and dispatches we received en route indicated continued use of this area by the Japs. The position of Wewak Harbor was determined as behind Kairiru and Mushu Islands on the northeast coast of New Guinea through the interest of D. C. Keeter, machinist mate first class, U.S. Navy, who had purchased an Australian "two-bit" school atlas of the area.

With everything ready and "loaded for bear," the skipper adjusted the speed to arrive off Kairiru Island prior to dawn. On January 24, at 0300 hours, we dived two and a half miles north of Kairiru Island and proceeded around the western end to investigate Victoria Bay. As dawn broke, LT O'Kane sighted a small tug with a barge alongside and a few moments later two *Chidori*-class torpedo boats. As this patrol was under way, we maneuvered to avoid, then came back for a better look into the mile-deep bay. There was no other shipping spotted.

At 1318 hours, we sighted an object in the bight of Mushu Island, located about five miles farther into the harbor. The *Wahoo* commenced approach at three knots. As the range closed, the aspect of the target changed from that of a tender with several small ships alongside to that of a destroyer with *RO*-class submarines nested, the latter identified by the canvas hatch hoods and awnings shown in ONI 14. The scant observations we could make proved insufficient for positive identification and the objects alongside may have been the tug and barge first sighted at dawn. It was then the captain's intention to fire high-speed shots from about three thousand yards, which would permit us to remain in deep water and facilitate an exit. However, on the next observation, when the generated range was 3,750 yards, our target, a *Pubuki*-class destroyer was underway. We had indicated angle on the bow 10 degrees port, the range at 3,100 yards. Nothing else was in sight. Maneuvered for a stern tube shot, but on next observation, target had zigged left, giving us a bow tube setup.

At 1441, the exec fired a spread of three torpedoes on 110 degrees starboard tack, range 1,800 yards, using target speed fifteen, since we had insufficient time to determine speed by tracking. Our sonar operator observed going aft as sound indicated eighteen knots, so fired another fish with enemy speed twenty.

The destroyer avoided by turning away, then circled to the right and headed for us. Everyone in the boat could hear the sound of thrashing screws growing closer. LT O'Kane kept the bow pointed at the Jap destroyer. He delayed firing our fifth torpedo until the destroyer had closed to about twelve hundred yards, angle on the bow 10 degrees starboard. Then to ensure the maximum chance of hitting him with our last torpedo in the forward tubes, the exec withheld fire until the range was about eight hundred yards. The last fish, fired at 1449, clipped the destroyer amidships in twenty-five seconds [running time] and broke his back. The explosion was terrific! It shook our boat up somewhat, but we sustained no damage.

Topside, on the destroyer, Japs covered turret tops and filled the rigging. Over one hundred members of her crew must have been operating as lookouts. LT O'Kane ordered several pictures taken and then we went to 150 feet and commenced a nine-mile run out of Wewak. We heard her boilers let go, in between the noise of continuous shelling from somewhere, plus a couple of aerial bombs. They were apparently trying to make us lie on the bottom until their patrol boats could return.

We slid out of there without trouble even though piloting without observation. After we cleared Kairiru and Valif Islands, we surfaced at 1930. We cleared the area on four engines for thirty minutes while on a course of 0-0-0 degrees (T). Huge fires were visible in Wewak Harbor. We speculated that the enemy had purposely created these fires to silhouette us, in case we tried to escape out of the harbor. If so, they were way too late.

At 0530, January 25, we passed between Aua and Wuvulu Islands. We changed course for Palau and went to two-engine speed (eighty to ninety revs), continuing a crisscross search for enemy shipping. At 0830, the COB fired a Tommy gun [.45-caliber Thompson sub-machine gun] across the bow of a small fishing boat, and we brought him alongside. None of our Chamoro or Filipino mess boys could converse with the six Malayans in the boat, but by sign language we learned that they were originally nine in number, three having died. One of the remaining six was apparently blind, a second quite sick, and a third obviously suffering from scurvy. We gave them food and water after we learned they had none, and then continued our search for the enemy.

On January 26, we sighted smoke on the horizon, swung the ship toward the vessels, and began tracking on the surface. We adjusted course and speed to get ahead of the enemy. After three-quarters of an hour, when we had reached a favorable position with the masts of two ships just coming over the horizon, from the bridge LT O'Kane ordered, "Dive! Dive!" and we went down to begin a submerged approach. In the control, we tracked the two freighters at ten knots on a steady course of 0-9-5 degrees, which puzzled those of us familiar with this piece of ocean, because it led from nowhere to no known port. During our approach, Captain Morton determined from the TDC that the best firing position would be 1,300 yards on the beam of the lead ship. The torpedo data computer gave him a solution of about 15 degrees right gyro angle on approximately a 105-degree track on the leading ship, with about 30 degree left gyro angle and 60 degree track on the second ship a thousand yards astern in column. However, at 1030, the exec, on the number one 'scope, found that we were too close to the track for this two-ship shot, so reversed course to the right and gained an identical setup for a stern tube shot.

At 1041, the order to fire came and we loosed two torpedoes at the leading ship and, seventeen seconds later, two more at the second freighter. The first two torpedoes hit their points of aim in bow and stern. We learned that there had been too little time to allow for the gyro setting angle indicator and regulator to catch up with the new setup cranked into the TDC for the third shot. This torpedo passed ahead of the second target. The fourth hit him.

On LT O'Kane's command, we swung left to bring the bow tubes to bear, in case these ships did not sink. At 1045, both LT O'Kane and the COB took sweeps around to ensure the setup at hand and were surprised to see *three* ships close around us, now heading directly at us although at a slow speed, and the third was a huge transport, which had evidently been beyond and behind our second target. Our first target was listing badly to starboard and sinking by the stern. The second was bow-on and headed directly at us. At 1047, when the transport presented a 90-degree starboard angle on the bow at 1,800 yards' range, LT O'Kane fired a spread of three torpedoes from forward tubes. The second and third torpedoes hit and stopped the ship. We then turned our attention to the second target, which was last observed heading for us. She was still coming, although reported down from the conning tower that she was yawing a lot, but quite close.

We fired two bow torpedoes down his throat to stop him, and as a defensive move. The second fish hit, but he kept coming and forced us to turn hard left, duck and go ahead at full speed to avoid a deadly collision. After that, we heard so many explosions that it was impossible to tell just what was taking place. Eighty minutes later, we came back to periscope depth. After reaching eighty feet, we observed that our first target had sunk, our second target still going, but even slower and with evident steering trouble, with the transport stopped but still afloat.

We headed for the middle of the transport ship, but our torpedo failed to explode. The transport was firing continuously at the torpedo with the same setup, except that the transport had moved ahead a little and turned toward us. That presented us a 65-degree angle on the bow. The torpedo wake headed right for his stack. The explosion blew her amidships section higher than a kite. Troops commenced jumping over the side like ants off a hot plate. Her stern went up and she headed for the bottom. Our COB took several pictures. At 1136 hours, we swung ship and angled toward the cripple, our second target, which was now going away on course zero-eight-five degrees. Tracked her at six knots, but could not close her, as our battery was getting low.

At 1155, LT O'Kane on the number one periscope sighted tops [masts and spars] of a fourth ship to the right of the damaged cargo ship. Her thick masts in line had the appearance of a light cruiser's tops. We kept heading for these ships hoping that the last one sighted would attempt to pick up survivors of the transport. When the range was about ten thousand yards, she turned right and joined the cripple, her masts, bridge structure, and engines aft identified her as a tanker. Decided to let these two ships get over the horizon while we surfaced to charge batteries and destroy the estimated twenty troop boats now in the water. These boats were of many types: scows, motor launches, cabin cruisers, and other nondescript varieties. At 1315, we made hasty battle surface and manned all guns.

We in the gun crew fired the four-inch gun at the largest scow loaded with troops. Although all troops in this boat apparently jumped in the water, small-caliber machine guns returned our fire. Then we opened fire with everything we had. During this surface action, one man received a severe cut to his right forearm, which required closing. It took seven stitches. Two other men received injuries by a twenty-millimeter explosion, when our gun misfired. In one of these cases, it was determined necessary to amputate two toes of the right foot. Due to a shortage of surgical instruments, our corpsman used a pair of sterilized side-cutters to cut away portions of the shattered bone. Because the bones of the second toe were completely shattered, he did not suture it closed but left it open to allow free drainage. These guys received a generous amount of Sulfa drug to help prevent infection. The other wounded man had a hole in his shoulder but no lead or foreign body could be located. Three sutures were used to close the cut. This man was back to duty in three days with no complications. These guys were incredibly lucky and the only injuries we had on this patrol. After securing from battle surface, Captain Morton set course of 0-8-5 degrees and went to flank speed to overtake the cripple and the tanker.

At 1530, lookouts on the periscope shears [small, rail-secured platforms, port and starboard, at the base of the periscope array] sighted smoke of the fleeing ships a point [1 degree] on our port bow. We quickly changed our course to intercept them. Closed until the mast tops of both ships were in sight and tracked them on course 3-5-0. They had changed course about 90 degrees to the left in an effort to give us the slip. We maneuvered by mooring board to get ahead undetected, but kept mastheads in sight continuously by utilizing number one periscope and locating lookouts on top of the periscope shears. At 1721, a half hour before sunset, with the two ships' masts in line, we dived and commenced submerged approach. Target speeds made it necessary to maintain a very high submerged speed to close the range. Someone said the pitometer log indicated ten knots. Our exec decided to attack the tanker first, if the opportunity permitted, since she had not yet been damaged. At 1829, when it was too dark to take a periscope range, we fired a spread of three bow torpedoes with generated range of twenty-three hundred yards, on a 110-degree port track. One good hit was observed and heard one minute, twenty-two seconds after firing. That apparently stopped him.

We surfaced twelve minutes after firing and went after the freighter. We were surprised to see the tanker we had just hit still going and on the freighter's quarter. With moonrise not until 2132, we considered ourselves most fortunate to have a dark night, and to have targets that persisted in staying together. Our only handicap came from having only four torpedoes left, and those in the stern tubes.

We made numerous approaches on the tanker first, since he was not firing at us. Captain Morton even attempted backing in at full speed, but the ship would not answer her rudder quickly enough. After an hour and a half, we were able to diagnose their tactics. We tried something they might not expect. We closed in on the tanker from directly astern, and when they zigged to the right we held our course and speed. When they zigged back to the left, we were on parallel course at about two thousand yards range. At once, we converged a little on the tanker's port beam. Then we twisted left with full rudder and power. That gave LT O'Kane a stern tube shot, range of 1,850 yards on a 90-degree port track. At 2025, we fired two torpedoes at the tanker. The second torpedo hit him just abaft of his midships, breaking his back. He went down in the middle almost instantly.

Immediately after firing, we changed course to head for the freighter and went ahead at full speed. The *Wahoo* passed the tanker at 1250, by SJ radar, at which time his image occupied the full field of a pair of 7×50 binoculars. That fixed his length at about five hundred feet. Only the bow section was afloat and its mast canted over when we left him astern. At 2036, eleven minutes after firing on the tanker, we commenced an approach on our last target. It quickly became quite evident that this freighter had a good crew aboard. They did not miss an opportunity to upset our approach by zigs, and kept up incessant gunfire to keep us away. Much of their firing was at random, but at 2043 hours, they got our range, placed a shell directly in front of us, which ricocheted over the heads of those on the bridge, and forced us to dive.

As an aside, I think our "gun club" could take a lesson from the Jap powder manufacturers. It was truly *flashless,* a glow [from the target] of about the intensity of a dimmed flashlight being the only indication that a projectile was on its way. It is somewhat disconcerting when a splash is the first indication you have of taking fire. Now, back to what happened on January 26.

We tracked the freighter by sound until the noise of shell splashes let up, then surfaced at 2058 hours, fifteen minutes after diving, and went after him. Two minutes later, a large searchlight commenced sweeping sharp on our port bow, its rays seemed barely to clear our periscope shears. The captain assumed that this was from a man-of-war and that the freighter would close it for protection. Our attack obviously had to be completed in a hurry. We headed for the searchlight beam and were most fortunate to have the freighter follow suit. At 2110, when the range was 2,900 yards by radar, the captain had the boat twisted to the left for a straight stern shot. We stopped and steadied.

69

Three minutes later, with angle on the bow of 1-3-5 degrees port by radar tracking, LT O'Kane fired our last two torpedoes without spread. *They both hit!* The explosion jarred even those of us who were not on the bridge. As the lagging escort came over the horizon, it silhouetted the freighter in her searchlight. We headed away to the east and then five minutes later, to the north. Fifteen minutes after firing, the freighter sank, leaving only the destroyer's searchlight sweeping a clear horizon. It had taken four hits from three separate attacks to sink that ship.

At 2130, LT O'Kane—who was also navigator—set course of 3-5-8 degrees for Fais Island. At 2345, Captain Morton had me send a dispatch sent to ComSubPac relating our new route and the engagement.

On January 27, we sighted smoke over the horizon at 0720. LT O'Kane had radar commence tracking and changed course to intercept. At 0801, masts of three ships came into sight. We dived and continued approach. LT O'Kane plotted our main course as 1-4-6 degrees, with the whole convoy zigging simultaneously 30 degrees to either side of base course. At 0830, the tops and stacks of two more freighters, and those of a tanker with engine house aft, came into sight. It was LT O'Kane's first intention for us to intercept one of the lagging freighters, which did not appear to be armed. However, a zig placed the tanker closest to us. We surfaced with a range of about twelve thousand yards.

Captain Morton went to the bridge and the exec manned the plotting table in the control room, while the engineering lieutenant stood by the TDC in the conning tower. We headed at full speed to cut the tanker off. The captain had the big gun trained sharp on starboard bow, then sent pointer and trainer below, to stand by with the rest of the gun crew. The convoy sighted us in about ten minutes, commenced smoking like a Winton [a brand of cigar no longer made], and headed for a lone rain squall. Only two of the larger freighters opened fire and their splashes were several thousand yards short. Their maneuver left the tanker trailing, just where we wanted him.

At 1000, when we had closed to 7,500 yards, a single mast poked out from behind one of the smaller freighters. One lookout in the periscope shears sang out as, almost immediately, the upper works of a corvette or destroyer came in sight. We turned tail at full power to draw the escort as far as possible away from the convoy, in case we were forced to dive. This would greatly shorten the time he could remain behind to work us over—a welcome thought to the whole crew. Captain Morton ordered a contact report sent out. Unfortunately, the radioman could not raise anyone.

To the captain's surprise, he found that our engineers could add close to another knot to our speed when they knew the enemy closely pursued us. We actually made about twenty knots, opening the range to thirteen or fourteen thousand yards in the first twenty minutes of the chase. In fact, the enemy was smoking so profusely that the crew called this vessel an "antiquated coal-burning corvette." Their black watch evidently just lit off more boilers because, seventeen minutes later, he changed our raucous tune by blowing over the horizon to swing left and let fly a broadside at estimated range of only seven thousand yards.

We had no doubt as to his identity then, especially when the salvo whistled right over our heads. The splashes landed about five hundred yards directly ahead. The captain cleared the bridge and we dived. As we passed periscope depth, the whole crew felt shell splashes directly overhead. We went to three hundred feet some fifteen minutes later and received six depth charges that detonated inboard. They sounded loud but did no damage. We lost sound contact at 1120 hours. With some forty miles to go to reach his convoy, the DD must have made that one run and left to rejoin them. Captain Morton decided to lay low and catch our breath, so we remained deep until 1400, when we surfaced and commenced running for Fais. At 2058 hours, we sent a contact report of the convoy to ComSubPac.

At 0830 on January 28, we lookouts sighted Fais Island fifteen miles ahead. We dived twenty minutes later, proceeded on a ten-mile circle, and closed the island at four knots. We took soundings at ten-minute intervals, and tried echo ranging on the reef. These soundings agreed closely to those on chart 5-4-2-6. We found no evidence of a sound listening post and the trading station was just as shown on the chart. We continued around the southwestern end of the island at one and a half miles from the beach and located the Phosporite Works, warehouses, and refinery on and inshore of the prominent point in the middle of the northwest side of the island.

Our captain immediately made plans to shell these works that evening at moonrise with our few remaining four-inch rounds, since the large refinery, warehouses, and all offered, as he put it, a "perfect target." This plan was prevented by the arrival at 1400 of an Inter-Island steamer with efficient-looking gun mounts forward and aft. She swung and moored to the buoy off the refinery point, where she would have made a nice target for one torpedo. We estimated her tonnage at two thousand. At 1600 hours, the captain decided to leave well enough alone and, after taking several more photographs, he set course that would allow us to clear the northern end of Fais Island. At 1800, we surfaced and went ahead on three main engines, taking the prescribed route to Pearl Harbor. We arrived at Pearl on February 7 at 0830. That ended my first patrol with the *Wahoo*.

Many times, during this patrol and the others, we were under attack by enemy aircraft. Mostly they used bombs, and primarily depth charges for when we dived quickly. They never damaged us to any extent, and were lucky they didn't manage to drop torpedoes. But, especially the first time, it's frightening. Depth charges sound like hell. It's as though someone put a bucket over your head and began to pound on it with a hammer. That first time, you tend to wet your pants. Eventually you get used to the sound and you know when it's not very close. When you get to that point, you realize it's probably five hundred yards away and it is not going to hurt you. I don't mean to imply that it is routine, it's definitely *not* routine, but at least you're not afraid of it. We would dive down deep below where the depth charges were set to detonate. The water compression at that depth was like an ice cream cone. The explosion would follow the line of least resistance, with the greatest force shooting upward, while the bottom edge got pressed outward and flattened. The most depth charges we ever took in one run was, I think, about forty charges. I'm not aware of how many charges they carried, but the smaller escort vessels, destroyer escort type, couldn't have carried very many—probably fifty or sixty.

During surface attacks, the merchant ships fired on us, but their crews were merchant seamen, not experienced gunners, and they could not hit you unless they were pointing directly at your forehead from about six inches away, so they weren't much of a problem.

We saw a lot of good action. We sank small ships, sampans, and one pretty good-sized ship with gunfire. That's also how we got our Jap submarine.

It was sitting on the surface; it couldn't dive for some reason, but we didn't know why. Anyhow, it made a perfect target for us—it was a sitting duck. We fired one torpedo and blew it right in two. We couldn't have asked for better.

My last war patrol was aboard the *Burrfish*. It was another monotonous trip. They assigned us a certain area—a grid, they called it—we had a grid of so many square miles of ocean and another ship would have a grid beside ours. We couldn't cross, we had to stay within those confines, and if you went into the shipping lanes, you ate, went on watch, slept, ate again, and went on watch, slept, etc. And as I said, later on in the war there wasn't anything to shoot at. The air force out of Clark Field was pounding the islands up there and what ships they [the Japanese] did have went back to Tokyo and tried to hide.

On the lighter side, I crossed the equator twice and I became an initiated shellback. Even with the cramped quarters of a submarine, we had a court [King Neptune, his Royal Queen, the Royal Barber and the Royal Baby]. We had to do all kinds of crazy things; we had to drink some tobacco juice, eat all kinds of nasty things. And then the baby, who was the biggest, ugliest guy on board, had his stomach painted with grease and we had to kiss his belly. The second time it was even more fun because I was a full-fledged shellback.

I never served on any of the snorkel boats, only the diesel-electrics. Now, when it comes to the modern navy, or the new navy as it's called, I think this present crop of sailors needs to be better and more knowledgeable technicians than any of us. I'm sure all the systems are nine times more complicated than ours were. That's especially true when it comes to operating the radio. They don't hammer a key anymore. They just sit at a typewriter and send it wherever they want it to go. It's an e-mail-type thing, which is so much more highly technical than we had. It's still a submarine and it still has the same function. It still has the same purpose. One of our submarines from right here [Pearl Harbor] fired the first Tomahawk missile into Beirut. We wouldn't be able to do that in 1942, of course. So it's entirely two different worlds, I'm sure. It's just night and day. If I were of an age to be able to do it, I'd want to serve on one of the nuke boats. Absolutely.

They're the cream of the crop in the navy . . . in my estimation, but then I'm a little prejudiced. I got that way over the years.

During my time, most of the guys in submarines were real characters, me included. As for standouts, Morton of course was in a class by himself. The COB on the *Wahoo* was a man named Lemmox. He was really a father figure to the young kids, and we *were* kids, with the average age of twenty. I was eighteen. But in their individual ways, they were all characters. They were all *individuals*; they were all capable and knowing people. We didn't have any flunks; they were weeded out early.

A lot of the people who applied for submarine service didn't make it. We went through extensive batteries of examinations: psychological tests, mechanical aptitude tests, and various other tests. So, anyone who went through the school qualified at his job. They didn't keep anyone who couldn't. We would have chunked him overboard—no, not quite. But he would have been gotten rid of right away. Even so, everyone was a character in one way or another, each had his own little quirks, yet we worked together beautifully. Like a machine, and a well-oiled machine at that.

Some of the real characters I sailed with were the mess boys. African American sailors could only serve as mess boys in those days. Some of the others were Filipinos, but they were segregated, I guess you'd have to say. But those kids were real characters. We had one mess boy who could play the banjo; he used to do the minstrel thing. Another claimed to be the son of the king of Haiti. Each one was a character in his own right, but good people. It was an honor to be with guys like that. Through most of the war I was happy to be with people like that. I could trust them. I knew that if anything was going to happen to me I had good people all around. Of course, when you were eighteen nothing bad could happen to you, anyway.

We were at sea when the war ended, and when we made port in Pearl Harbor, we didn't have a lot to do. We'd stand muster at 8 A.M. and then you were free to go until the next morning at 8 A.M. There was a lot of celebrating, of course. We also had to consider our futures. I was regular Navy, while most of the others were Naval Reserve. The reservists got points in those days for being overseas for a specified amount of time and such. On the other hand, as a regular, I had a couple of years left until my enlistment ran out. So while they counted up their points to get out right away, I went to check what was open. Also, at that time they had a system whereby, in your rate—I was a radioman first class—you could go to the personnel people and if there was a first class on the East Coast who wanted to come to the west coast, they'd swap you. Anyway, I wanted to go to one of the U.S. East Coast sub bases because at that time we were having bases in Scotland, and in the Mediterranean, and I'd never been on that side, except for Portsmouth, New London, and Key West. I thought that if I had a couple of years to do, I'd get over there. They arranged for me to transfer and I went back to Portsmouth. I got immediately assigned to a ship named the *Sennet,* and discovered it was preparing to go under the South Pole. I went back to personnel and said I'd like to go back to the West Coast.

In December 1945, I was assigned to a boat called the *Seafox.* We left in January from Pearl Harbor and we were at sea for eight months. We went to every island in the South Pacific: Australia, back up to Bougainville, Guadalcanal, literally every island, even some that were not even on the map. We had two guys from Graves Registration with us. They were looking for someone from a ship that had sunk or somebody from an airplane that had been downed and might have survived on one of those remote islands. They never did find anyone alive but they were hoping to. They did find graves. Almost all of those islands had a priest of some kind on them—Belgian, French—Catholic priests there for the natives, and when they had a body wash up, they'd bury it. They'd keep the dog tags and everything they could preserve. The guys with us recorded some eighteen or twenty such incidences. I wish I had made a video of it. It would be worth a million dollars today.

All in all, it was kind of a fun trip. The trim dive came up in the morning, and then we'd put up an awning and, if you were not on watch, you could come up and look around. Some of those islands had a freshwater lagoon in the middle, which made them kind of interesting. The natives would sometimes have a radio that was not working. We'd fix their radio, or if they needed something we had, we'd fix them up. I'm glad I never went to the South Pole. We were sort of ambassadors of goodwill on this trip. I never got to the Atlantic. Actually, we didn't have much [submarine operations] in the Atlantic during World War II. That was all German territory. They actually came right off the Florida coast. But they didn't have any shipping. We had the shipping for them to shoot at. There wasn't any submarine action, other than convoy escort duty, in the Atlantic during the entire war.

For the remainder of my enlistment everything was pretty dull. It didn't improve during my recall for Korea, as I think I mentioned before. Korea simply was not a submarine war. But I still treasure the time I spent in submarines.

4

ENNIS CRAFT MCLAREN
COXSWAIN (THIRD CLASS PETTY OFFICER), USN (RET.)

Although naval operations in the Atlantic from 1942 to 1945 could not properly be considered a submarine war, one submarine—ironically it was the captured Italian sub, the *R-9*—that participated in gunnery practice and antisubmarine warfare, was instrumental in the destruction of the German sub *TJ-515* and subsequent isolation and capture of the *U-505*. Admiral (then Captain) Daniel V. Gallery, forced the surrender of the *U-505* from his aircraft carrier, the *Guadalcanal (ACV 60)*. The German sub (*U-505*) now rests in a concrete cradle at the Great Lakes Naval Training Center outside Chicago. For a number of years, it rested outside the Museum of Modern History in Chicago near the University of Chicago campus. The capture of the *U-505* is a fascinating story to rival any of the other war tales of our submariners.

After her shakedown training and pilot qualifications out of San Diego, California, *Guadalcanal* departed November 15, transiting the Panama Canal and arriving in Norfolk, Virginia, on December 3. *Guadalcanal* became the flagship of antisubmarine Task Group 21.12, and set out from Norfolk with her escort of destroyers on January 5, 1944. They were to search for enemy submarines in the North Atlantic. On January 15, aircraft from *Guadalcanal* sighted three submarines fueling on the surface and, in a rocket and bombing attack, succeeded in sinking the German submarine *U-544*. After the task group replenished supplies and ordnance at Casablanca, they headed back for Norfolk to make repairs, arriving on February 16.

After repairs and refitting, *Guadalcanal* was back at sea again on March 7, transiting uneventfully to Casablanca. They transited from there to Madeira. West of the Spanish port, aircraft from the *Guadalcanal* spotted the German submarine *TJ-515* and closed in for the kill. *Guadalcanal*'s aircraft, aided by destroyers *Chatelaine, Flaherty, Pillsbury*, and *Pope*, made several excellently coordinated attacks on the enemy with rockets and depth-charges throughout that night. When the German sub lost depth control on the afternoon of April 9, it forced the *TJ-515* to surface amid the waiting ships. Instantly trashed by direct rocket and gunfire, the *515* wallowed in the troughs of waves. As Wildcat fighters from *Guadalcanal* strafed the submarine, her captain, German Ace *Kapitanleutnant* Werner Henke, ordered Abandon Ship and she went to the bottom.

It proved a busy time for the *Guadalcanal* and her task group, because on the night of April 10, the group caught the German submarine *V-68* on the surface in bright moonlight three hundred miles south of the Azores, and sank her with depth-charges and rocket fire. The convoy arrived at Norfolk on April 26, 1944. *Guadalcanal* underwent repairs and refitting and went back to sea on May 15, 1944. For two weeks, they received no contacts. Captain Gallery decided to make for the coast of Africa to refuel. Ten minutes after reversing course, the destroyer *Chatelaine* detected a submarine, later identified as the *U-505*. The destroyer commenced a depth-charge attack and, guided in for a more accurate drop by orbiting aircraft from *Guadalcanal*, soon made a second run. This last pattern blasted a hole in the outer hull of the submarine, and rolled the U-boat on its beam-ends. Shouts of panic from the conning tower led her inexperienced captain to believe his boat was doomed. He blew his tanks and surfaced, barely seven hundred yards from *Chatelaine*. The destroyer fired a torpedo, which missed, and the surfaced submarine then came under the combined fire of the escorts and aircraft. The volume of fire forced her crew to abandon ship. Captain Gallery had been waiting and making plans for just such an opportunity. Having already trained and equipped his boarding parties, he ordered the *Pillsbury*'s boat to make for the German sub and board her. Under the command of LTJG A. L. David, the party leaped onto the slowly circling submarine and found it abandoned. Risking unknown dangers below, David and his men quickly captured all important papers and books, including the ship's log, while closing valves and stopping leaks. While *Pillsbury* tried to get a towline on her, the party managed to stop the *U-505*'s engines. By this time, a large salvage group arrived from the *Guadalcanal*. They began the work of preparing *U-505* for towing. After securing the towline and picking up the German survivors from the sea, *Guadalcanal* started for Bermuda with her priceless prize in tow. Fleet tug *A. J. Abnaki* rendezvoused with the carrier task group and took over towing duties. The group arrived in Bermuda on June 19.

For their daring and skillful teamwork in the extraordinary capture, *Guadalcanal* and her escorts shared in a presidential unit citation. The captured submarine proved to be of unbelievable value to American intelligence, and they kept its true fate secret from the Germans until the end of the war.

Thanks to the invaluable training from a little submarine that belonged to an enemy when captured, the antisubmarine prowess of the *Guadalcanal* won the big prize.

Among our submarine sailors, a coxswain was an extraordinary rank. Generally, the rate signified a master small boat handler. On a submarine, a coxswain was a man of many trades, and many hats. More than any other enlisted member of the crew, a coxswain had to be highly knowledgeable in nearly every duty assignment aboard, and expert in some. Our next subject served during World War II and mostly had two principal jobs he frequently preformed.

I had already been in the navy awhile when I left from here [in Hawaii] to attend submarine school. I was originally from Oklahoma, and I went to New London, Connecticut, for the school. The requirements they expected us to meet were very, very strict. You had to be able to withstand certain depths of water—twelve and a half feet, I think it was, for minimum, maximum being one hundred. We took it [preliminary tests] in Hawaii before leaving and then again in New London. Then we had a day and a half with a psychiatrist, and another day or so with a medical doctor. Our training was either on the "Y" or "S" boats for the most part. There was one modern-type submarine, as a diversion from the regular fleet-type boat, called a Marlin. Except for being smaller, it was the same as the fleet-type sub used during the war. The Y and S boats were from World War I and in between [the wars]. The classroom work rounded out our schooling. I went into the school as a seaman first class. When I completed sub school, I went on to a training school and later on I made coxswain. However, I got busted down and made seaman again, then made coxswain again. While in the boats, I had various duties.

Most often I stood lookout watches. At battle stations, generally I was on torpedo reload. It got hot down there, both in temperature and in tension. Some [other] times I was on the bow or stern planes. At battle surface, normally I would be assigned somewhere on a gun crew. I served in three boats—one of them very famous [the *Tunny*].

The *Sculpin*, the *Tunny* and *Bluegill*, in that order. Mostly, in those days, the boats traveled on the surface.

When on the surface, lookout watches were four hours on, eight hours off. Normally, when you got off [watch] you went to your bunk because there wasn't that much to do. The only recreation area you had was the mess hall. We could go in there and play cards or whatever. And there'd usually be food laid out. One good thing about it, if the cook wasn't in the galley [to serve up food], we could go in the refrigerator and get whatever we wanted, just so long as we cleaned up after ourselves.

Lookouts were a very important part of the crew in those days. The radar in the forties was just not that good. Very often, lookouts spotted things *l-o-ong* before radar even thought about it.

We had port, starboard, and after lookouts, in most cases. We would take one sweep of our sector with the glasses [binoculars] we took from the guy we relieved. Then we'd take another sweep when [after] we adjusted them to our own eyes. Then we'd make three sweeps with the glasses and one fast sweep with only our eyes. Then we'd put the glasses back on the horizon and make the next three sweeps. It was a very accurate way of keeping abreast of what was

USS *Bluegill* (SS 242) WWII battle flag patch.

Courtesy of United States Navy

going on. Using lookouts, it took us very little time to go to Battle Stations.

We engaged in very little surface action. On the *Bluegill,* we surfaced a couple of times. It was always a fishing boat or disguised [as a] fishing boat. We would take them out easily, but it would be suicide to surface and try to take on a destroyer. If we got one hole in the pressure hull, we couldn't dive and that's our main defense. In fact, during the whole war, I made only four war patrols. On the *Sculpin,* we were mainly up in the Yellow Sea. In the *Tunny,* we were in and down around the Channel Islands [now the Indonesian Archipelago]. On the *Bluegill,* we were in the East China Sea mostly, up around [the area of] Borneo. One time, we made a landing on Pantagus Island, about 180 miles northeast of Hong Kong.

We had two commandos on board. I was overload man alpha. I took care of their gear and made sure it was all there, then stowed it for them, that sort of thing. The commandos were there to get some prisoners. They got the word off to the officer of naval intelligence (ONI) and we broke out six rubber boats that were to go over. I was in the first boat, but by no means did I participate in any commando activity or anything. We rowed ashore and saw all the soon-to-be prisoners there, and they had a little bit of food and a little ammunition and we gathered up that. They also had a radar tower, which we [the commandos] blew down. This all happened near the end of the war, near the summer of '45. The enemy needed the kind of ships they rarely had [anymore]. It turned out to be one of the more exciting patrols we went on. Our patrols averaged forty-five to fifty days. [What ended them was] we'd usually run out of torpedoes or fuel and we'd have to go back in.

I'd say [to name] the skipper I would consider the best, I'd have to choose between two really great skippers I served under. That would be Harry Prior on the *Bluegill* and John Scott on the *Tunny*. [Bottom line] I think I'd have to go with John Scott. The most exciting patrol I went on had to be the fifth patrol of the *Tunny*—John Scott was skipper then—and was my second war patrol. We had a lot of action on that one. We sank two tankers, and as I remember, two destroyers, a submarine, and we put three torpedoes in to a prime battleship of the *Haitachi* class. That was our greatest patrol and we got the presidential citation for it.

Well, we had sunk the submarine, and Halsey's Third Fleet was making their first air raid on Palau [Island], east of the Philippines. But before that happened, and we'd made that run two times, this task force came on. There was a cruiser, some destroyers, of course, and the battleship. We had only four torpedoes left. We decided we had better do it.

I was doing the attack plot then, so I said, "Okay, you guys run an azimuth and lock on when Sound [sonar] picks them up."

We managed to evade the destroyers. Sound gave us the bearing and we managed to lock on and run the problem through the TDC. It didn't take long—though it seemed like it. With all of those destroyers around, most of the guys were really sweating it, although we were certain they would never detect us. The OOD ordered a spread of three fish, which we put into the battleship, but that didn't sink it. And of course the destroyers were coming in and we had to get down real quick. By the time we got back to the surface again, that battleship had completely disappeared. For some reason, Sonar never picked up any sounds that would indicate the ship breaking up. We never did figure out how they got out of there that soon, yet we saw not a sight of them. We learned from Intelligence later that we had damaged the battleship to the point that the seaworthiness was in question and the crew had to abandon ship.

Now, the captain didn't call me into the wardroom very often, but this time what I learned was that she was hurt so badly that they put her out of commission and she never sailed again during the war. In the meantime, the destroyers were coming after us again, so we had to go deep to get away from [them]. I think they were out to relieve the [troops] on Palau, to reinforce them. Our attack prevented that. To take that further, I don't think I ever had a boring patrol. Truth to tell, the whole experience—the whole war—was exciting to young kids like us. My only regret is that I did not put in thirty years before getting out. I could have easily made master chief.

Now, let me stick out my neck. To my way of thinking, the modern nuclear submarines are *Disneyland* [which he did not mean in a derogatory manner]. Things we never dreamed of have come to be standard equipment and operations aboard the new subs. I love the Islands, but if I [was now] the age when I entered the navy, I'd sure bust my butt to get into a fast attack or a boomer.

5

C. J. GLASSFORD
CHIEF TORPEDOMAN: USN (RET.)

On June 25, 1949, six North Korean infantry divisions, supported by armor and artillery, crossed over the thirty-eighth parallel, thus beginning the Korean War. The same day, the United Nations Security Council adopted a resolution that condemned the North Korean invasion and demanded an immediate withdrawal. Prior to that, the United States Submarine Service was making history of its own.

On April 5, 1950, the USS Guppy II-type submarine *Pickerel* (SS 524) completed a record-breaking underwater transit on snorkel. She departed Hong Kong on March 16 and surfaced off Pearl Harbor on April 5. Under command of LCDR Paul R. Schwartz, USN, the *Pickerel* had snorkeled continuously for twenty-one days, one hour, and traveled 5,194 miles. Remarkably, the submarine suffered only slight damage to the deck structure; they lost both emergency buoys and sustained other underwater destruction during the long journey.

A submarine figures prominently into the Korean conflict only one other time. On August 14, 1950, the *Pickerel* departed Yokosuka, Japan, for a photoreconnaissance mission off the eastern coast of Korea, north of Wonsan. The photographs later served to select a point for submarine-landed commandos to attack North Korean rail lines. These became the only U.S. submarine operations against North Korea during the conflict.

The next year, on February 10, 1951, the USS *Grenadier* (SS 525) was commissioned with CDR Henry G. Reeves Jr. as skipper. It was the last of the navy's World War II submarine building program to be completed. From December 7, 1941, until August 15, 1945, a total of 202 submarines had been built at such boat works as Electric Boat Works, Portsmouth Navy Yard, the Philadelphia Navy Yard, Manitowoc, and other builders. Their construction resembled a generally similar design to the *Gato* (SS 212), *Balao* (SS 285), and *Tench* (SS 417) classes. Nine of the *Balao* class, and thirteen of the *Tench* class were not completed until after the war.

Later the same year, on November 10, the first U.S. submarine of post–World War II design and construction, the *K-1* (SSK-1), was put in commission at the Electric Boat Works yard at Groton, Connecticut. Her first commanding officer was Frank A. Andrews, USN. She was a small 765 ton, hunter-killer submarine, intended to lie in ambush and destroy Soviet subs transiting straits and narrow sea lanes.

Meanwhile, snorkel conversions began in several shipyards due to the successful transit of the *Pickerel*. Such technology put the U.S. Navy far ahead of any potential enemy, and even most of our allies. The snorkel's superiority would remain in the world of submarines until the advent of the nuclear-powered submarines.

There is an old saying: "Join the navy and see the world." That saw is true also for submariners. Many of them went from boat to shore to boat again, visiting all sorts of exotic, as well as mundane, places. From San Diego, California, to New London, Connecticut; Key West, Florida, to San Juan,

Puerto Rico. Or from Norfolk to Rota, Spain, and on into the Mediterranean, to Greece and Italy. Not to omit Pearl Harbor to Brisbane, Australia, Midway Island, Manila, the Philippine Islands, Holy Loch, and many more. Such an individual is C. J. Glassford, who spent his entire military career in the submarine service.

I joined the navy in 1943 in Detroit, Michigan. I've been in and around submarines my entire naval career. After the war was over, I got out, spent almost two years [as a civilian] and found I didn't like civilian life, so I came back into the service. I served on nine diesel boats—great submarines. The boats I served on were the USS *Blower* (SS 325), USS *Catfish* (SS 339), USS *Aspro* (SS 309), and the USS *Pomodon* (SS 486). These boats were all in the San Diego area and from there I went to shore duty at Whidbey [Island], Washington. Ironically, being a submarine torpedoman, my shore duty was as an instructor in crash fire-fighting. I was teaching Airdales [navy slang for aircraft crewmen] how to put out fires in their aircraft.

This was somewhat of a surprise to the commanding officer at inspection when he would look at those dolphins and asked me what I did. When I told him, he couldn't believe it.

When I completed shore duty, I went to New London and caught the USS *Tench* (SS 417). From the *Tench*, I transferred to the USS *Spikefish* (SS 404) and went to Key West, Florida. While I served on the *Spikefish*, I had the privilege and honor of being on the boat in May 1960, when she became the first submarine in history to make ten thousand dives. It's rather an honor; they call it the "Original Ten Grander's Club." I was still aboard when we put the *Spikefish* out of commission. After leaving the *Spikefish*, I went to the USS *Picuda* (SS 382). After leaving the *Picuda*, I went to the USS *Balao* (SS 285) and put her out of commission in Charleston, South Carolina. After leaving the *Balao*, I went back to Key West and rejoined the *Picuda*. We made several cruises, none of which turned out to be very exciting. From there, I put in for shore duty at Great Lakes, Illinois. While I was in Great Lakes, I was also a part-time policeman for a local suburb of Chicago. After my time at Great Lakes, I went back to the West Coast, to San Diego, and went to the USS *Bugara* (SS 331). We went to WesPac and did a couple of patrols off the southern coast of Vietnam. They were routine and dull and, like most submarines over there, we saw no action.

To my regret, I never did make a war patrol during World War II. I was with a unit in Darwin, Australia, that serviced submarines. We'd overhaul torpedoes, and act more or less in the capacity of a relief crew. The one war experience I had on a boat came when I logged on as a passenger, instead of a member of the crew, so I never had the distinction of being a member of a boat in combat.

After World War II, while I was aboard the *Catfish* in 1950, we were in Olongapo [a city outside of Manila]. We had anchored at Subic Bay in the Philippines when the Korean War broke out. Our first duty, naturally, was to make all of our torpedoes ready for shooting. We provisioned and loaded ammunition aboard for the surface guns and set out on a war patrol of sorts in the Lipa Straits, off mainland Japan.

While on this patrol one day, the Russians sent us a message. It read, "*Catfish*, surface and clear the area, or you will be sunk."

Our Captain, C. J. Mendenhall, said, "Well, just ignore that." The next thing we here is rumbling in the distance, which, of course, we knew came from depth-charges dropped by the Russians.

Then the captain said, "Maybe we should surface and clear the area." Which, being sensible, we promptly did. After that, there were no more incidents or close calls. Korea just wasn't a submarine war.

In the Vietnam War, I was on the USS *Bugara* and made recon patrols on her, as I mentioned earlier. The North Vietnamese didn't have much in the way of a navy, but we were chased a few times. I have no idea to this day if they were North Vietnamese or Chinese, but they came damned close. Other than that, it was all just run of the mill.

I have the greatest respect for today's sailors, and although I've never had the opportunity to serve on a nuclear submarine, I'd really like to. I believe they are the greatest deterrent to another major war that we possess. Submarines are getting to a state now that they are so advanced, it is almost unbelievable. I recently got an opportunity to go out on a daily cruise operation and I was amazed, *astounded*, at the things that boat could do. In a way, it's a different navy, yet it's still submarines. Submarine sailors are sort of a rare breed. They choose to spend their careers inside of a steel tube, most of the time under water. These days, they don't see daylight often.

Speaking of our social life, naturally your first concern when you came into port, if you're married and have a wife and children, was to see your family. The next thing, especially on the old diesel boats because of the permeation of diesel fuel, coffee, body sweat, a few miscellaneous items—like our dirty laundry—had to be taken care of. The first thing you want to do is wash your clothes and take a shower. A submarine shower used to consist from wrist down and neck up, because your water supply was *very* limited. The next thing, for the single guys, was to hit the bars in San Diego or some other liberty port. The beer flowed freely and there was a lot of tension to release. I was a torpedoman and proud of it. People laugh about torpedomen, but we had an old saying: "We were done with all our work and ready to take a nap by the time everyone else got started."

Although there were numerous incidents with the Russians after the war, even in the old diesel boats, most have never been revealed, and I don't feel at liberty to discuss them. Now, when it comes to the nuclear boats, the sailors on them can't say *anything* about operations they are involved in because that's all classified. Even we, as well as them, received medals and awards for things and never learned about what they represented. The citations that went with them never showed a latitude or longitude.

The country does owe a tribute to the people who build our submarines. If you look at the history books, as far as the losses of our U.S. submarines, they are very, very low compared to those of other nations. The safety factors that are incorporated into the building of our submarines for the safety of the crew are much desired. Our hats are off to the men of Electric Boat Works [EB] and all the other shipbuilders in the United States.

In 1966, I made my twilight cruise and retired to civilian life in Poway, California, with my wife of fifty years. Now, I have been married for fifty-nine years, I'm the father of eight children, and I have thirteen grandchildren and six great-grandchildren. Otherwise, I'm kicking back and enjoying life.

I'm very active in submarine affairs, involved in anything that happens on the base.

I've been on the Veterans' Council of San Diego County and had the good fortune of receiving a nomination for, and becoming, Veteran of the Year for the City of San Diego.

We remain a close-knit organization and most of us [vets] know each other by name. It's very seldom that, if you're walking down the street wearing a hat that signifies submarines, some stranger doesn't say, "Hey, I was on that boat," or, "Did you know so-and-so?"

It's a very tight group. We depended upon one another for our life, that's why we're so proud. When you check aboard a submarine, they don't just *issue* you a set of dolphins. You *earn* 'em. Once you've earned that set of dolphins, you know how to take over every man's job. That's why it's [the submarine service] so respected. I have to say, though, that I should have gone for thirty instead of getting out at twenty years. The way it is, I missed out on the nuclear boats. I really regret that.

6

GERALD "JERRY" DRUM
ENGINEMAN FIRST CLASS,
USN, LATER, LIEUTENANT, USN (RET.)

The addition of nuclear-powered vessels to the navy's arsenal changed the submarine service forever. That technological advance came close to fruition on June 25, 1953, when the STR Mark I—prototype reactor for the submarine *Nautilus* (SSN 571)—reached full power at the navy's test facility at Arco, Idaho. The reactor had previously achieved sustained critical mass on March 30, 1953. In June, the first full-power run lasted ninety-six hours, which was the equivalent of the submarine making a submerged run of 2,500 miles (across the Atlantic). In July of that year, the *Tunny* successfully launched the first Regulus missile fired from a submarine.

Albacore (AGSS 569), a U.S. research submarine, was commissioned on December 6, 1953. It was a 1,242-ton diesel-electric boat, the first modern submarine with a "tear drop" hull design. She served until 1972, when she was decommissioned on December 9, as an underwater test platform. Her first commanding officer was LCDR Kenneth C. Gummerson, USN. A high-speed vessel, she reached speeds above thirty-five knots several times during her career. Her exact top speed—which remains classified—would not be outdone by any U.S., or any other nation's submarine at any time prior to 1998.

Negative feedback invaded the submarine world immediately when, on January 3, 1954, the *New York Times* ran an article quoting an unnamed "institutional" representative of the navy saying the *Nautilus* (SSN 571), which was being outfitted at the Electric Boat Works, would remain a test vehicle. "I doubt that she will ever fire a shot in anger," the disdainful naval officer remarked in the article. Ironically, this arrogant declaration proved to be true until the time of the first Gulf War. The awesome power of our nuclear fleet kept the peace for thirty-six years. Other navy "experts" claimed that the *Nautilus* was "too big" and far "too unmaneuverable" to perform effectively as a frontline combat vessel. That, of course, was before she went under the Arctic ice and surfaced at the North Pole, then transited to the Bering Sea.

At last, ready to enter the water at the Electric Boat Yard in Groton, Connecticut, our first nuclear submarine—the USS *Nautilus*—was christened by Mrs. Mamie Eisenhower, wife of the president. In addition, in May 1954, the Regulus missile was certified as operational on board the USS *Tunny* (SSG 282) while serving with the Atlantic Fleet.

More bad news came on September 4, in the form of an announcement by the Navy Office of Information regarding the size of the Soviet Union's navy. They were known to have 350 submarines, 13 cruisers, and 125 destroyers. Our navy stated that, "the USSR could supplant the United States as the preeminent naval power in ten years, at their present rate of expansion." A Soviet representative was also quoted as declaring that the United States' claims of Soviet strength were exaggerated and that it was simply an alarmist effort "to get larger appropriations for the U.S. Navy." Our mainstream media—of questionable loyalty even then—immediately seized upon this declaration and embellished it.

By no coincidence, the world's first nuclear-propelled submarine was put into commission at New London, Connecticut, on September 30. Her first commanding officer was CDR Eugene P. Wilkensen, USN. Sixteen days later, the Chief of Naval Operations, Admiral Robert Carney, USN, announced that the number of nuclear-capable shipyards would be expanded, starting with the Mare Island Naval Shipyard in Vallejo, California. In his announcement, Carney stated, "the yard [*Mare Island*] should prepare for a significant role in the atomic age program."

His prediction came close to fruition when, on December 30, the power plant of the *Nautilus* was fired up for the first time. On January 3, 1955, the *Nautilus* departed from New London. On board was Rear Admiral Hiram G. Rickover, USN. Although a minor difficulty developed in the starboard reduction gear, it was soon corrected. Commander Wilkinson had the signal sent: "Under way on nuclear power." Their sea trials took them through Long Island Sound and out into the Atlantic.

Surprisingly, a large number of submariners did not come from families with a strong naval service tradition. Some, in fact, were the first to enter any military service. With the success of the *Nautilus* and the advent of nuclear-powered submarines, a whole new era opened with, seemingly, no upper limits. Such is the case with Jerry Drum, who had family that served in the Civil War and two uncles who served in the navy in WWII aboard surface ships. He took his basic submarine training and, later, nuclear power school in New London, Connecticut. As a nuclear sailor, he had the opportunity to contribute to the breaking of records, and to extensive engagements in coastal surveys of enemy, or potential enemy, countries. He also participated in surveillance missions of Soviet naval elements.

After joining the Navy in 1948, and completing Basic Training, I was first rated as an engineman and assigned to a boat pool in

Inchon [South Korea], where we did faishon [engine refitting] operations. Therefore, when I attended Basic Submarine School at New London Naval Base in Connecticut, they knew that I knew engines and I never went to an engineman's school. For me it was all "hands-on" training when I went to sub school. I had a rating as a fireman at the time, a sort of engine tender. It was only a short course, as I recall, about ten weeks. It did include a lot of classroom work, reading, and tests, also a couple of trips out on a school boat to get some hands-on experience and to prove that we knew how to perform our expected duties. Later, I also attended Nuclear Power School in New London. My only other school was Conversion School at Treasure Island, in San Francisco Bay.

My first homeport was in San Diego, where we tied up next to the *Sperry* and the *Narius*, tied downtown in the stream. One thing you never got away from was the smell that went with both the old diesel boats, and the snorkel boats as well. In San Diego, we had what you'd call locker clubs. We kept our civilian clothes there because we could not take them aboard. When we'd get in port, first thing we'd do was head for our locker club, get a good shower and clean up, then get dressed in civvies and go out. But, in truth, you could never get rid of the odor.

One day I was on a bus after doing this and this woman sitting next to me said, "You're a submarine sailor, aren't you?"

I answered, "Yes, ma'am. How'd you know?"

She went on, "My husband rode them during the war and I'll never forget the smell."

I went back there years later on different subs, too. I was married by then and my wife went with me to new stations on several occasions. We had three children, two boys and a girl. The first boat I went to when I returned to the submarine service was the *Segundo*

(SS 398). I picked it up in San Diego in early 1952. Right away, we went to Hunter's Point Naval Ship Yard and the *Segundo* converted from a fleet boat to a snorkel boat. In those days we were sent to snorkel school, which was up at Mare Island [San Francisco Bay, California], where they taught us how to snorkel.

In later years, I served on the *Bugara,* which was in Pearl Harbor. My brother was on it, so we arranged a swap so we could be on the boat together. Then, I went to shore duty in Hutchinson [Kansas Naval Air Station]. This is something unusual for a submariner. Then I went to the *Sea Leopard* in Norfolk, Virginia. I was only on there six months and they shipped me off to electronic tech [ET] conversion school because all of the ETs and fire control techs were getting out of the navy, and they wanted upper [grade] petty officers, second class and above to convert over. I went off to the school and from there to the *Volador*. The boat was then undergoing an overhaul in San Francisco. I was on the *Volador* for almost four years. It was home-ported in San Diego, also. That was the first boat I was on when we made some major WesPac runs.

Speaking of life aboard a sub, some of the things we had to put up with weren't all that nice. I mentioned the diesel fumes problem. Then there was the odor of sweat and human bodies. Worse, God help us, when we had ham and beans served. Even a lot worse came from the sanitary tanks where all the human effluent went. They were contained, yet when they got full, we had to blow them with air. If you were submerged and you blew them, you vented it *inboard*. That wasn't very pleasant, especially if it was around mealtime. On the surface, it was easy. There, we could vent overboard and get rid of the waste. Another thing that did not change was the size of the boats. When the production models of snorkel subs came out, the *Segundo* was exactly the same size as the existing fleet boats, 312 feet long. They later added a stubby

USS *Salmon*
(SS 182),
March 1943.

Courtesy of United

States Navy

step sail, which was high enough in the stokes that it was a step down to where the officer of the deck was, only a step up from the main deck. The beam was also the same as on old diesel boats. Some of them, like the *Connie* and the *Perch*, converted to where they could carry troops and missiles; they [the missiles] were more like an airplane [based on the German V-1 rocket]. They extended the length on some of those, and then they had SSRs, like the *Salmon*, where they put an extra length in there that amounted essentially to a radar control center. They could pick up a missile after launch and guide it from there.

When it comes to the critical duties of a submarine crew, I would think that the most important were the control room people who were on the hydraulic manifold—which is normally the chief of the watch—who would order them [the control room crew] to do whatever, along with the diving officer. Such as close the vents and have the floods open, and the person on the air manifold would put the air into the tanks. All of those in the control room were key people, as were the officers and the quartermaster [QM] up in the conning tower, all of who kept track of where you were and what else was around you. In the old boats, they also ran the TDC from there. That was quite a thing in itself.

In the early days before the TDC, they used to have a thing called an "Is-Was." It was like a huge slip stick [slide-rule] and they could figure your angle. The QM would run intercept courses and whatever, in order to get a good torpedo shot. When the data computers came out, they were huge, with vacuum tubes, bulbs, and such, and had three sections: a section that was an angle-solving section, a position-keeping section, and a torpedo track determination section. We had people on board who would get periscope sightings, angle on the bow and such, and then they could track and get the speeds with the plotting parties that they had. They made a big difference in accuracy.

The plotting party had a table set up inside the wardroom so, when the COB or duty officer yelled "Battle stations," those involved would go in there and start figuring courses and speeds so we could get good angles and intercepts. Like, if you had to take off fast and run at night on the surface in order to catch them [enemy targets]. That's what you'd do in World War II.

Most of the officers were excellent. The greatest skipper I ever served under was Admiral R. L. J. Long. He was my skipper on the *Sea Leopard* and the *Patrick Henry* (SS 599). While on the *Sea Leopard*, Admiral Long was a lieutenant commander and I was a second class engineman, but he didn't know me too much because I didn't get into trouble and, if you're not a troublemaker, sometimes the skipper doesn't really remember you. Although when I was out in Idaho at the nuclear power training unit in Arco to be taught to be a nuclear reactor operator, he [R. L. J. Long] came through out there and he was the prospective commanding officer of the *Patrick Henry*.

He recognized me and asked me what ship I was going to when I left and I said, "The *Scamp*, the SS 588, at Mare Island."

Then he said, "No, you're not, Drum. You're going to the *Patrick Henry*."

So that's where I went and I served with him on there for about three years. I made chief on the *Henry*, too. From there, he recommended me for a commission, which I received while on the *Henry*.

I missed World War II and Korea [as a submariner] so I never went on a war patrol as you normally think of them. I was on surface ships during the Korean times and we did the invasion at Inchon. That was hairy enough. The reason I got into submarines was that the boat crew we had was home-ported out of Sasebo, Japan, and we had a chief engineman in there, his name was Dallas, he had been a submariner during World War II and a prisoner of war of the Japanese. He was kind of my mentor.

He told me several times, "The thing you should do is to go aboard submarines. You'll love it."

That's when I put in for submarines. Even then, my favorite liberty port was Yokosuka or Sasebo, Japan, and remained so when I was in submarines. I never made it to Taiwan or Bangkok. Hong Kong was a good liberty port, too. Of course, when we were out of Charleston, we had Dunoon, Scotland. We could go to Dunoon, get the ferry, and go across to Glasgow.

I did make four Cold War patrols in the Pacific and made two deterrent fast boat missile [FBM] patrols [above] the Arctic Circle. Some of the patrols in the Far East were for intelligence gathering. We had some intelligence types along who did the real work. However, mostly they were about keeping an eye out on what was happening in other people's countries. Normally, we'd go out on one of those and it would last for thirty to forty-five days. One time we were on one that lasted over sixty days. Well, we started running out of chow in a hurry. What's worse is, when the good chow is gone, you start gettin' the cans and after the canned stuff is gone, you start getting a lot of tuna and cold sandwiches. Yet, if you have a good cook aboard and a lot of flour, you've got it made.

During these patrols, for the most part, everyone remained pretty laid-back. On a normal day, we would stand our watches, eat, do something for recreation and sleep. If something *would* happen, it got very tense. The one thing that we were all afraid of big-time was fire. If you are submerged and have a fire on a submarine, you don't have any good air to breathe and it gets tough—especially on a nuke sub, which rarely surfaces, or if you have somebody above you [enemy craft] that you don't want to know that you're there. You still have to come up high enough to get the snorkel going and draw some air into the boat, get some ventilation, control the fire, and put it out. Our fire-fighting apparatus was limited. About the only thing we had in those days were a few CO_2 extinguishers and, of course, a pressurized piping system that we could use—the Trent System. You could pressurize it and hook up to that. Other than that, there weren't a heck of a lot of ways to fight a fire. Flooding is probably the next biggest thing. We thought about these situations a lot every time we went out on patrol.

I'd say that the most boring patrols were when we went out on FBM patrols where you would get into a routine. They were all sixty-day patrols. You'd go out and cruise around, with nothing happening, then turn around and come in and do a turnover [exchange crews, i.e., Blue and Goldcrews]. Then the other crew would take it out. When we'd go out on one of these, it was too easy to fall into a routine.

Other than the drills, it was always the same thing, day in and day out. We'd have a lot of time to play cards, to play Acey-Deucey, talk, and write letters. We even had a small gymnasium in the missile compartment where you could keep fit. Nevertheless, it was a good life. I really enjoyed it.

The one combat drill that scared me the most, we used to have a thing they called "Snap Shot."

The sonar men—if they could hear what they thought was another submarine with the doors on the torpedo tubes for somebody to shoot us, they would holler, "Snap shot!", which meant that a couple of torpedomen had to get a tube set up and ready to shoot that torpedo back at the bad guys. That way if they got you, you would get them in return.

The *Patrick Henry* was the first FBM to go into Scotland. Prior to that, while I was aboard the *Patrick Henry*, we had an unusual event happen. We were down at Cape Canaveral doing the missile tests. We were trying to prove the system out because it was getting ready to deploy. We made what was supposed to be a routine firing and one of the birds we shot malfunctioned. While we watched, it went up, turned, and came back down and hit us just aft of the sail. It struck on one of the [launch] tubes and broke apart. It did some minor damage, which we repaired on site. Admiral Burke told Admiral Rayborn to have four missiles prepared so we could go out and do a "wide ocean" test to prove that the missiles were all right. In those days, getting the missiles ready for the *Washington* and the *Henry* to deploy, there was a big problem. There weren't many spare missiles around.

Admiral Rayborn said, "I don't have any."

Admiral Burke replied, "Well, you get 'em, because we're going to do this test." We stayed at the Cape—in those days, it was Canaveral

Admiral Arleigh Burke in 1960.
Courtesy of United States Navy

instead of Kennedy. So we loaded up the birds, went out, and did a wide ocean shot. It proved out the system. When fully loaded, we carried sixteen missiles with sixteen tubes—no refills. Anyway, when we got a full complement of missiles we put to sea and headed for Scotland.

One time we were going into Holy Loch after a patrol and everyone was looking forward to going home.

Suddenly the sonarman sang out, "Snap shot! Snap shot! This is not a drill."

We all thought it was the real thing and we were scared. However, it ended up that it wasn't a big threat so it worked out fine.

We were lucky, I guess. We never had any close encounters with the Russians. Most often, they never made contact with us. When their sonar did, they weren't able to close to lock on and fire. I don't know of any time when Chinese submarines discovered us. The same goes for surface ships. Just lucky. We received no ramming, no depth-charge attacks.

The only war shot I was present for was on our way to WesPac one time. We fired on this island, and the missile ran sweet and straight and hit where we aimed it. It exploded as it should and that was it. Unlike the old boats, the nuclear subs do not carry any surface gunnery. We had Thompson sub-machine guns and rifles, but there was no need for us to have a five-inch thirty-eight or a twenty-millimeter. For sinking sampans and other small craft, there were enough aircraft those days with enough range to take care of that. All we had a need or a use for were missiles and torpedoes.

When it came to our patrol destinations, like in the old diesel boats, most of the crew had no idea where we headed or where we were when we got there. When we went on patrols on the Polaris boats we knew we were going to be in the Arctic Circle. That's all we knew. We had no idea how close we came to Russia, our enemy at that time. We literally knew nothing. I have no idea if I was ever under the Arctic ice. Nobody ever did. If you were, say, a reactor technician and you went and asked the quartermaster where the boat was, he wouldn't tell you. We were a single steel boat and on our own. But I do know I am a member of the Arctic Circle Yacht Club. That's what the crews and everyone else used to call the FBMs, those that went up into that area, anyway.

I made chief on the *Patrick Henry* and had my chief's initiation at sea. The only thing I am disappointed about is that I'm not a duly-initiated shellback. I never crossed the equator during all my naval service. I miss it, too. Everybody tells me how great it was to go down to Australia.

I believe this about the modern submarine force: I think the nuclear submarine navy today has some of the best-trained, honest young men that there are. The officers are outstanding. You know, a lot of the trouble we had in what I call the old submarine force was drinking. You know, you'd drink when you went on liberty, you'd have beer ball games, and many excuses to drink. And drinking can cause a lot of other problems. It could lead to dissention among the crew, car accidents, and everything else. These people today, if they go somewhere and they're going to have some [drinks], they have a duty driver and a van and they'll haul them places so there's not a lot of these chances of people getting in big trouble or whatever. However, the majority of them today . . . I don't think they indulge too much in the drinking aspect of it. A lot of them take college courses to improve themselves, and they have better things to do other than to go out and indulge in the drinks.

Sometimes, crew problems extended beyond the norm. We had a gent who came aboard when I was supply officer on the *Segundo*. He was my storekeeper. He was an ex-army man, and had had a hard time. For some reason, he tripped out and raised some hell. We had to take him off in a straitjacket. Actually, he was the only one we had any problems with—at least when I was part of the crew. However, I can say one thing. When it comes to colorful shipmates, one who always comes to mind is a gent named Cy Manning. He retired from the Navy after forty [!] years.

In one story about his retirement, which he related later on, he went home and told his mother and she said, "I knew you could never hold a job." This was even though he had worked his way through the ranks! He was then a warrant officer and he made JG [lieutenant, junior grade], and he retired as a commander. He was skipper of one of the ammunition ships, the *Pyro*. He was the DivCom [division commander] for a mine sweeping group. He was a superb people person. Whenever they had a problem, they'd call him in to unofficially solve a ship's problems.

Another real character was Stan Nicholls*; he came up through the ranks. He was the first yeoman to make master chief, and Manning was the first one to make radioman master chief. Stan never said a bad word about anybody and he would go out of his way to help you. He was the kind of person everyone would like for a shipmate. [He was] one nice person.

For the most part, we had a lot of off-duty activities with which to release pressures. We had acey-deucey tournaments and pinochle tournaments. Many people were poker players. I was one of them. We had a group who played nonstop. Sometimes we would go a long time without sleep after being at the poker table. We had movies. We had one every evening. They'd rig them in the mess hall or the forward torpedo room. The officers had their own movie projector in the wardroom. We also had a stationary bicycle and a treadmill. There may have been some dumbbells there, but I didn't use them. I don't recall any free weights at all. I learned that one of the other FBMs, same class as the *Henry*, had a piano aboard.

One of our off-duty activities was Field Day. We'd be assigned a clean-up or repair activity by the COB and we got at it. Then we also had Captain's Inspections. In addition, those kept the boat clean and squared away. The galley and mess deck area were always sparkling clean. There was a big difference between the mess deck on an old diesel boat and the nukes. The old boats didn't have much space, so we'd eat in three settings. First call would be for the oncoming watch.

*See pp. 27–52 for account of LCDR Stanley Nicholls.

They'd line up, start going through the line, and as soon as they finished, people would be lining up to follow them, and you'd just go until everyone had eaten. We had three meals a day, plus what we called "by-grats," when the cooks put out sandwich making materials and whatever.

On the *Segundo*, I had one cook who was a good friend of mine. He was a baker and he would bake some of the best pastries, which went out to the mid-rats and then what was left we'd eat for breakfast. Altogether, the food was outstanding. It was excellent on every boat I was ever on. There was no exception to that, other than the bigger the boat, the more and varied stuff you could carry. Getting the best stuff—the filet mignon and lobsters—depended on how well the cook could work the books. If they were familiar with Volume 8 of the supply manual (that's what it was when I was supply officer) they'd say, "Hey, we can take this stuff here and we can throw it away because it is spoiled and rotten and write it off." A little "book making," and if they knew how to do it and stay out of trouble, everyone could eat real good—better [than many]. On the *Henry,* we had an ice cream machine and a Coke machine. There was still nowhere you could go to buy candy bars and stuff like that, but the soda machine and ice cream made up for that. Other aspects of life aboard included the fact that some of the crew still bunked out on top of the torpedoes.

A big difference between the old diesel boats and the nukes is how they are steered. Boats like the *Bowfin* had a huge wheel on them, and that was for a good reason. If we ever had to switch to hand power, it's tough and we'd need the big wheel to get a grip on to control the direction of the dive. When we dove on the old boats, we had two lookouts on the bridge, plus the officer of the deck. The OOD would come down and take over as diving officer, and the two lookouts—one could take the stern planes and one the bow planes.

They'd have to rig the bow planes out so when the lookout came down and hit a lever and they'd rig out, and he's the one who would control the depth, and the guy on the stern plain would control the angle [of descent]. It was up to the diving officer to determine the trim of the ship. He had to determine whether he had to pump water from fore to aft or vice versa, blow water or take water on, in order to get down. What set the gradient was this pumping back and forth until the diving officer could see that it all agreed with the set of bow and stern planes. It was quite a trick. Of course, in those days, too, when we snorkeled, we wanted to keep the depth to where we didn't have too much pipe [snorkel induction pipe] sticking up out of the water because it made a radar target.

We had a skipper who [when he] set the depth, he'd say, "The depth I want you to be is where you can hear it cycle." What that meant was the snorkel device had an electrode on it so that when it got wet, it would shut the head valve. If that head valve shut when we had two diesels running back there, it kind of pulled suction on you so that when it released, it would pop your ears.

However, he insisted, "That's where I want to be. Right where I can hear that head valve cycling."

Unfortunately, in a rough sea it's kinda tough when you're rockin' and rollin', to try to maintain just the proper depth. If we had too much pipe showing, we made a target of ourselves. If you got too much vacuum, it automatically shut the engines down. I was in one diesel boat that was a snorkeler and we were in doing a little snooping [from his hesitancy to say where, it can be surmised that the "bad guys" spoke Russian] and we flooded out the four main motors. Worse, there was an incoming tide. When you have a zero ground, it's somewhat hard to put some juice to an engine. We were trying to get at least one of them up, and they were splashing fresh water on it and got it up. We finally got out to where we felt comfortable to proceed out of there. So we headed back to Japan, had the motors worked over, and we all agreed that was one scary deal.

Another thing I had some fun with started on Christmas Eve of 1967. At the time, I lived in navy housing. I was the division engineer for Submarine Division 71, and we had the *Barb, Plunger, Flasher,* and *Guardfish* as the four boats in the division. The *Guardfish* was coming back off a spec op [special operation] and we knew she was due in on Christmas Eve.

I'd sat there [at home] and had a few, and the phone rang, and it was my division commander and he said, "Get your uniform and come in."

And I said, "What for?"

To which he said, "Get your uniform on and come in."

So I went in and asked, "What's the problem?"

He said, "It's your job to go out on the pier there at sub base and tell all of those dependants out there that the *Guardfish* isn't comin' in tonight. She's gone aground just outside of Pearl Harbor."

After telling the *Guardfish* crew's families, I spent a few days with the squadron engineers, and they had to send some salvage ships. Admiral Rickover was not a happy person. Luckily, the main seawater section—although it had many chunks of coral in it—was still giving water enough to keep the reactor cooled down. So that, too, turned out not to be a big problem. What we later learned was one of the navigational lights had the same flash as 1-PH [One-Papa-Hotel, the outer channel marker buoy], and in the confusion of coming in and in getting rigged for surface and everything, they got off onto that other light and ran aground. It did quite a bit of damage to the bottom of the ship, not quite as bad as the *San Francisco* that, later, got its bow stove in.

Admiral Hyman George Rickover.
Courtesy of United States Navy

On the nuke boats, that's not a problem. As far as steering goes on the nuke boats we had steering controls like the yoke on an airplane, so you can turn all of your controls over to one person. He can control the depth of the boat and the course. By just throwing a few switches around you can change the whole thing over.

On the *Patrick Henry*, we had a specific living quarters that was in the midships compartment. In the early days, they had a huge gyro in there and we used to call it "the Monster." It was supposed to stabilize the ship, fore and aft, side to side. Later, when they took it off, we had nice sleeping arrangements on there [the *Henry*]. The chiefs had a good one. They had some up in the forward torpedo room, so there was still some sleeping around the tubes. However, times change and the submarines do also.

All of the old OS submarines that had sixteen missile tubes are gone now. They're all chopped up and gone away. They were the

"Forty-four for Freedom" Fleet subs. They've been replaced by the Trident-class submarines and they have twenty-four missile tubes. Those are magnificent machines. My guess is they can fire a salvo of missiles from a depth of one hundred feet. I was a reactor operator and was more interested in providing power to the boat than in what they were doing in missile country. Let me tell you that the reactor school is a surprisingly stringent school to begin with. What you'd have to learn not to do is bring your control rods out too fast if you're going to heat up because you get metal fatigue, so you have gradient curves you have to go by, and head-up rates to follow to get up your water and pressure. Once you're up and operating, then you have standards you have to adhere to. Like pull the rods out a little farther, or leave them where they are. That is all done with electric switches.

I give a lot of credit to Admiral Rickover. His program was excellent. We never had a major problem with any of our reactors. Some of the civilian reactors had problems, but the navy was fortunate and he [Rickover] kept his thumb right on everybody, too. I can't wait to see what comes next.

Let me get in a good word here about the submarine service in general and its veterans. The submarine service is one of these organizations where the camaraderie is really high. On active duty or not, we stick up for other submariners. We have an organization, the United States Submarine Veterans, Incorporated, with almost twelve thousand members. To join that, you have to be entitled to wear either set of dolphins: silver [enlisted] or gold [commissioned]. You can be retired, active duty, whatever. Nevertheless, with these local chapters, all the individual ships also have their reunions, and they normally schedule them with the national reunion we have. We've held them in all sorts of places.

In 2006, we're going to have a cruise to Alaska. We're trying to get the whole ship. And then we're going on to Fort Worth, Texas. Of the ships we have, the *Patrick Henry* has a reunion every five years, which is too long. We've lost many dear friends since the last one, including the two skippers we had on there, Sheer and Long.

Now, for the *Segundo*, we have a reunion every year and, of course, it includes guys from the time of the ship's commissioning until it went out and was torpedoed and sunk. She was one of these things we had to give up when the nukes came in.

They came around and said, "Instead of salvaging that thing, we can use it for target practice." So that's what they did. Now it's gone. Yet, it's nice to get with the old cronies and talk about the good time we had and the bad times.

In addition to the *Bowfin*, the museum out here [*Bowfin* Submarine Museum, Pearl Harbor, Oahu, Hawaii], has artifacts from the *Swordfish*. They have the diving stand from the *Swordfish* and a section from the missile control center, and they have a section of the ballast control panel in there. The sail for the old *Perch*, which was one of the more famous boats of World War II—they have it down at the old sub base in Pearl. The conning tower is out here [at the museum] on display, so you can go into it and look at the 'scopes, see where the helm was, which gives you a good feeling. The conning tower sat right on top of the control room. It was a self-contained unit and that's where they looked through the 'scopes, and the plotting

USS *Swordfish* (SS 579).
Courtesy of United States Navy

party was there, the TDC, the helm was up there and the radar so you could make all of your approaches from up there. If something happened, you could seal it off and not lose the boat, though you'd lose the people who were up there. I think this tour of the museum is a good place to stop. I never regretted for an instant that I had chosen to be a submariner. All of us old guys feel that way.

7

ROBERT A. BROWN
MASTER CHIEF TORPEDOMAN, USN (RET.)

Experimentation continued on torpedoes into the 1950s. Eventually the navy ordnance department developed the MK-48. Still considered the *sine qua non* of torpedoes, the Mark 48 soon proved excellent in all instances where fired. They run, as torpedomen say, "hot, straight and normal." Powered by an improved propulsion system, their gyros prevent not only deviations from the set bearing, but also porpoising, or vertical deviation that could broach a torpedo or send it down under the target. Although there has yet to be an MK-48 fired in anger, they continue to perform perfectly. Torpedomen found them to be excellent and never tire of extolling their virtues. In the following account, we cover this situation through the eyes of a master chief torpedoman.

Meanwhile, advances in submarine activity continued in other areas. On May 29, 1955, the navy added a suffix to ship designations to denote nuclear propulsion. Thus, nuclear-propelled missile submarines then obtained the designation of SSG(N). The next year, the navy dropped the parentheses for the sake of simplicity. We were not alone in making progress in submarine armament and warfare.

On September19, 1955, the Soviet Navy launched the first ballistic missile from a surfaced submarine when a Soviet Zulu IV–class submarine fired an SS-1 ballistic missile. The test was successful. This would become significant when, four and a half years later, the United States launched the first Polaris missile. The disturbing thing to our intelligence services and the navy brass was that the SS-1B was a liquid-propellant, nuclear-capable missile with a range around eighty miles. After this success, each Zulu-class sub carried two missiles, which were mounted in the sail. They were then elevated before firing.

On the home front, the only midget submarine built for the U.S. Navy went in service on October 10, 1955. The X-1 weighed twenty-nine tons, a design intended to operate in coastal waters only. Built by Fairchild Engine and Aircraft Corporation, its primary function was to assist in the development of harbor defense procedures. Her first CO was LT. Kevin Hanion, USN. The X-1 enjoyed service in several U.S. overseas ports, as well as in the United States.

November 1955 saw the establishment of the National Ballistic Missile program, created by Secretary of Defense Charles E. Wilson. It was a joint project of the army and navy for the development of Intermediate Range Ballistic Missiles (IRBMs). The navy chose to concentrate on the Jupiter liquid-propellant missile as a potential fleet ballistic missile (FBM). Naturally, submarines received serious thought as launch platforms. Their strategic advantage—covert approach to within firing range of an enemy installation or military harbor—could not be overlooked, even by an openly pro-surface Naval Planning Board.

The era of the missile submarine came closer on the second of December that same year when the Chief of Naval Operations, Admiral Arleigh Burke, announced his program for the development of the Polaris missile. This appeared in a memorandum to his staff. It was then, *and for the future of submarine warfare,* a remarkable revelation. It read as follows:

"If Rear Admiral Rayborn runs into any difficulty with which I can help, I will want to know about it at once, along with his recommended course of action for me to take. If more money is needed, we will get it. If he needs more people, those people will be ordered in. If there is anything that slows this project up beyond the capacity of the Navy Department, we will immediately take it to the highest level and not work our way up [the chain of command] for several days. In taking this type of action, we must be reasonably sure we are right and at least know the possible consequences of being wrong, because we will be disrupting many other programs in order to make achievement in this one, if we are not careful. That is all right if we really make an achievement." Two days later, Admiral William F. Rayborn received appointment to head the Navy's Special Projects Office (ordered into being by Admiral Burke in October 1955).

By January 3, 1956, the nuclear age made a giant leap forward. Predictably, our navy's first nuclear power school opened at the submarine base at New London, Connecticut. Then, on March 20, the Ballistic Missile Committee of the Office of the Secretary of Defense gave approval to establish a navy program for solid-propellant motors, slated for use in ship-based ballistic missiles. This little-publicized event led directly to the development of the Polaris missile.

Further progress came on April 14, when the *Sailfish* (SSR 572) was put into commission. It was a radar picket submarine, and the first SSR of new construction—the earlier versions of this submarine were conversions of WWII fleet boats. Her first CO was a very pleased LCDR Stanley R. McCord, USN.

May 29 saw the first flight of the navy's Regulus II land-attack missile. This definitive missile, scheduled to be operational in 1960 at an as then unspecified date, led our way for a decade. The Regulus II was a turbojet-powered missile, which could reach almost Mach 2, with a maximum range near one thousand miles at lower speeds. The design incorporated the ability to carry a nuclear warhead.

On June 18, in response to a direct request from CNO Arleigh Burke, the think tank–like Committee on Undersea Warfare came into being at the National Academy of Science. It commenced a three-month, antisubmarine warfare study. Sixty men and women were involved in the project—called Nobka—at Woods Hole, Massachusetts. The brainstorming project, organized by Columbus Iselin, produced several submarine advances, while their deliberations greatly advanced the Polaris missile system. One-third of those involved were from the officer corps of the navy and civilian experts, two-thirds from the scientific community and from industry, primarily ship-building.

Although the "fly-boys" appeared to have seized the navy early in 1956—their plans centered on the new, modern aircraft carriers—progress continued near the end of 1956 with the assignment of Rear Admiral William F. (Red) Rayborn, of the Special Projects Office, the responsibility to develop the Polaris missile system, including the missile submarines.

Torpedomen are a special breed of submarine sailor. Over the ages, since WWI, there has been a plethora of jokes about their profession—some amusing and colorful, others insulting. Even the modern nukes carry torpedoes, in some cases the nuclear version of the MK-48. Danger from compartment flooding due to damaged outer tube doors was a constant. However, as related by others, the greatest fear for torpedomen was fire. An electric or chemical fire could prove almost instantly fatal and, like all the crew, the denizens of the torpedo rooms learned how to respond instantly. The following account takes us from the diesel boats to the nuclear navy.

I had attended Tiffin High School in Tiffin, Iowa. It's a little town about seven miles outside of Rapid City, Iowa. The population was

150 people in those days. I was in one of the largest classes graduating; we had thirteen people my year. The grade school I attended my first eight years was a one-room schoolhouse, with all eight grades taught at the same time. It was in Coreville, Iowa, which was also just about seven miles from Rapid City. We had one teacher and she rode a little interurban train, a local railroad there. That poor lady would have to get off at the train station and walk about three hundred yards through snowbanks and everything. First thing, she'd have to fire up the furnace. Either my dad or my uncle would go down on Sunday evenings and light the fire so we'd be at least halfway warm on Monday morning in the schoolhouse.

They expected one teacher to teach all eight grades. The main way she did it was that, naturally, when you got older, in the sixth, seventh, or eighth grades, you were qualified to teach the little tots math, reading, things like that. Not any of the graduates from that little country school had any problem going into high school. From my high school, about half of the graduates went on to college and never had any trouble with the entrance exams or anything. Parents *cared* in them [sic] days. We went to school at eight in the morning and got up at four o'clock to get ready. We got out at four in the afternoon, and had to go home and do chores. To and from school for me was a mile. We walked whether there were snowdrifts or rain, but we *went* to school.

When we got home, we had chores to do; after we got them done we studied. In those days, there was no television and such things. My folks had a radio but the only time that was on, generally, it was when the area had electricity. What we had was a battery radio, and the only thing we'd use that radio for was when Joe Lewis was fighting. Or on Sunday night, when we had *Fibber McGee and Molly* and a couple of other shows. Life was rough in rural Iowa in those days. Luckily, my dad agreed with my wish to join the navy.

I went into the Navy in 1953, right out of high school. First, I went to boot camp and learned basic seamanship. Near the end of the school, I requested submarine duty. The reason for that was, when I was a kid, my father had a friend who was a submariner. All he talked about was submarines. However, at that time, in 1953, they didn't need any submariners; so consequently, I ended up on a destroyer.

I was on that destroyer about a year and a half and one day we pulled into Okinawa.

The OOD said, "Mr. Brown, this will be the last time we stand watch together."

I asked, "Oh, how's that?"

He replied, "Tomorrow I'm leaving the ship. I'm going to submarine school."

I said, "Oh, I sure wish I was going with you. I applied while I was in boot camp, but they weren't taking any people at that time."

Even so, the next morning over the MC comes an order—for me to report to his day room. In those days, if you served on a tin can [destroyer] and you were told to report to the day room, usually you were in trouble.

Anyway, I went to his stateroom and he said, "Brown, do you still want to go to submarine school?"

I said, "Yes, sir."

Then he told me, "Get your bag packed. You're going with me."

Just that easily, we went to submarine school. Every Friday at the school we'd have a test that covered the week's work we had studied. Every Friday afternoon there would be a note on the bulletin board for me to report to his room in the bachelor officer's quarters [BOQ]. I'd go up there and he would [always] ask, "How did it go this week?" We would have a couple of beers and talk about what we had done that week.

Then he'd say, "Now, if you ever have a problem whatsoever you come and see me. We don't want to take a chance on you getting dropped out of school."

As a result, I finished submarine school, graduated at the top of the class, and received orders to Pearl Harbor, Hawaii. I was to report to the USS *Bass* (SS 551) [K-2]. I reported to there, I believe it was in 1956. I stayed on there for about two years, took her to San Diego, and put her out of commission in early 1958. We put orders in, about four or five of us volunteered to go back to Pearl Harbor, and as luck would have it, three of us got selected: Brown, Jones, and Smith—the three most common names in the whole crew I ever served with in the boats. They assigned me to the USS *Cusk* (SS 348).

However, back to the K-2. Our skipper was Black Jack McAddams. We had a very small crew—I think about four officers and thirty-four or thirty-five enlisted. The K-2 wasn't very powerful even when we were running on diesel on the surface. One day we set out and were going to the far corner of another island, Maui or Oahu, I'm not certain which one. We departed from Pearl Harbor about 8:00 in the morning and by 11:30 we still hadn't made much headway because the wind was blowing so strong that we couldn't reach the Diamond [Head] area. Therefore, we went back into port and tied up next to the pier.

First thing, the lieutenant of the boat that had tied up next to us yelled across to Captain McAddams and asks, "What's the matter, Captain, are the 'fog cancel' warnings out?"

The old man went berserk and yells to our exec to get on the phone and call the captain of that boat and [tell him] to report to him immediately on the pier. Anyway, that was the big, big problem with the K-boats—they didn't have enough power.

Returning to the *Cusk* (348), it and the *Carbonero* were guidance boats for the USS *Tunny* (282), which was one of the first Regulus boats. We'd go on patrol, the *Tunny* would shoot the missiles, and the *Carbonero* and *Cusk* would be downrange where the targets were, because in those days we had to be within visual or at least radar contact so that we could guide the Regulus onto the target.

We had several successful runs on the *Cusk* and in 1959, I received a transfer from the *Cusk* to the submarine base torpedo shop. I stayed there for three years, then ended up in San Diego as the instructor in the Leadership School. [After that] I had orders to transfer to Key West, Florida. My orders said to report to the submarine school.

When I went to report in I told the yeoman, "I know there's been a mistake made here, because I'm supposed to be across the island at the torpedo school."

The OOD when I was checking in said, "Well, we know there's been a screwup in your orders, but we need instructors also."

So consequently, I received an assignment to teach basic electricity and electronics at the fleet sonar school there. About a year and a half later, someone finally found out I was over there from the gun shop and they transferred me over to the 8-11 shop [torpedo operation and repair shop]. I taught the Mark 37, the SUBROC [torpedo tube-fired rocket depth charge], and Aster there. Then I had orders to go to Guided Missile School at Dam Neck, Virginia. About the time I was going to accept these orders and go to Dam Neck, ComSubPac said they needed an instructor immediately on the MK-37, Aster, and SUBROC. I was the only man qualified to teach all three, so they cancelled those orders and I reported to Ford Island and set up a torpedo school there. I talked to Boomer sailors who had just come off a patrol out off Guam and were coming through the school and so I wound up doing four more years teaching there.

It was an interesting arsenal we had in missiles. The top of the line was the Regulus and, at the time I was serving, it was very, very secretive. We had a special place on the submarine base at Pearl Harbor always closed to us. They allowed only those who had a desperate need to know in this area to be working on this Regulus missile. The *Tunny* had this big tank on the back to load the missile in. I don't believe there ever was one deployed in a bad situation. It wasn't a very accurate missile and half the time the tanks wouldn't work right and it [the missile] would splash down [short of the target]. It wasn't the fault of the missile itself. Our guidance systems weren't the top of the line. They saved the best guidance, radars, and satellite systems for the space program. Torpedoes still led the way in submarines.

The regular torpedoes we carried on the *Cusk* were the Mark 27-4, the Mark 18, and Mark 14-C torpedoes. At that time, we'd go out for our exercise shots and fire, and then we'd have a torpedo boat—a boat from the marine base—that would retrieve the torpedoes. But the boat was capable of retrieving and reloading its own torpedoes alone.

Now, the SUBROC was another type of missile that we never fired in combat or warfare. It was a very, very hard missile to take care of; it was so delicate. Since we fired it through the torpedo tubes, there was a great concern at that time that, in case we did have to fire one, we had to have a backup system. There was a lanyard attached to the missile and tied to the torpedo tube to self-ignite the projectile. When you fired—*impulse-ejected*—the missile, there was always a great fear the missile would self-ignite in the tube. That would be all she wrote for the sub, because it would mean we would burst the rear door of the torpedo tube and, with the outer doors open, we'd flood. We just didn't know for sure. Again, let me say that it was never fired in combat, but we did have—we did carry on war patrols—then, well after, it was the Mark 45, which had a nuclear warhead also, and the SUB-ROC missile.

In 1958, I left the school on Ford Island and went to Pascagoula, Mississippi, for new construction on the USS *Puffer* (SSN 652). We commissioned that boat in 1969, and after sea trials, we were on our way to our home port in Pearl Harbor, Hawaii. On route between the United States and Hawaii, our rudder pin snapped and we had no rudder control. Without the rudder, the only way we could steer the boat was to lower all the outboards and the wake on the outboards would switch the rudder right or left. Therefore, we came into Pearl Harbor more like a sailboat, yawing to the right, then left, right and left. The maximum speed we were supposed to make using the outboards lowered was 5 knots. I think we exceeded that a few times in order to get into Pearl Harbor.

Everything had been set up for a "Welcome Aboard" greeting and party, and we wound up with a two- or three-day delay. Even so, everybody—the wives, families, and so on—were waiting for the boat to come in and it disturbed them quite a bit when we were so late. The *Puffer* was probably one of the finest submarines on which I ever served. On a K boat—the K-2 especially—you were lucky if you could shower once a week. The *Puffer* primarily was much better because the stills would put out enough water. The batteries came first, we had to have water for the batteries, and the second priority was the coffeepot. Thirdly, if there was any water left over, we could take a shower. It usually resulted in the chief of the boat turning on the water for three seconds. We could soap down and when you wanted to rinse off you got five seconds of water.

Being torpedomen, we were quite lucky. We had enough alcohol in the forward torpedo room. When we needed to clean up, we'd run the alcohol, and take a rag and soak it up. The only drawback was making sure to keep your rear end area clear, because if you got your butt wet with that alcohol, it hurt for a while. Another reason the *Puffer* was great was because I made chief on her.

I made my first WesPac in 1971 and I had a very successful operation on that tour. I was in Hong Kong when we finished our WesPac cruise. I received notification of my father's death, so I caught a flight out of there and went to the funeral. When I reported back on the *Puffer*, we took her to Seattle, Washington. As a matter of pride, the *Puffer* became the first boat qualified to shoot the MK-48 torpedo. It was a brand-new weapon at that time.

In 1972, I got transferred to Iowa City, Iowa, and the recruiter tried to get me held on shore duty as long as possible as a recruiter and [in fact] I ended up being chief recruiter for the 9th Naval District in Omaha, Nebraska. While there, we first switched to the all-volunteer service. It was very, very hard to make quota there in the midwest. Those farm boys were smarter than heck. But that farmer—if he'd been on the farm long enough, when the kid got out of high school, he went to college and got an agriculture degree, or else he took over the farm.

My father used to say, "Every year, you'd either have a good year or a poor year and you'd never know when which one would happen."

That farmer, once he got so tired of taking the losses along with the profitable years, he wanted nothing other than for his boy to take over for him. He sure didn't want him to go into the navy or the army or any other service.

Regarding war patrols, I'm not sure that I'm yet allowed to say where we went, and not often did anyone in the crew, other than the officers, the COB and the quartermaster, know where we were headed or where we would be when we got there. One thing I can say is that the people where we went spoke a lot of Russian. None of the patrols I went on could I consider boring. I think that of all the patrols I went on, there was only once or twice that we weren't sure we'd come back. We weren't at war, but we were playing war games all the time. That was with the Russians and there weren't any rules.

Their skippers would try to prove how good their boats were and our skippers would try to prove how good ours were. Whenever we made contact, they or we would run and hide. On one patrol, we had a periscope get bent over and an antenna broken. One of their destroyers hit them. We had to pull into Alaska to make repairs.

We always operated under secret orders when we went anywhere close to Vladivostok. We were there for several Russian operations. It was high priority to get underneath one of them [Russian subs] and take pictures of their screws and all of the things along the keel. What we called a "trail." We'd get ahold of one of their boomers going out on patrol—their patrols were much like ours—and follow them. One of our goals when we operated up north was to get contact with one of their boomers going out and follow them as long as we could. Many of our American submarines were capable of following and doing a trail, so in case something bad happened, we would demolish that missile boomer before it could get all four shots off. In order to accomplish that, the captain and crew had to be efficient enough to get four shots off; if they [the Russians] launched on us, we got them, too. I'm not aware of anything like escape pods that would allow a Russian crew to make escapes from under the keel. That's all Hollywood stuff. However, we did observe a large number of their missile shots.

One evening—we always carried aboard what we called "spook people"—they were all Americans, but very fluent in the Russian language. They were ONI, or CIA people, something like that. We would stick up an antenna and we could monitor what was going on. The spooks would translate the communications between one Russian and another, and we'd be ready to shoot if something went wrong with their missile. We were underneath and around them while they fired their missiles.

I don't think they [the Soviets] had so many disasters with their missiles. It was more a case of aborted shots that makes me think their missile technology was way behind ours. Initially, when we had our first boats, the Polaris had only one warhead. Then they advanced and we had multiwarheads. The Polaris had three weapons in each warhead at the time. I'm not sure how far they've gone, I was not in fire-control systems, but I think they have sixteen warheads, known as Multiple Reentry Vehicles. They're all MRVed, often set up with sixteen warheads per missile. It's a known fact now that [when visualizing nuclear weapons] everybody always thinks of a 10 KT or 12 KT or 15 KT bomb, such as Big Boy that we used on Nagasaki. Those were one big warhead. Now, we're talking megatons.

When they came out with the multiwarhead missiles, you might have a megaton all together, but each individual warhead might be only 10 KT. I've even heard talk of a multimegaton payload. When you fire a missile, it can only make a person so dead. I mean, if you can kill him with a .22, why use a four-inch or five-inch gun, let alone a hydrogen bomb?

Their strategy now is to pattern a target. Instead of having that one big warhead, they have all of these little ones all around, and destroy the target and everything around it. It is much more efficient. I took care of the ditty (log) books on the warheads and weaponry and it got to where I knew the warheads very well. It paid off whenever we went to battle stations.

Speaking primarily of the *Puffer*, when you're out to sea just training, training, and training, you always get a couple of guys that just ain't hacking it. If you have an inspection or something like that, you always try to hide these two or three little boogers. It's hard when you try to train anyone like that; they really do screw up. But in an actual crisis, if we had a fire or an emergency leak, or something of that nature—it was surprising but the little guys you always hid or didn't think would be worth a shit, all of them little boogers would come through in the event of an emergency. It really makes you proud when you train, train, train and this little guy you thought would never amount to anything, when an accident occurred he would be Johnny-on-the-spot and do exactly what he had been trained to do.

We never had a lot of accidents at sea but, when you are deep, any mishap is dangerous, especially a fire. The air manifolds are full, of course, but if there is a fire, there's so much damage that can occur that would affect the surfacing of the sub or the steering of the submarine or multiple sorts of things like that. We had minor fires on the *Puffer*, usually from electrical circuitry breaking down, but nothing dangerous.

Now, if you're in certain waters and you have a nuke and only one screw [because of a fire or system failure], the last thing you want is to be discovered in those waters. Therefore, you have to work your butt off to keep off the bottom and keep from broaching so you don't expose yourself. Actually, while I was on the *Puffer,* we did a bow bump. We hit a sudden, uncharted rise in the seabed. Fortunately, nothing was damaged. Naturally, there was a big investigation on it. Nevertheless, the captain was not relieved nor the quartermaster nor the navigator. We didn't even hit hard enough to bounce.

I want to say one thing about being on the *Puffer*. Our second skipper on the *Puffer* was Daniel Cooper. Shortly after reporting aboard, he went to sea with us for about a week or so with our old skipper. The first time we went to sea with him [Cooper], we had an old patrol boat and I was the duty non-commissioned officer [DNCO]. He'd come off a boomer and I was pilot officer on the *Puffer*. We got out off Honolulu one morning, and when we got in deep enough water to dive, and they called me into the control room to dive the boat.

I told him, "While I was walking to the control room I had to pass your stateroom."

The staterooms have shelves and they have this bar across them so that, in case you dive and take a down-angle of so much, it's so that all the books don't come bouncing down.

I told him, "I noticed when I went past your stateroom that you had a bunch of books laid out and the bars weren't in place."

Now, he was a boomer sailor and I was fast attack. There's always friction between boomer sailors and fast attack, so when I dove the boat I took about a twenty-five or thirty down and I hear this *bang! bang! bang!* Right then, I thought, *Oh, shit, what's going on in his stateroom?* The next thing I know, I'm getting down to depth and leveling off when a hand comes over my back. I looked around and it's Captain Cooper.

He says, "All right, COB, I got your message. I'll have them secured when we go to sea."

He went on to become the number three admiral in the navy and was in charge of the Atlantic fleet. [He was] a very good man. Our initial skipper, Captain Will, has passed away now. In those days in fast attack, we didn't have the Outlook program. The COB's wife and the captain's wife acted basically as ombudsmen. Captain Will's wife and my wife got along real good [sic] and did a terrific job of taking care of the families of the crew.

The new counseling system is all right, Outlook that is, and it provides more services than the wives could do. Yet, our old way made for closer-knit families I think. The truth is, I enjoyed counseling the younger guys in the crew and their families. Helping those kids and their families was one of the best things I did in the navy. Of course, that is outside of the snapped rudderpost, and the excitement of the ramming by the Russians and being chased by them.

8

THOMAS INNOCENTE
FIRE CONTROLMAN FIRST CLASS,
USN (RET.)

On March 30, 1957, the nuclear-propelled attack submarine *Seawolf* (SSN 575) was commissioned with CDR Richard B. Laning, USN, as her first skipper. Only the second U.S. submarine to do so, the *Seawolf* used liquid sodium as the heat exchange medium, rather than pressurized water used in the *Nautilus* (SSN 571). The *Seawolf*'s plant was not successful and technicians replaced it with a pressurized water plant.

On December 9, 1957, the Secretary of Defense, Neil H. McElroy, authorized an increase in the development rate for the Polaris submarine-launched missile. The new goal was to produce an operational weapons system by 1960, a full five years ahead of the original date for a surface-launched and seagoing missile system. Later that month, on December 23, the nuclear submarine *Skate* (SSN 578) was commissioned and became the lead ship of the first class of production nuke submarines. Her first commanding officer was CDR James F. Calvert, USN.

On March 7, 1958, LCDR Hugh G. Nott, USN, became the first

One submarine tender and sixteen decommissioned nuclear-powered submarines are shown including the USN *Seawolf* Class Attack. Submarine USS *Seawolf* (SSN 575). *Courtesy of United States Navy*

commanding officer of the diesel-electric submarine USS *Grayback* (SSG 574), which was commissioned that day. The *Grayback* was the first U.S. submarine to be built in a guided missile design. It fired the Regulus. Exactly a month later, the first Soviet nuclear-powered submarine, the K-3, was placed in commission after highly secret sea trials. The K-3 was later renamed *Lenensky Komsomol.* The NATO-class designation for this new class Russian sub was *November.* The first commander of the K-3 was Captain of the First Rank L. G. Osipenko.

The U.S. submarine *Stickleback* (SS 415) received severe damage on May 28, 1958, when she collided with the escort ship *Silverstein* (DE 534) during exercises off Pearl Harbor, Hawaii. During the course of the maneuvers, the *Stickleback* had broached and the *Silverstein* struck her amidships

Grayback (SSN 574) with Regulus 1 missile mounted.

Courtesy of United States Navy

between the forward battery room and the control room. Rescue operations recovered all of the crew and the sub sank late on May 29, despite tremendous efforts to keep her afloat.

Submarines were in the news again on July 1, when the CNO established Submarine Squadron 14 to develop plans for operational logistics support, crew training and rotation, patrol doctrine, and refit procedures for Polaris missile submarines. This first Polaris squadron served well through the Cold War until disestablished in 1992. It became the first and last to carry the Polaris-Poseidon missiles. To this day it is still theorized that the true ultimate deterrent to a war with the Soviet Union was not the ICBM, but the missile submarines that could get up close and personal.

The USS *Nautilus* (SSN 571) made history when the nuclear-powered submarine commanded by CDR William R. Anderson became the first ship to reach and pass under the North Pole. Their four-day, 1,830-mile journey under the ice took them from the Pacific to the Atlantic Ocean. The *Nautilus* surfaced at last on August 7. Then, on August 11, the nuclear attack submarine *Skate* (SSN 578), commanded by CDR James F. Calvert, USN, became the first submarine to surface at the North Pole. Then she repeated this amazing feat again on August 17 as part of an Arctic voyage of exploration that lasted from July 30 until September 22, 1958.

In September, intelligence sources indicated that the government of the Soviet Union had decided that they would not continue a long-range strategic strike role. With their future strategic missile submarine building halted, the Hotel-class SSBN's component parts were shifted to the Echo II SSGN program and the already-planned Yankee SSBN design was temporarily put on the shelf.

The navy conducted the only launch of a Regulus II land-attack missile from a submarine on September 16, 1958. The USS *Grayback* (SSG 574) fired the missile off the coast of California. Flown by radio command, the missile served as part of a simulated attack on Edwards AFB, California. The results were short of expected performance, and redesign was directed for the Regulus II, but the entire project was cancelled on December 12 by Secretary of the Navy Thomas S Gates Jr. Although the Regulus II had flown forty-eight test flights, thirty of them successfully and fourteen partly so, proving nothing significantly wrong with the missile, the decision was made to proceed at full speed on the Polaris submarine-fired missile. This compelled the navy to cut several other programs in addition to Regulus II.

Another signal year for submarines was 1959. On April 15, the attack submarine *Skipjack* (SSN 585), the lead ship of a new class of high-speed submarines, went into commission under command of CDR William Behrens Jr., USN. The *Skipjack* joined nuclear propulsion with the advanced hull design of the USS *Albacore* (AGSS 569). It produced a high-speed (thirty-three knot) but, unfortunately, noisy submarine.

The submarine *Barbero* (SSG 317) began the first Regulus I deterrent patrol in the North Pacific on September 21, 1959. She carried two of the surface-launched, land-attack missiles. From this time until August 1964, the Regulus-armed submarines continuously patrolled in the North Pacific, their missiles programmed for targets in the Soviet Far East. One or two submarines would carry a total of four or five Regulus missiles. Forty-one Regulus deterrent patrols were conducted in that period. Although the number of

USS *Spikjack* (SS 184) in 1943.

Courtesy of United States Navy

missiles on station was small, it did permit sufficient coverage of specific targets with nuclear weapons. The biggest plus factors were the ability to remain unseen, and that these patrols did not require the presence of an aircraft carrier task force in the area or basing nuclear-armed aircraft in Japan or South Korea. Both nations were adamantly opposed to nuclear weapons on their soil. Yet our navy was able to strike at desirable targets in the Soviet Union.

Another one-of-a-kind achievement came on November 10, when the nuclear-propelled radar picket submarine *Triton* was commissioned with Captain Edward L. Beach, USN, as CO. Beach had formerly been naval aide to President Dwight D. Eisenhower. The *Triton* was 447.5 feet (136.5 m) in length. It was the longest U.S. submarine built to this day and the only one powered by two reactors.

On December 30, in Groton, Connecticut, the U.S. Navy's first ballistic missile submarine, the nuclear-powered USS *George Washington* (SSBN 598) was put into commission. CDR James B. Osburn, USN, served as the first Blue Crew commanding officer, with CDR John L. From Jr., USN, commanding Gold Crew. The crews would alternate operating the submarine, their color designations deriving from the blue and gold of the crest of the navy seal.

As technology raced forward through the 1960s and beyond, some equipment and functions remained somewhat primitive, among them, Basic Submarine School at New London and photography through a periscope.

Our next submarine sailor experienced some of both. He also served on the nuclear boats and participated in a hair-raising action that provided invaluable intelligence on the Soviet Union's submarine service.

Critical to satisfactory performance by a submarine are the men who have served as fire controlmen. Their duty is to direct the firing of torpedoes, and in the case of nuclear submarines, the launching of missiles. It is a highly specialized position that calls for high intelligence, a critical eye for detail, and a determination to *never* make a mistake. Here is an account by a fire controlman whose experiences far exceded his expectations.

Well, I was the first in my family to enter the navy. I went to boot camp in San Diego and then to fire control technician A-school in Bainbridge, Maryland, and then on to submarine school in New London, Connecticut, in 1962. The training we received in submarine basic school at New London was primitive compared to today's standards, judging from what I've seen. We took our sea school on the old fleet boats [from the 1920s and '30s]. At the time I went through, power school for nuclear boats did not exist and, at that time, I think the *Swordfish* was the only nuclear submarine in the Pacific. There were others—the *Nautilus,* the *Sargo,* and the *Seawolf,* but all in the Atlantic.

After submarine school, I went to Mark 106 underwater fire control school. The 106 Fire Control system was what they were using on the old fleet boats at the time. I went from there to the *Rasher* (SS 269). The nuclear power program was short on fire controlmen, so they pulled nine or ten of us off. We were all on San Diego–based boats. They sent us to sea school for the 101 underwater fire control system at Great Lakes [Naval Training Station]. Then they shipped us out to Pearl Harbor and we all went to various submarines at Pearl.

Among them, the *Halibut*, two of us went to *Swordfish*, one went to *Barbero*, which was a Regulus boat at the time, one to *Snook*, and *Permit*. They were all named after fish [traditional in the submarine service].

Pearl Harbor became my home port. Later I served on the *Tiru* (SS 426), too. Our captain was Commander Frank Adams, who was the executive officer on the *Nautilus* when they went under the ice. Rickover thought highly of Frank Adams. The captain is dead now, killed in a car wreck, from what I understand.

Rickover gave him the *Swordfish* as the first nuke in the Pacific. He had a good status; in fact, our pier was Sierra-1-Alpha, which was the *prize* of the docks, if that means anything. As far as status goes, the pecking order was that he could come into port first and got the choice of piers. Sierra-1-Alpha was the closest to everything. We were the key boat of the squadron and [though] we never got the Gold "E," we had the "E" with three hash marks on it. We went into the shipyards before the fifth year, which is when our boat finally got the Gold "E" awarded to it, which was a permanent one, which meant we were the lead submarine for four years running. Life on the nukes was good.

The comparison [between the nuke and diesel boats] was like night and day. I guess the only way you can accurately describe a nuclear submarine is to have served on a diesel submarine. I first qualified on the 269, the *Rasher*, which was one of the World War II boats that had a commendable war record. Take just one item: water. The *Rasher* had two one thousand-gallon distillers—or stills, as we called them—so the maximum capacity [of fresh water] was two thousand gallons per day. However, the downside of that was that one of them was *always* broken. Therefore, we'd have one on line and be repairing the other. When we got that one fixed, we'd tear down the other.

It was a constant maintenance thing. When it was brand-new, it produced a thousand gallons of water a day, but when we got aboard, maybe it was seven or eight hundred gallons. That made life a little uncomfortable.

The rule of thumb was, for whatever time you were going to be at sea, you took one pair of underwear, one pair of socks, and one set of dungarees for every week at sea. We'd roll them into little balls. You'd lay the trousers out and put in the shirt and other things [and roll them up]. By the end of the week, you'd throw the underwear away since there was no way to clean them, but the dungarees you'd keep because they cost too much to throw away.

However, the sweat and body odors were rampant and showers were nonexistent, unless your mission allowed, [then] we could go up and take a saltwater shower. We'd come up and open the deck hatches. We could get in the superstructure and we'd go under and wash off like that. They had some saltwater soap they'd give you. It was kinda like Lava soap, and it could scrape the skin right off of you. The saltwater took the smell away but the problem then was that you had the salt on you and you had no way to get it off. Therefore, you smelled better but the salt sure as hell itched.

By comparison, when I first walked on board a nuclear submarine, I saw washing machines and dryers. I thought, Well, hell. If you have the luxury of a washing machine, I guess that means you have water enough to take a bath. The water wasn't endless on the first nuclear subs, but even so, if you took a shower on a nuclear submarine once a week, that was paradise compared by the old standard. I could tell you horror stories, like this one: I can still recall getting on buses and sitting down beside someone and they would sniff loudly and get up and leave because, even though you were clean, that diesel fuel just permeated into the wool uniform—the navy blues—and there just wasn't any way to get it out. What you smell on a nuclear submarine they call "Amnie" [amniotic crystal] filtering. It's a crystallized substance that they use for filtering out [odors in] the air.

While I'm on the subject of the nukes, let me say that the greatest skipper I ever served under was Frank Adams on the *Swordfish*. I think he was the best skipper I ever saw anywhere. I don't go back far enough to compare him to guys like Fluky, Beach, or some of those guys who were in World War II; certainly, they had to be something. Although the things I saw Adams do, you can't imagine. They'd scare you to death, if you didn't have the confidence in the man to do such things.

I recall one of our missions—frankly, when I got discharged I signed a paper that I wouldn't reveal any of this stuff for eighty-eight years—yet, one time I was telling my wife about it while she was sitting in the living room watching TV. All of a sudden, this movie came on—*Blind Man's Bluff*—and she said, "Isn't that the patrol you've been telling me about?"

I said, "That's the stuff I signed a paper saying I wouldn't reveal for eighty-eight years." What a joke.

One of the things we did, one that I recall offhand and that scared me to death—we trained for it, we practiced for it—we went to Vladivostok, Russia, and waited for a new construction submarine to come out of Vladivostok Harbor. When it came out, we got up under her and the skipper put up the 'scope. We were submerged, but we had the 'scope up partway. The whole front of our submarine was underneath theirs. Our conning tower—our *sail*—was close enough to it for a clear view. Our job was to take pictures of the propellers of the Russian submarine. We went in until our 'scope was within feet of the propeller—I don't remember if it was one or two propellers. I was a fire controlman at the time and on fire control watch at the time. We were taking pictures of it [the aft quarter of the Russian sub] and at the time we didn't have video cameras, we had Polaroid cameras mounted on one of the 'scopes. Anyway, the captain was on the attack 'scope and we had the Polaroid camera on the number two 'scope.

He said to me, "Come over here and pull these pictures off. Make sure you're getting them." Then he says, "Here, look through the one 'scope." I looked through the one 'scope and he asked, "See what we want?"

There was the belly and the screws of that damned Russian sub.

I said, "Yes, sir."

Then he said, "Okay, that's what we want pictures of." He went back to the one 'scope and said, "All right, start runnin' them off the two 'scope." The Polaroid pictures in those days came in a roll of sixteen or twenty pictures. As fast as we could shoot them he would say, "Shoot."

I'd push the button and pull it off and put it up [to self-develop]. It took sixty seconds for the thing and then he'd ask, "Did you get it?"

When I'd say yes, he'd say, "Get another one."

I guess we ran a couple of dozen pictures of that new sub. That's just one example. I didn't understand it at the time, but apparently by the propeller rotation they could tell the speed that the thing could do and the engineering people could tell what the boat's maneuvering capabilities were just by the size, shape, and definition of the propeller blades. Of course, our sound wasn't as sophisticated as it is today, but we were also making tapes of the propeller noise to identify that particular one [class]. It wasn't as clear as it is today. They were lucky if they could identify subs, for the most part, as a class of submarine; whether it was a Victor or Echo or later a Whiskey or whatever we were fooling with at the time. Today, they can take the signature and identify one particular boat, which is remarkable.

Some incidents became so routine that the crews considered them noteworthy. However, in truth they were. Well, the bumpings and the rammings were kind of commonplace. They [the Russians] played tag with us. We came back to Pearl [Harbor] one time with our entire sail crushed in. Our 'scopes and our radar had all been crushed. They [the harbormaster and pilots] wouldn't let us back in because all we had to navigate by was sonar—we had come back from Japan to Pearl Harbor by sonar. They didn't want to give us clearance because they didn't want us to be recognized. They brought us in at night, about two o'clock in the morning, as I recall. They had a dry dock—a *ship dry dock*, not a land dry dock—a floating dry dock. I can't remember the name of the damned thing, but they had one flooded down and brought us right in and tied up. They threw camouflage netting over the boat and pumped out the dry dock. Within an hour they had everything cut off. They had welders standing by, so they had everything cut away before daylight. They didn't want anybody seein' that. All of our Cold War patrols were exciting, like that one.

We felt we were doing something significant for the country. That raised the level of excitement—I don't know if you could call it joyous excitement, though. I guess you could call it *anticipated* excitement, for lack of a better term. It gave us a sense of accomplishment or something to that effect, so it was excitement in that respect. Of course, there was excitement of the unexpected. You had no idea what the hell might happen to you out there.

We got a navy unit citation for infiltrating a Russian war exercise. They had Russian war games going on. They were dropping live depth-charges and they had their submarines working. They had their screen out. Our job was to get in and penetrate it. We got in all right and stayed with it. It was like a ten-day operation. We hid right in the middle of their war game exercise. We recorded everything we could.

Certainly, the crewmembers didn't know the specifics of what all were going on. When I read my Unit Commendation it said "for exercises," very nonspecific. Only then, if you see it on *Blind Man's Bluff* or read books about that kind of stuff, you say, "Gee, I did that."

We knew we were in their exercise, but I never knew the specifics of it. The details were not related to the crew. Very few men actually knew what we were doing. For instance, I don't know if we ever had an encounter with Soviet or Chinese aircraft. Maybe they were there, and they may have detected us, but I didn't know about it. Surface ships and submarines were another matter. As I said earlier, they were dropping depth-charges in the exercises and, as far as I could tell, the Russian ones were just as good as any of ours. A depth-charge is a depth-charge. [Laughs] I mean, nobody argues about what it is when it goes off.

Anyway, the way these operations usually began was that we would leave from Pearl Harbor, dive, and transit to Okinawa. There we would pick up supplies and spies. They were mostly communication techs [CTs]. All of them were Asian-looking guys. Obviously we assumed they spoke another language other than English as their first language: Korean or Chinese or whatever. They all came on board, no rank showing. I was a friend with the yeoman, and I learned from him there were little indicators you could pick up. We could identify the marines; they were mostly marines and sailors.

The civilians had no identifiers; we couldn't pick up what they were. The thing that gave the civilians away was that they were older. One guy, about forty, came aboard with a sailor's uniform on. Anyway, they locked them away pretty good. They socialized with us, but only on a nonprofessional level; they wouldn't talk about anything they were doing. They stood all of their watches in the radio room and the sonar room, and they never got loose with their hands-on stuff. They were mostly intercepting radio transmissions.

These types of operations were highly stressful. We never had anyone become worked up enough that they got deep-sixed. We had some guys who had a problem, mostly not related to what we were doing. Other factors usually came into play. There was one guy in particular, a very good friend of mine. His infant child died while we were at sea. The CO and Exec contemplated if they would tell him or not. Once he found out, he went into a kind of recessive shell; he kind of curled up in a ball and didn't communicate with anybody. It wasn't job-related, it was only personal.

On a lighter side, our chow was the best food in the navy. On the *Swordfish*, the captain again—his position, his authority and the way he was respected in the submarine corps—he got whatever he wanted. He handpicked his cook, a man named Smoky Miles; he was a first class cook. We had an old saying that may be a little gross, but we'd say, "Smoky could make a turd taste good." *And he could*. He was one hell of a cook. He made gourmet food out of [shrugs] whatever. He was never satisfied with the meats that the navy provided, so the captain got him a special chit—I don't know where he went—but he'd go downtown. He went to some warehouse and selected his own meat. He'd bring it back [to the base] in a Volkswagen van. That's how selective he was.

He'd say, "I wouldn't cook that military crap."

Submariners' food was always exceptional, the best food in the navy by far, not only in quality but in quantity. I don't know how the hell they do it today with the navy's weight control program. How do they expect a guy to go out to sea for ninety days, eat and drink like a pig, not alcohol, but consume the quality of food, yet maintain a weight control program? Anyway, when we were in San Diego, the submarine base was at Ballast Point [at the bayside foot of Point Loma], and we had the submarine tender *Sperry* and she had a nest on both sides of her. When I was on *Rasher*, we were in a nest of six or seven on either side. Moreover, it's literally a pain in the ass, because you put a gangplank from the brow of one submarine to the next. Depending on what your status was in the nest, you would have to go a long ways, from one boat to another, if you wanted to get to the tender, and then back again.

[When asked about colorful characters he served with in the boats the response came through a big, hearty laugh.] When it comes to funny or weird shipmates, the name that comes to my mind is "Lovely" Linus Day. He was a colorful character. Linus was a genius, for want of a better word. He could quote verbatim any verse you chose in the Bible. He could talk about electronic subjects, like computer standards today, just off the top of his head. He was a boatswain's mate on surface craft and decided he wanted to come on submarines, so he changed his rate from boatswain's mate to electronics technician, and was able to cross-rate from—I think—a second class boatswain's mate to a second class electronics technician, just by reading books. He later went to nuclear power school and made first class and chief the first time up.

Linus was such a tremendous contrast. In one way, he was this phenomenally intelligent guy and on the other side he was just a *boatswain's mate*. I don't know how to picture a guy like that. On one hand, he could be the grossest man on earth, with some of the dotty habits and whatever. He had this goofy laugh. He'd laugh out of the side of his mouth and go [demonstrates] "Haw-haw-haw! How do you like that, kid?" If you challenged him or criticized him in any way, he would shift gears into the intellectual. He was like a character from *Three Faces of Eve* or *Jeckyl and Hyde*.

We called him "Lovely" because some of his habits were [more laughter] hard to describe without becoming really graphic. I guess you'd have to say that this constant back-and-forth sway of going from the epitome of boatswain's mate to the epitome of electronics technician described his style. I guess you have to understand what a boatswain's mate and what an electronics technician are. However, he knew that nuclear reactor inside, outside, upside down, and backwards. We were fortunate to have him. As a chief petty officer, he was top shelf. As an example for young kids to follow, Linus left a lot to be desired.

Well, we had this guy named Shit-Tank Willie. His name was Williams, a second class sonarman. He'd transferred over from a surface craft. To the best of my recollection, he did not go to submarine school. Well, Williams came on board and he didn't understand how submarine heads [toilets] worked. So he went in the head and went to the bathroom. It [the head] was just forward of the crew's mess on the *Swordfish,* between the crew's mess and the forward torpedo room.

Unbeknown to him, they were blowing the sanitary tanks at the time. The way you empty a sanitary tank on a submarine is that you put a pressure in it greater than the seawater. First, you seal everything up and put a pressure in the tank, then you open the outboard valves and compressed air blows the waste overboard, as long as the pressure exceeds that of the seawater. There's pressure in the tank and it will be there as long as you open one of them. Submarine toilets have a flapper valve. You pull a lever and it's sort of like a half-moon escape valve that opens up.

Well, Williams went to the bathroom and to flush this valve you literally have to stand up and turn around and face it. Your face is toward the toilet bowl when you pull the valve. Well, Willie pulled the valve and took about fifty to a hundred pounds of sanitary waste in his face. That's how he got the name Shit-Tank Willie. He was that from then on. It was so comical, because when he came out of there, he was crap from his head to the bottom of his shoes.

Actually, it was a lot more serious than that, because some of the waste product went up under his eyelids and in his nasal passages. So, while it was comical to the old salts, it was tragic also because we had to rush him up to the hospital [Pearl Harbor]. I'm not sure of the name of where they took him. They used all kinds of antibiotic stuff to clear out from under his eyelids and square away his nasal passages. Only at seventeen years old, you don't recognize the seriousness, all you see is this guy dripping with toilet paper as he came out of the head.

Speaking of navy hospitals let me say a little about our corpsmen. To be a corpsman on a submarine, you have to be a minimum of a senior second class, actually a rank of senior E-5. Once you made E-5, they sent you to training in New London at that time, called Submarine Medical Technician [SubMedTech]. It was like a sea school for corpsmen. A corpsman on a sub had to be a hell of a lot more proficient than just a run-of-the-mill, surface-ship corpsman. Because you then had the opportunity to go and say, "Hey, Doc, what about this?" In effect, he was your doctor. They received necessary intensified training because of that. I never ran into a corpsman that I didn't have tremendous respect for. A very good friend of mine was one, Doc Sloane. He's another story; he went on to be chief and I think he made senior chief before he retired. I was always under the impression that a corpsman was, by the Geneva Convention, barred from a combat position, but he ended up being COB, not on the *Swordfish*, but on another boat.

When it comes to my preference of nuke over diesel and vice versa, I really don't know. You can make an argument for either one. The old diesel subs had the advantage that you went to a lot of places.

When you went to WesPac, you had the advantage of many liberty ports. The nuclear-powered boats of the time were prohibited from going into a number of ports. Like the *Swordfish* was the first nuclear-powered boat to go into Japan. They wouldn't let it into Yokosuka, which is the traditional navy port. They sent us to Sasebo to lessen the impact. Japan was the only nation to sustain a nuclear attack and we're taking a nuclear submarine into there. Now it's run of the mill but, at that time, the liberty call on nuclear submarines was very limited. We used to go on R&R flights. We would pull into Okinawa, by way of example, and from there they'd fly you to Hong Kong, or fly you to Hawaii or to Japan or Thailand—something of that nature. So the ports of call were quite different from on the old ones [boats].

Okinawa was my favorite port of call. What was our greatest attraction? That's a silly question to ask a seventeen-year-old kid. [Regaining composure] It was freedom of the no-holds-barred climate in *Naha*. They let you do whatever you wanted—within reason. Of course, the young ladies were the main attraction. By far, the best liberty port according to cost was Olongapo, Philippines. Anything a sailor wanted, he could get it in a night and not even spend ten dollars. That was [always] quite an attraction. However, I liked *Naha* the best.

Of course, during World War II, the submarine force was the mainstay in the Pacific. We didn't have much in the way of a surface fleet after Pearl Harbor and, in that respect, the submarine force was the elite of the navy. Further, I think that those who carried on during the Cold War era were the *most* elite in that they kept the lid on. Deterrence through force must have worked because the balloon didn't go up for forty years. Nobody shot a rocket at anybody for those forty years, so the fact that the submarines were out there keeping the lid on, maintaining the checks and balances, the nation has—the world, for that matter—owes a tremendous debt of gratitude to those people.

By today's standards, I think we're into a new role now, into the covert stuff and the shallow-water submarines. Particularly in the area of insertions, Special Forces small-team insertions, the SEAL teams, lockouts, and all that sort of thing. I guess the jury is still out on the effect of Iraq on the navy and our country. Having worked with SEAL teams in the 1960s, if they are anything today like they were then, I can't imagine the things those people do. They are just phenomenal men and phenomenal attributes to our nation. I can't give them enough respect, even though they're scary. They're so good they're truly scary. Taken all together, I can best sum up my activities in the navy and in the submarine service during the Cold War era as acting forcefully with restraint. I love the navy and I loved the sub-

A SEAL swimmer ascends from the nuclear-powered submarine USS *Kamehameha* (SSN 642) to the surface breathing on a pony SCUBA bottle. *Courtesy of United States Navy*

marines. My only regret is that I didn't go on and obtain commissioned rank and do thirty years.

USS *Halibut* (SSGN 587) was commissioned on January 4, 1960, as the U.S. Navy's first guided-missile submarine with nuclear propulsion. CDR Walter Dedrick, USN, became her first commanding officer. The *Halibut* turned out to be the only SSGN completed by our country. The remainder of the Permit-class subs was completed as fast-attack submarines. Originally the Permit-class ships were designed to carry the Regulus II strategic attack missile.

The nuclear-powered attack submarine *Shark* (SSN 591) was launched at the Newport News Shipbuilding and Dry Dock Company in Virginia on March 16, 1960. She was the first nuclear submarine constructed at that shipyard. Prior to that, the shipyard had built diesel submarines, including some constructed for Russia, in the early 1920s and '30s. Two days later, the first test firing of Project Hydra was conducted at the Naval Missile Center, Point Mugu, California. The 150-pound rocket successfully ignited underwater and launched into the air, thus demonstrating that it was feasible to fire missiles while they floated upright in the water.

Success came quickly in 1960, as the first successful launch of a guided missile occurred aboard the USS *Halibut* (SSGN 587) on March 25. It was a Regulus I, fired during an exercise off Oahu, Hawaii. Next, on May 6, the United States came close to the brink of war with Castro's communist Cuba, when the Cuban cutter *Oriente* fired on the U.S. submarine *Sea Poacher* (SS 406) in San Nicholas Channel. Cooler heads prevailed and the United States did not launch the incredibly superior force of our Navy and Air Force against Castro's belligerent Communist nation.

The nuclear-propelled submarine *Triton* (SSRN 586), commanded by Captain Edward L. Beach, USN, established a new record on May 10 when she completed a totally submerged circumnavigation of the world. The

Triton's historic voyage lasted for eighty-four days and covered 41,519 miles. The only exception to the total underwater mode of travel was off the coast of Spain, when the sail broached the surface to allow a small boat to approach and take off a sailor having a severe kidney stone attack. On May 10, Captain Beach received congratulations from President Dwight D. Eisenhower and the Secretary of the Navy, William B. Franke.

On July 20, the nuclear-powered missile submarine *George Washington* (SSBN 598) engaged in the first launch of two Polaris A-1 ballistic missiles while submerged, which marked the first time a missile was fired from a submerged U.S. submarine. The pair of Polaris missiles were launched at an interval of two hours, fifty-two minutes, and broke surface without wobble or trajectory deviation. Likewise, they did not have trouble as they streaked more than 1,000 nautical miles down the Atlantic test range. When the Soviet Union learned of this accomplishment, they responded with impotent anger at the United Nations.

They falsely claimed that the United States had violated nuclear weapons test limitations. Since there was not a nuclear warhead aboard the missile, the United States chose to ignore this outburst. There was more to come.

On August 25, while charting the Northwest Passage through the Canadian archipelago, the U.S. nuclear-propelled submarine *Seadragon* (SSN 584) surfaced at the North Pole. In a moment of giddy celebration, the crew cavorted on the polar ice and played the first game of baseball at the North Pole. Though not as spectacular as the voyage of the *Nautilus* (SSN 571), *Seadragon* received a navy unit citation for their accomplishment.

By October 21, Great Britain was able to launch its first nuclear-powered submarine, the *Dreadnaught*, from the Vickers-Armstrong Yard at Barrow-in-Furness, and christened by Queen Elizabeth II on the anniversary of the battle of Trafalgar, Nelson's historical victory over the French. The *Dreadnaught* had a modified U.S. 55W reactor plant and employed several other minor U.S.-designed systems. Eleven days later, Prime Minister Harold Macmillan announced that the British government had decided to allow U.S. Polaris submarines to be based at Holy Loch, Scotland.

Nine days later in the United States, the last of the small, hunter-killer-type submarines to be built, the *Tullibee* (SSN 597), was placed in commission with CDR Richard E. Jortbert as her skipper. Following on November 11, the U.S. ballistic missile submarine *George Washington* (SSBN 598) sailed from Charleston, South Carolina, on its first Cold War patrol—the navy's first Polaris deterrent patrol. Her armament consisted of sixteen Polaris A-1 missiles. This initial deterrent patrol concluded on January 21, 1961, when the *George Washington* returned to New London, Connecticut, after a submerged cruise of sixty-six days, ten hours. Another record was broken in that this voyage was the longest submerged submarine operation for a U.S. sub made to this date. It is believed that the longest totally submerged operation was likely that of the German diesel-electric submarine *U-977*. Using a snorkel, she traveled submerged for sixty-six days from the coast of Norway to the mid-Atlantic, heading for Argentina after Germany's surrender in early May 1945. Intelligence sources considered it likely that this was the sub traveled in by Adolph Eichmann in his flight to avoid retribution for being the architect of the "Final Solution."

Coming quickly on the heels of his swearing-in as president, John F. Kennedy made his first State of the Union address. He announced that he had given instructions to the Defense Department to "reappraise our entire defense strategy." Kennedy also revealed to the public that he had issued orders to accelerate the Polaris missile and submarine programs. This news delighted Admirals Lockwood and Rickover.

More progress arrived on March 8 when the Polaris-armed submarine *Patrick Henry* (SSBN 599) entered the harbor at Holy Loch, Scotland, after completing her first deterrent patrol. The sub resupplied and was serviced by the submarine tender *Proteus* (AS 19). It was the first time an American submarine replenished overseas, accompanied by a crew exchange of a ballistic-missile submarine.

On the same day as the failed Bay of Pigs invasion, CNO Arleigh A. Burke, USN, testified before the Senate Armed Services Committee, with the shocking information that, "A Soviet version of our Polaris-firing submarine must be expected in the near future." In fact, the Soviet Navy already had a primitive ballistic missile submarine. The Soviet Polaris-type system became operational in 1967. It consisted of Yankee-class submarines and SSN-6 missiles.

On June 23, communications with submarines at sea greatly improved, when the new U.S. Navy radio station at Cutler, Maine, commenced operations. It became the navy's major low-frequency transmitter station, used to exchange signals with the Atlantic Fleet's ships and submarines. A belated Independence Day celebration followed the arrival of the USS *Robert E. Lee* (SSBN 601) at Holy Loch, Scotland, on July 9, after a record-breaking submerged operation of sixty-eight days, four hours, fifteen minutes.

First in the second class of Polaris ballistic missile submarines, the USS *Ethan Allen* (SSBN 608) was commissioned on August 8, 1961. Her first commanding officers were CDR Paul L. Lacy Jr., USN, commanding the Blue crew, and CDR William W. Bahrens, USN, who skippered the Gold crew. Later, on October 23, the *Ethan Allen* launched the first Polaris-2 ballistic missile from a submarine. The test was a remarkable success, with the missile's flight down-range of 1,400 nautical miles before the reentry cone fell into the sea.

With his usual bluster, Soviet Premier Nikita Khrushchev warned Great Britain on October 31 that their practice of allowing the United States to establish bases for submarines would make the British "among the first" to undergo a nuclear attack in the event of war. Conservative Party Prime Minister Harold Macmillan responded with the typical British "stiff upper lip" reserve, in effect telling the braggadocio Khrushchev to "bring it on."

A New Year's baby arrived on January 1, 1962 for the navy. The chief of naval operations authorized the first US Navy Sea-Land-Air (SEAL) teams that day. Their primary function was to conduct unconventional warfare operations. In the future, their missions would be carried out in restricted waters and river areas. This also marked the navy's entry into special operations with personnel and units especially trained for this role. From the inception of the SEAL program, it was determined that *submarines* would figure largely into the SEAL actions, providing covert transportation to their areas of operation. Prior to this, submarines had delivered covert operatives only from the Office of Naval Intelligence, Marine Corps Raiders, and Army Special Forces personnel.

A frequently sought-after situation arrived on January 27, 1962, when Vice Admiral H. G. Rickover, head of the navy's nuclear propulsion program, turned sixty-two, the statutory retirement age for the navy. However, due to his invaluable ability and knowledge, he was retained on active duty until January 1982, coincidentally at the age of 82.

The New York Shipbuilding Corporation launched the nuclear-powered attack submarine *Pollack* (SSN 603) on March 11 at Camden, New Jersey. She had the honor of being the first nuclear submarine built in that yard. Prior to that, the yard had produced only one diesel-electric boat.

On May 4, the United States' defense capabilities received a big boost when the government committed five Polaris ballistic missile submarines to the North Atlantic Treaty Organization (NATO) during an intense three-day ministerial session of the Atlantic Council meeting in Athens, Greece. The ministers accepted one proviso: The submarines would remain under the operational control of the U.S. Navy.

Operating as part of Joint Task Force 8, near Christmas Island in the Pacific, the nuclear submarine *Ethan Allen* (SSBN 608) fired the first Polaris missile with a nuclear warhead that detonated. It turned out to be the only test firing of the full-system of either a land- or sea-based U.S.-made nuclear missile. The May 6 test was code-named Operation Frigate Bird.

Mrs. Jacqueline Kennedy, the First Lady and wife of President John F. Kennedy, launched the U.S. ballistic missile submarine *Lafayette* (SSBN 616) on May 8. The launch took place at the General Dynamics Electric Boatyard in Groton, Connecticut. *Lafayette* is the largest undersea vessel ever produced by a Western shipyard to date. Later in the month, on May 10, the navy made history again when a Sparrow III air-to-air missile fired from an F4H-1 Phantom II (the designation H-1 was later dropped for all services), successfully destroyed a Regulus II in a head-on attack while both were flying at supersonic speed. This test, at the Pacific Missile Test Range, was the first in which a head-on attack launched by an aircraft scored against a surface-fired missile. The message to submarine captains was loud and clear.

After extensive sea trials, the nuclear submarine *Ethan Allen* (SSBN 608) sailed from Charleston, South Carolina, to begin the first deterrent patrol with the now-proven Polaris A-2 missile. Submarine activity accelerated on August 1 when the second U.S. Navy Polaris missile submarine, assigned to SubRon 16, was commissioned at the Naval Submarine Base at New London, Connecticut. Although no Polaris submarines operated from New London, the staffs of SubRon 16 and the individual crewmembers were stationed there.

On the next day, the nuclear submarines *Skate* (SSN 578) and *Seadragon* (SSN 584) created another moment in history as they rendezvoused under the polar ice and surfaced at the North Pole, making this the first such submarine operation at the Pole. August remained busy for submariners. On August 7, an advanced version of a Polaris A-3 missile was fired from the launch facility at Cape Canaveral, Florida. It proved a remarkable success. With a range in excess of 2,500 nautical miles, the missile was slated to replace the A-1 and A-2 missiles in U.S. submarines and the Royal Navy's strategic missile submarines. The Polaris A-3 was significant in that it had one of the first Multiple Reentry Vehicles (MRV), incorporating a warhead that shotgunned three nuclear projectiles into a target. Currently the MRVs have advanced to twelve, fourteen, and sixteen warheads in each projectile, with a 10 KT payload, equivalent to the bombs dropped on Hiroshima and Nagasaki.

President Kennedy and British Prime Minister Macmillan started a three-day round of meetings at Nassau, Bahamas. One subject of discussion was the U.S. government's intention to cancel the Skybolt air-launched strategic missile, which was intended for use by Britain. Kennedy offered Macmillan the Polaris missile—minus the warhead—for use in the British nuclear deterrence arsenal. Britain immediately accepted the offer.

9

GEORGE E. BONHAM
YEOMAN CHIEF,
USN (RET.)

To many people, the name yeoman signifies only a fancy navy name for a secretary. *Au contraire*, as a famous entertainer delighted in saying. A yeoman, especially on a submarine, has many duties. He might have a duty station as sonarman, signals radioman, as diving planes operator, or—in the old days—TDC operator. Of course, we cannot overlook that old standby, lookout. Everyone from the captain to the mess cooks received training as lookouts. More yeomen have been lost overboard in high seas, shelled by enemy surface fire, or depth-charged to death while manning the TDC, radio, or sonar, than they ever did pounding a typewriter.

Yet the bottom line remains: a yeoman is a secretary or, in a less pejorative way, a records keeper. A submarine had (and has in the nukes) a stores keeper, a mess chief, a chief torpedoman, and a morale and entertainment officer (usually a noncommissioned officer on subs). Also a chief medical officer (even if he's only a first class petty officer), chief engineer (usually a master chief, until the nukes came along), and a full complement of strikers for these positions. Readers may recall that LCDR Stan

Nicholls began his career in the boats as a yeoman. So, likewise, did our next subject.

I served in the submarine force from 1954 to 1974. While I was still in submarine school, our class went down [to the lower base at New London] and commissioned the *Nautilus* (SSN 571). I can't remember what lady broke the bottle on it. After I got out of sub school I served on the diesel boats and started out aboard the *Pomfret Deputy Able* (SS 391). On our first cruise, when we were on our way to WesPac on the *Pomfret*, we stopped off at Saipan. We anchored out and a little ol' boat came out and got us. There were some army guys there and about ten or twelve navy guys. They had this old flatbed truck, so they loaded up what guys had liberty. We rode out into this sort of jungle until we got to this little grass hut. They had an icebox there with sixty beers. We'd drink all the beer they had and then we'd drive on to the hut. We drank all the beer they had in Saipan.

While still on the *Pomfret* we anchored out over in Japan someplace. Ensign Marks—he was a captain when I left ComSubPac—went over to Saipan on liberty. When he came back on one of those little sampans—one of those little one-lungers, he had three or four military nurses with him. They wanted a ride back to Yokuska [Yokosuka]. Ah, the old man was hot.

Chas. K. Smith was our skipper. I didn't think much of him, but he wasn't very happy with Mr. Marks. Only, they [the nurses] were already there; however, we couldn't send a sailing report. When we'd leave a port, it was my job as yeoman to submit a sailing report. It listed everybody who was on board the submarine. I'd submitted one when we left wherever we were last. Of course, these four nurses weren't included. So if we'd gone down and never came up, nobody would have ever known where those nurses were.

We had some great liberty ports while we were at WesPac. I guess the best was Yokosuka. Although there was one time when we anchored out at this island. I don't know for sure where this was in WesPac. A little boat came and got us and we went in. They had this gigantic—well, pretty good-sized—hotel. The top floor revolved very, very slowly. You could look out at the submarine at sea and, half an hour later, it would be back around. It [the floor] revolved on a wooden spindle, probably ten feet across. I don't know *what* turned the wooden spindle. It [the hotel] was four stories tall. Still, I didn't know where we were, never was told the name of the place. The rooms were kind of pie-shaped. We sat around on the floor drinking and they had big windows, from floor to ceiling, covered with fancy cloth of some kind. It was so nice.

There was another time on the *Pomfret* when things got sort of hairy. We were up around Russia checking out their radio transmissions. Anyway, this Russian destroyer came out after us. They used the underwater telephone to contact us.

They said, "Unidentified submarine, identify yourself."

Well, our skipper, Chas. Smith said back, "We ain't no submarine; we's a school of fishes."

Then we [Yeoman Bonham and the COB] said, "You'd better surface."

In the meantime, the XO is getting us turned around and we're crawling out of there as best we can. So they kept on [us] on the surface.

The old man was saying, "Load up the torpedo tubes."

At the time, the XO was saying, "No no no. We don't want to do this." Even so, he kept on it until, pretty soon, we got out deep enough so that we could go down under some cold water [thermal cline] and get 'em off our back. I think that was about the *Pueblo* [Incident]

157

time. No, I'm wrong, it was *before* the *Pueblo*. Had we surfaced, they'd have hauled us in. We stayed at WesPac for about six months and came back.

Well, another narrow escape came in San Diego. We were shadowing the submarine school off the coast. We were to show them [the students at sub school] a snorkeling submarine. The school was on a destroyer and we were gonna cruise alongside of it and show them what a snorkeling submarine looked like, what it sounded like. Well I guess the Destroyer Escort (DE) thought we were getting too close. As a result, he [the OD] puts a little left rudder on it and they were going like *this* [illustrates with hands a position that shows the "sub" headed for the DE] and the old man thinks he's getting too close so he goes like *that* [illustrates with "sub" hand pointing out away from "DE"]. If our cap'n had went [sic] with him [the DE], we'd have been all right. As it turned out, the destroyer came at us, hit our periscope, and knocked off part of the snorkel and the periscope. I was lying down in my bunk and it knocked me out of my rack onto the floor. The old man laid that on the senior quartermaster on the helm, but it wasn't *his* fault.

I went to shore duty. I was the yeoman for the chief of naval air training. I was the only submarine sailor down there. That was at Pensacola, Florida. Then the yeoman for the Blue Angels went on leave, so I went out and yeomanned [sic] for them for a while, which was somewhat different for a submarine sailor. Then I went to the National Rifle and Pistol matches at Camp Perry, Ohio, while on my way to a submarine out of New London, Connecticut. But I didn't want to go to Connecticut, so while I was in Ohio at Camp Perry, I got my orders changed to a submarine down in Key West, Florida. I went back and got on the T boats.

Back in '59 they had some small boats they called the T-1, T-2 and T-3. They had names, but I can't think of them. The galley was tiny; they could only feed about four men at a time. They were only about a hundred feet long and had about twenty-some men on them. They were of the cigar-shaped hull design, so they looked like a nuke sub, but they were just little propane subs. Later on, we gave the *Pomfret* (SS 391) to the Italian Navy as a NATO ally. Some foreign group came over and we showed them how to operate the thing for about a month, then they headed out in it. I heard later that they sank it. I don't know whether that was true or not.

When I got back to Dago [San Diego], the *Nautilus* had come around and I went aboard her for a little bit. But while I was down at Key West, they were putting together a submarine squadron over in Rota [Rianjo], Spain, so my boss got permission to go to Charleston to gather a personnel office and put together all the paperwork, all the books and everything, to set up a submarine squadron.

So [when that was done], he says to me, "If I'm going over there you have to go with me."

We got on a plane and flew to Holy Loch, Scotland. We had a submarine tender there and we took it to Roha, Spain, anchored out because they wouldn't let United States ships harbor there until we paid Franco [General Francisco Franco, dictator of Spain at the time.]. It cost X amount of dollars and anyway they [finally] got all of the money taken care of and we pulled into the harbor. After that, the SS-BNs started working out of there, Submarine Squadron 16. I was taking care of the vault that contained classified documents and I'd ride helicopters to deliver their secret orders. But on the way out of port, I'd ride the submarines out a ways and I'd give them their orders, then the helicopter would come out and pick me up. Then, when they came back in from their patrol run, they'd surface at about the same place they had dived. I'd ride the helicopter out and pick up their patrol report and we'd go back.

I'd go over to the submarine tender and type up the patrol report and have it ready before the submarine actually got in, so they could have a conference. They got those three-pronged deals that you ride on to go down to the submarine and I always had a briefcase in my hand, and one time I was scootin' out of the helicopter and the submarine was below us sixty feet or so. The ol' kid running the winch line, instead of taking up the slack, he hit the wrong button and started letting the slack out. The COB was waiting for me on the deck. He wanted to get me quickly aboard because the decks were almost awash.

He was looking up at me and later said, "I was hoping that you didn't get out there before the kid got the slack taken up," because I would have dropped about four feet and I would have flopped out of there and fell on that submarine and I wouldn't be here to talk about it.

They had two crews (the Blue and Gold) on all the fleet ballistic missile subs. I think they had about 137 crewmembers and nine officers on each crew.

I spent four years in Spain and then I went back to Charleston and caught the *John C. Calhoun* and rode her for three patrol runs. In fact, I made chief on one patrol. Actually, we [the crew] weren't supposed to know where we went. We'd submerge outside Charleston and run to the Russian coast. We'd just be one SSBN up there and another a thousand miles behind us coming on. Anyway, when we went out of Charleston on patrol, we worried about the Russian fishing trawlers, which were spy ships, identifying us. We'd have a diver along and we'd go ahead and dive at a shallow depth and send the diver out. He would go down and put some baffles on our screws so our signature would not identify us. Then when we got out to sea a ways, we'd come back up to a shallow depth and let the diver out to take off the baffles. Supposedly this kept the Russians from getting an ID on our screws. [As a sonar operator] I thought that to be a good idea.

When we got where we were going, we would be on the west side of Russia, I guess you'd say. I don't remember ever learning . . . well, we weren't supposed to know. We'd just go along at about three knots where we'd keep our cable out to get messages. We had a floating antenna and it would slide along in the water.

There was one time . . . I was on sonar and there wasn't anything, not any traffic out there. All at once, the boat came to a complete stop.

The OD says, "What's going on here? All ahead two-thirds."

About that time, the sound of motors and propellers engulfed us. I mean, they were all around us. We thought we had run into a [Russian] fishing trawler. They were just camped out there. They had their lines across, from one to another and, the fact was, we'd run into their cable and it caught us right about where the conning tower joined the hull. It was about an inch-thick steel cable. All kinds of racket broke out. The old man brought us up and went to the periscope to take a look because we had kinda pulled that one ship over, and he made sure there was someone there to take care of them. When we came up to periscope depth, he could see that everyone was all right, even those in the water, because we had actually tipped both of those trawlers over. There were other trawlers around and Captain Sertel saw that the others took care of them.

Satisfied, we got out of there. We went on our merry way until we pulled back into Charleston. We still had that cable dangling on both sides of us. It just broke and we took off with it still on board. That made the trip more than a little exciting. After we hit that cable, I knew that Captain Sertel had so much humanity about him that he just had to come up to periscope depth to make sure no one was drowning or such.

161

When I departed from Charleston, I went to New Orleans and recruited out of there. The CO of the recruiting program had kicked out our officer programs lieutenant. I was a chief, so I took over the lieutenant's job. Assuming the program officer's duties, I went about Louisiana recruiting OCS candidates. I tried to retire down there, but they wouldn't let me. They sent me to SubPac, Pearl [Submarine Force Pacific, Pearl Harbor]. The chief who ran the personnel office there was retiring and they needed someone in there, so they hooked me for another three years. We went over there and I ran the personnel office. Of course, you had to ride a submarine for so many submerged hours each month to receive your submarine pay. I'd just catch one going to San Diego or some place and I'd get three months worth of hours in and then fly back. Right before we left, our chief of staff (he was on the *Pomfret* with me, my first submarine and his first. Only now, he was a captain and I was a chief) told me they needed a yeoman to bring back a submarine from Guam.

Their yeoman had gotten sick, so I said, "Hey, can I go?"

He thought a second and said, "You ain't got anybody you can send?"

"Yeah, I've got people I can send," I told him, "but I want to go. I haven't been there in twenty years."

Then he said back, "Yeah, if you can get somebody to run the office."

I said, "Okay."

That's how I went to Guam. I got on this fast attack boat, an SSN, and we were getting ready to come on back. We got out there and they were trying the emergency power, which was a Fairbanks 500 diesel. They had to keep it up. In case something happened to the nuclear power plant, we'd have one diesel to run on. Well, we got into some heavier outboard pressure because of the bow structure—exhaust pressure has to be greater than the sea pressure or, instead of the exhaust going out, the sea water comes in.

I was laying there in my rack and the chief came and got me, and said, "The XO needs you. We've gotta change operations on the outgoing."

I told him, "All we've got to do is to build up more pressure here than what we've got out there." We changed it and went back into port.

We went back out the next night, and we flooded again. We flooded it for three nights, in the engine room, before they could get their wording right, instead of just saying build up the pressure greater than it is on the outside. It was ridiculous. It didn't hurt anything—the little engine room for the Fairbanks was watertight. However, you just didn't want it happening. That engineering chief wasn't the brightest bulb.

The truly bright one was the best skipper I ever served under. His name was Frank Sertel, skipper of the *John C. Calhoun*. He was an ex–white hat, a noncommissioned ranker, a hawse-hole climber. He came up through the ranks. He made commander, and then I guess he went on to make captain. He was good with men and he sure knew his submarines. He was just so much of a man's man, it was just real nice being on that submarine. Everybody in the squadron, if they could have gotten orders to be on the *Calhoun*, then they sure would have been. The thing is that we never had any bad patrols. Even the routine ones went well—just normal, run-of-the-mill patrols. There was one time, off Vietnam. We dropped some SEALs off one night, and they took a rubber boat and went in. We were supposed to pick them up two days later at the same place. We were back there two days after, but the SEALs weren't. We never did know what happened to them. These SEALs had ridden with us from where we picked them up in Hawaii.

In fact, there was another time we stopped off in Yokosuka and picked up a couple of civilians. They gave the impression they were from Washington, D.C. [CIA headquarters is just across the Potomac River from Washington.] They brought on some kind of radar detection equipment that told them what sort of radar was operating. Anyway, they put their equipment aboard and we headed up toward Russia. All the while, we were going along making note of exactly what type of radar the Russians were operating along the coast. Then we were inside the ten-mile limit, I think, but outside the three-mile limit. Back then, the three-mile was what you had to go by. Only the Russians had a ten-mile limit, they said, but it was not the international limit.

About that time, this Russian destroyer came out looking for us. It thrashed around and evidently never got a solid fix on us. The OD eased us out to the east, I think it was. Anyway, we moved toward deeper water, and we pulled the same sort of trick on them that we had done on the *Pomfret*. There are these layers of water, alternating cold and warm, and sonar or subsurface radar cannot penetrate them with any sort of accuracy. Not at all, in fact, when it comes to sonar. Looking back on it, there was another tense moment.

We went to Hong Kong one time and that's when you went past the river—the *Twinging*—what was the name of that place? Kowloon, is it? I volunteered for shore patrol duty when we were pulling into Hong Kong. A lieutenant j.g. and I went over to Kowloon because they had an imaginary Red China–Hong Kong line on the northern part of Kowloon. None of the U.S. sailors could go past that line. If there were some bars they wanted to go to, they had to be on the British side of the Kowloon line. So we sat in the British officer's club, this j.g. and I had us a few drinks and the Limeys were supposed to go into town and one of our guys would come over and say "Hey, we've got one of your guys and he's in such-and-such bar, but he's okay." When we got on back to Hong Kong, we got on a boat and went back to the submarine. I didn't realize while I was there that just right across the street there was the line. The thing is, those Brits couldn't hold a candle to some of the characters we had aboard the *Pomfret* or the *Calhoun*.

On my first submarine, we had one black person, a first class quartermaster, one smart dude. He was from California. We called him "Ratchet Jaw Williams." He ran his mouth all the time. He's the one who taught me to play pinochle. He didn't have much luck getting a pinochle partner, so I was his partner. He was actually the assistant navigator of the submarine. He was officer material and he should have been commissioned. He just didn't have the college education to go with it. Nevertheless, he sure had a good high school education.

We were on our way to WesPac, and we had Filipino mess cooks and stewards for the officers and they [officers] ate in the forward battery. We ate in the after battery. The control room was divided in two. So when the officers got done eating, the mess stewards had to take the bowls and whatever back to our mess to wash up. Then they had to take bowls of beans and corn and steaks into the control room, into the forward battery, and into the officers' mess.

My office was back about twelve inches from the watertight hatch between the control room and the rear battery, and I had a sliding door on it. I just had enough room to step in and sit down to get to my typewriter. But to get up, I had to put my foot out in the aisle to get out of the office. One evening, I put my foot out just as the steward was coming through the hatch with a tray full of food. He splattered on the deck, the food splashed, and the dishes broke. Was he mad! He went and got himself a knife and I saw him coming back so

I went and closed the hatch to the control room. One of the officers got ahold of him and talked to him.

We put him off at Pearl when we got back home and the old man said, "We don't need you anymore." He couldn't handle it. It was an accident, but we had to move him out because he was crazy. Oh, on the nuke subs we also had a genius.

He was smart, like graduating number one at the nuke school. He was a second class, I think, but he didn't have any common sense about him. He was making wine on the nuke sub somehow. He had this—we called them "poopie suits"—they had Velcro and they were blue. No buttons on them, because they might pop off and fly into something, hence the Velcro. He had sewn pockets on the inside of his poopie suit and had little plastic bottles of wine in them. Anyway, the COB got after him, so they kicked him out of the nuke part and put him to doing laundry on board this SSBN. Well, one day I'm on the sonar and heard a noise.

I poked the OD and said, "I'm hearin' a noise and I don't know what it is. It must be ship's noise. Either that or somebody's in our baffles or something like that."

"Okay," he says, "I'll clear the baffles."

When you clear the baffles, you go this way [demonstrates a movement off a straight line fore-to-aft] and then you can hear behind you. That's because you can never hear *straight* behind you. On a 180, you only hear screw noise.

So he did and I said, "I-I don't hear it from outside, but I still hear this noise."

He got a couple of people and they went through the boat trying to find what the noises were. Well, this ol' kid was down in the head where we had our washers and dryer. He had a vacuum cleaner and had it [the hose] over a pipe. That vacuum cleaner was running and vibrating that pipe. Through the entire submarine you could just hear that pipe going *umm-umm-umm*. That's what the ship's mystery noise was. No common sense at all. Anyway, aboard the *Calhoun* we learned to live with the oddballs, as well as the rest. That's about all I can say, except I spent twenty years in the navy, mostly in the submarine service, and never regretted a minute of it.

10

CHRIS KREISS
LIEUTENANT COMMANDER, USN (RET.)

With dramatic rapidity, 1963 opened with a string of successes and one terrible tragedy for the U.S. Submarine Service. The Department of Defense announced the deployment of the first of three Polaris missile submarines to the Mediterranean on March 28. Defense analysts look upon this as a substitute for the dismantling of U.S. Jupiter ballistic missiles in Turkey and Italy.

Then, on April 10, tragedy struck when the U.S. nuclear-powered submarine *Thresher* (SSN 593), commanded by LCDR John W. Harvey, USN, went down with all hands—139 officers, enlisted men, and civilian technicians—at nearly 240 nautical miles east of Cape Cod, Massachusetts. It appeared that the disaster resulted from a reactor shutdown ("scram") during a test dive to the submarine's maximum depth of 1,300 feet. The *Thresher* was the world's first nuclear submarine to be lost.

Four days later, the Polaris submarine *Sam Houston* (SSBN 609), which was the first U.S. ballistic missile submarine assigned to the Mediterranean, paid a visit to Ozmir, Turkey. This was the first call on a foreign port other than Holy Loch, Scotland, by a U.S. Polaris sub.

Three days later, on April 17, the first British nuclear submarine, the *Dreadnaught*, was commissioned with CDR B. F. P. (Peter) Samborne, Royal Navy, as the first commander. Six days after that, the USS *Lafayette* (SSBN 616) became the first of the third class of Polaris submarines to be commissioned, with her first commanding officers named as CDR P. J. Hannifin (Blue crew) and CDR James T. Strong serving Gold. On April 24 Secretary of the Navy Fred H. Korth announced that a Deep Submergence Review Group (DSRG) been established. Rear Admiral E. C. Stephan, USN, commanded it for the purpose of review and to formalize all of the navy's requirements. This included deep-ocean search, location, rescue, and salvage operations.

On June 7, a U.S. Court of Inquiry completed its work on investigating the loss of the submarine *Thresher*. All court records, along with its findings of facts, opinions, and recommendations, were delivered to Admiral H. P. Smith, USN, Commander in Chief, U.S. Atlantic Fleet, who was the convening authority of the court. Following an intensive review by Smith, the report was submitted to the secretary of the navy. Later that month, on June 20, the opinion of the court of inquiry was made public. Their conclusions stated that a flooding casualty in the engine room was now believed to be the most likely cause of the sinking. This accident was brought about by a piping failure in one of the submarine's saltwater systems.

The navy's deep-diving bathyscaph, *Trieste II*, searching for the sunken *Thresher*, recovered a peace of copper tubing and a fitting with markings from the lost submarine. The *Trieste II* made a total of five dives during seventeen days on station searching for the remains of the *Thresher*. Her support vessels returned to Boston with the *Trieste II*. Later, on the sixth of July, Secretary of the Navy Fred H. Korth directed an end to the operational portions of the search for the lost submarine. In his public declaration, he announced that "the location of structural parts of the *Thresher* on the ocean floor have been positively confirmed by the bathyscaph *Trieste II.*"

On October 20, the first Polaris A-3 missile launched from a submarine was fired from the *Andrew Jackson* (SSBN 619). The test proved a remarkable success. In mid-November, on the sixteenth, President John F. Kennedy, on the deck of the USS *Observation Island* (EAG 154), observed a launch of a Polaris A-3 from the *Andrew Jackson.* Again, the launch was extraordinarily successful.

On December 4, following the tragic assassination of President Kennedy, the U.S. Navy revealed the details of their new Submarine Rocket (SUBROC) anti-submarine weapon. The SUBROC had been undergoing testing at the Naval Ordnance Test Station at China Lake, California. Details described the SUBROC as an underwater-launched missile with a range of some twenty-five nautical miles, carrying a nuclear depth bomb. The missile was fired from a standard torpedo tube. It had a solid-fuel rocket motor that propelled the missile out of the water and through the air toward its target, whereupon it submerged and detonated on or near the intended target.

Early in January 1964, a new naval supply center, tasked with the responsibility of support for the Polaris missile weapons systems throughout the world, was commissioned at Charleston, South Carolina. Four days later, on January 10, 1964, the Military Sea Transportation Service (MSTS) placed in commission the first of several FBM resupply ships. The USNS *Norwalk* (TAK 279) was commissioned in New Orleans, Louisiana. It was a converted Victory freighter whose keel was laid in 1945 in Portland, Oregon. It was commissioned as the *Norwalk Victory.*

On February 1, Admiral H. G. Rickover, USN, assistant chief of the bureau of ships for nuclear propulsion, retired at the mandatory age of sixty-four, only to immediately return to active duty in a retired status. On February 5, the navy announced plans to base Polaris submarines at Charleston, South Carolina, and Melville, Rhode Island. In the event this plan was accepted, which it was, the Charleston base would be—and was—established as the only Polaris base in the continental United States.

U.S. submarine USS *Henry Clay* (SSBN 625) successfully fired a Polaris A-2 missile on April 20 while surfaced off the coast at Cape Kennedy, Florida. This was the first launch of a Polaris missile from a surfaced submarine and, at the time, no further plans for surface Submarine Launched Ballistic Missiles (SLBM) were announced.

After three and a half years of operation out of Holy Loch, Scotland, the USS *George Washington* (SSBN 598)—the first to deploy with Polaris missiles—returned to her home port at New London, Connecticut. During her period of extended service, the *Washington* undertook fifteen Polaris deterrent patrols in the North Atlantic and the Bering Sea. During an overhaul that followed at the General Dynamics/Electric Boat yard in Groton, Connecticut, the *Washington* underwent modification to carry the Polaris A-3 missile.

In a startling announcement on July 15, Chief of the Soviet Navy, Admiral Sergei G. Gorshkov, declared that the Soviet nuclear-powered submarines had operated in "distant areas of the ocean, beneath Arctic ice and in equatorial waters."

The Polaris missile assembly facility for the Pacific fleet was commissioned on September 8, at the U.S. Naval Ammunition Depot, Bangor, Washington. This 430-acre site, designated as Polaris Missile Facility, Pacific, served as the primary link between industrial producers of the missile and the fleet. A week later, the French government reported that a nuclear power plant of the type designed for planned nuclear submarines had operated for the past three weeks. On the September 28, the U.S. ballistic missile submarine *Daniel Webster* (SSBN 626) sailed from Charleston, South Carolina, for a two-month patrol in the Atlantic. This deployment represented the first for the A-3 Polaris missile.

On October 11, the U.S. Navy announced that the majority of the wreckage of the nuclear attack submarine *Thresher* (SSN 593) was located. A representative of the navy produced reasonably clear photographs of the wreckage of the submarine's diving planes and sail structure, with the hull number clearly visible, taken by the bathyscaph *Trieste II*. On October 27, the U.S. attack submarine *Seadragon* (SSN 584) arrived in Hong Kong. It was the first nuclear-propelled ship to visit any port in the Far East. On the last day of October, Japan formally notified the United States that U.S. nuclear-powered ships would be permitted to visit Japanese ports. Ships carrying nuclear weapons, however, were still officially prohibited.

November 12 saw two events of considerable importance. The USS *Seadragon* arrived in Sasebo for the first visit of a nuclear-propelled ship to Japan. Approximately two thousand of an anticipated fifteen thousand demonstrators were on the docks as the ship arrived in Japanese waters. In addition, France announced details of its five-year plan to construct a nuclear strike force, including Polaris-type submarines. One such submarine, they claimed, would be operational by 1970, with another pair under construction by that date. The United States Navy's nuclear experts did not take France's ambitious claims too seriously.

On December 26, 1964, the first ballistic missile submarine patrol began in the Pacific. The *Daniel Boone* (SSBN 629) departed Guam, armed with sixteen Polaris A-3 missiles. Although being unsure of their destination, the crew maintained a high state of enthusiasm over being the first in WesPac.

We have so far seen the lives of yeomen and torpedomen, of signalmen and sonarmen, radiomen and fire controlmen and enginemen, the denizens

USS *Tucson* (SS 770) sonar room.
Courtesy of United States Navy

of both diesel and nuclear power rooms. We have seen these duties through the eyes of officers and enlisted men. Now is the time to move to a completely new world, that of the quartermaster. A quartermaster wears many hats, much like a yeoman. They can be on the TDC one day, back in the WWII times, or on lookout, or operating the plotting table, or on the bow or stern planes, the diving control, or standing watch at the sonar station. In addition, they have the responsibility of keeping the lists of weapons and all other items aboard. They are more than number crunchers, however. They work closely with the COB to see to the needs, nourishment, and safety of the entire crew—a tall order for someone usually portrayed as a man with a clipboard in hand and pencil behind his ear. We'll hear from such a man next.

Chris Kreiss as an enlisted man.
Courtesy of Chris Kreiss

L̲ike most guys, I went through submarine school at New London.
Before that, though, I had made rank and was assigned to a surface ship. I had some difficulties while at my first duty station. I
needed to find some answers and a way around them [his problems]
so I wrote to BuPers [Navy Bureau of Personnel]. They arranged authorization for me to transfer and enter submarine school. That
changed the whole course of my life.

In my estimation, the New London school was not so hard as to
cause anyone to want to quit. Still, they kept you busy all the time.
When we weren't in classes, we were taking tests. Not just on the
subject we'd been studying that week, but personality tests and
psychological things. I made third class quartermaster shortly after

graduating from the school. No one else in my family had served in the armed forces, so I was doing something new to them all.

After the school, when I joined my first submarine in 1943 at Pearl Harbor, we patrolled off the coast of Russia. [Isn't it interesting that this early our navy intelligence considered the Soviet Union enough of an enemy to maintain surveillance on their activities?] Our intention was to remain entirely undetected. Sometimes that came to be almost impossible. There was one time when the seawater got loose in the engine room and the battery compartments. It was so cold that, even though it was still liquid, it froze many of the electrodes. We had to work hard and fast to clear up that mess.

That was bad, but I think the strangest patrol I went on was one while our boat was assigned to ComSubPac out of Midway. I was a chief quartermaster then and our skipper, Aaron Stevenson, was having some problems with his eyesight that interfered with his function as captain of a boat. He got worse until he sent a message to headquarters, ComSubPac, asking to be relieved. Ironically, they sent out his *brother* to relieve him, something unusual in the submarine service. Bill Stevenson became our new skipper, relieving his brother when we got into Midway. For that patrol, we got a navy unit citation, an award that covers the entire crew, the boat, everything. We had charted a lot of Russian activity and intercepted their radio signals, took photographs, and such. For all of that, we never got a scratch.

In the meantime, my promotion to ensign had come through. However, at that time they [the navy] had the policy of not letting people stay aboard when they went from enlisted to commissioned rank. Therefore, they transferred me off to the relief crew in Midway. I stayed around Midway and helped with the relief crew. When a boat

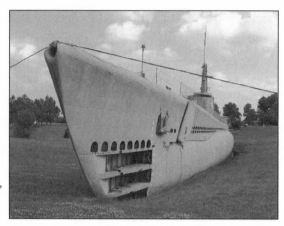

USS *Batfish* (SS 310) as now on display in War Memorial Park, Muskogee, Oklahoma.

Courtesy of Chris Kreiss

would come in off patrol, the crew would go off on R and R and we'd take over and operate the boat, to bring her in. We'd see that the shop crew did the repairs and charged them off.

Usually the ship's crew would make up a list of the things they wanted done. We'd just punch it and make sure it was completed. While I was in relief crew, I became acquainted with another officer named Jake Price. He was a lieutenant commander at that time and he was leaving for assignment to a submarine. About four or five months into my time there, Jake received an assignment to the *Batfish*. At that time they were having trouble with the *Batfish* skipper—so Jake went down there and he [the skipper] had to be relieved.

Jake took over in 1944, and when I found out, I said, "Jake, how about takin' me aboard? I'm tired of looking at the gooney birds out here." Which is about all the recreation we had out there on Guam. We'd watch the gooney birds dance. Did you ever watch the gooney birds dance? They go like this [indicates a wavy line] then they kind of line up, four of them, and they go like this [illustrates oblique zigs and zags] and then like that. I think it's what gave them their name.

So anyway, he [Price] arranged for it and took me aboard the *Batfish* as an ensign. I served there for a while. I sure liked it. Matter of fact, I liked most all the skippers I served with. I never got along with Barry Stevenson, but he was a good skipper on the *Tunny*.

Of course, we were used to the steel boats, so we served as a school boat at the school in New London. The only time we left there was to go to the Philadelphia Navy Yard for fitting up with some experimental equipment for making fresh water, called a Kleinschmidt; we were the first ones to get the equipment. Then they started to put them on all submarines.

Before that, the only way to make fresh water in the diesel-electric boats was to poke a hole in the line that came off the distillery that ran off the engine. They could make two thousand gallons a day [when in new condition]. Anyway, that's the sort of thing we taught at the school. That's when we'd take the students out. I like the thought that Sam Deley [inventor of the Kleinschmidt] himself would approve. And Self Childs, who was a great skipper, too, although they didn't serve in a wartime situation. Self Childs made a name for himself. He's still alive; he's living in Florida. He took the *Sea Devil* out and then made a name for himself on the *Prado*. Though I have to say that Jake Price was the one I knew the best and served with under wartime conditions.

I made one war patrol on the *Aspro*, and four on the *Batfish* with Jake Price. After our fifth patrol, we came into Pearl Harbor and went for R and R at the Royal Hawaiian, which was really something. When we went back out again, it was the *Batfish*'s sixth patrol and my fifth. We'd been patrolling awhile, and we'd been going up and down off the coast of the Philippines. New orders came and they sent us to an area called the Luzon Straits and the Pubuyan Channel. We learned later that the intelligence people got that the Japanese were bringing flyers out of the Philippines because we were gradually taking over the islands. MacArthur was leading the way back in.

There was a port at the north end of the Philippines called Aparri Harbor. The Japanese were moving their flyers up there and, eventually, taking them off by submarine and bringing them back to the mainland of Japan. They [the navy] sent us into the Pubuyan Channel for the purpose of intercepting them. We hadn't been there very long and we got contact. I might explain that the Japanese had radar, but they were very slow in developing it. It was mostly for aircraft, so we didn't know how well they could detect a ship. A submarine has a very small silhouette and it makes it hard to pick out one. No matter, radar puts out a signal that can be detected by other radars and we managed to pick up theirs on ours. It makes a sort of scrawly mark on the radarscope when another radar is coming in. Therefore, we turned our radar off.

We had some sort of equipment called an Electronic Counter Measure (ECM) but it was stationary, it would not rotate. We had to turn the boat to get a stronger signal and we sort of expected that; if it had been an American submarine, it would send a signal, because we could communicate by radar signals in the form of dashes and dots in Morse Code. Quickly, we homed in on them and, on this occasion, we took some ranges and bearings, and finally got close enough to fire on them. We'd definitely identified them as a Jap submarine. We fired—I think—four torpedoes. Only, they [the Japanese sub] speeded up. Consequently when our torpedoes reached the end of our approach, the torpedoes missed them.

We had the TDC up in the conning tower. Whenever we got a contact by sound or radar, or periscope reading, we'd get a bearing on the target, which they'd then put into the TDC. In addition, when we got the range, we'd put that in. Although somehow the data computer was supposed to solve the problem of enemy course and speed for us, we also ran a manual plot, and all the data on bearing, speed, and course, and put them on this manual plot.

I was the one working this manual plot. The reason I brought this up is that they didn't catch the change in speed because the number of inputs were too far apart. We actually proved them out on paper. I caught them in the end but it was too late to change bearings. After we missed, they went on by, so we turned out away from them and made a sort of end-around run. They stayed on the same course. They headed for the Philippines, so it allowed us to get around them and into position again. This time, we got their course and speed down good. We fired three torpedoes at them, but one of them hung up in our tube, while the other pair ran out normal and one of them sank the sub, which we later identified as the I-41.

The next night, approximately another day later, we contacted another sub, same rate. This one held a course to the south. The first one had been headed north, away from the Philippines, and the second one headed toward the islands. This time we did the same thing. Only on this run, when we got radar contact and came in close, we dove and kept only our radar out of the water. That way we could still take bearings and not expose our periscope. When we maneuvered into a firing position, we fired four torpedoes again. They ran hot, straight, and normal, and we sunk that one, too.

Come the next night, we did the same thing again. Another sub appeared, also headed south. This one dove just about the time we closed her and was about ready to fire. Only suddenly, she came back

Chris Kreiss as an officer.
Courtesy of Chris Kreiss

up on the same bearing. We wanted to make an approach on her. We lost some time because we had to swing around and fire torpedoes from our stern tubes. We'd run out of torpedoes up in the bow. We had to make our approach and then do a 180-degree turn in order to fire, which we did, and sunk that one, too. We had a regular feast of Japanese subs.

There was a book written called Batfish, *the Champion "Submarine-Killer" Submarine of World War II* by Christian Lauder. He was a radioman on board. He's since passed away. We had our wartime insignia made up by someone who would come to our ports and make designs for various subs. Anyway, these sinkings were confirmed by intelligence and, for that patrol, we received the presidential unit citation. The skipper was awarded the Navy Cross and several other officers and enlisted received other awards. I received the Bronze Star.

On one patrol, after we'd sunk several ships, we gradually began to work our way south. It was the same patrol when they sent us in to Hinan Island, which is off the coast of China. The only guided torpedoes we had during the war were these little short things and we could put them in the tubes and fire them. We called them "cuties." When we were down there off Hinan, we found some targets that were somewhat small. Well, we had some of those [guided torpedoes] aboard, so the skipper decided to use them. We fired them but they didn't do any good. In fact, there was always a lot of concern that the things would circle around and hit us. If that were to happen—not with the cuties I don't think, but there were some torpedoes that made circular runs. In the case of the *Tang*, that's what sank the *boat*. The same thing happened to the *Toffey*. In both cases, they were both lost at sea. Anyway, those guided torpedoes were the only ones I know of and the ones they had on the *Batfish* were the only ones they tried.

After that incident, we went down to Perth [Australia] for R and R. Fremantle is the port for the submarines to operate out of, we had a good time there. I think it was actually the best port because the folks there treated submariners royally. Our subs also went into Brisbane, on the east coast, closer to China.

We left there after our R and R and a week of training, went up the coast of Australia, and put into Exmouth Gulf. We had some special operations people we had to drop off there. In the meantime, we discovered that one of our periscopes was not operating good [sic]. It had developed scratches. Every time it went up, we'd see these score marks on the barrel of the periscope. As a result, as we headed north to our patrol area, they told us to put into Darwin, which is way up at the north end of Australia. We put in there and they had a navy tug that did a little bit of repair work and had a hone.

Chris Kreiss in command
of the control room.
Courtesy of Chris Kreiss

We stayed in there for twenty-four hours. They pulled our periscope, and discovered that while we were in Perth, some work-man had left a bolt inside where the bearings that guide the 'scope are located—there's twenty-one bearings that guide the 'scope. In be-tween the bearings there is a hollow area and this bolt had been left in there [one of these hollows] and it was rubbing against the 'scope and putting scoring marks on it. They took the bolt out and then honed the 'scope. However, whenever we used that 'scope after that repair, the water would run down quite strongly. The skipper would [he chuckles] have to wear a rain hat or the water would come down over his eyes. Even so, we managed to complete the patrol because it wasn't a particularly serious leak; it was only a troublesome leak be-cause it affected the use of the periscope.

On our way out from there, we went through some straits where the Japanese had frequently attacked submarines. It was a very narrow strait. We managed to get through that all right without any trouble. Later, as we were going north, out through the Zulu Sea, we suddenly saw targets; one looked like a big freighter. The skipper decided to come in on them on the surface. It was night and so we got just about in firing range and all of a sudden they opened up these fake covers on the deck—they looked like huge cargo boxes—they manned their guns and started shooting at us. [A trick the Japanese learned from the Germans, who had decoy ships they called "raiders" operating in the South Atlantic against surface ships, and both U.S. and British submarines.] Immediately, we turned tail, dove, and got down fairly deep. They came right after us, dropped depth-charges, and worked us over for a while.

We slowly edged down under a gradient. We had a bank of thermographs and could tell the temperature of the water. When it got colder, we could get underneath that depth layer; the sonar equipment on the surface craft would bounce off that gradient. They couldn't detect where we were. That's how we got away. We sneaked away, went up farther north through the Philippines, and looked for downed flyers. They were attacking the Philippines at the time and we had a couple of flyers reported, but we never could find them.

We also went by where the *Darter* went aground on the shoals off the Philippines coast on the western end, facing the sea that we would cross to go to China. The *Darter* went up so high and dry that they couldn't get her off. There was another submarine close by, the *Dace*, and it took all the crew aboard. Before that, the *Darter* crew destroyed all the equipment that the Japanese might have gotten and used. After they got all the crew off, the *Dace* fired at the *Darter*, trying to destroy as much of it as they could. So from then on, whenever a submarine was anywhere near, they'd go by and fire at the *Darter* to destroy it some more. We only did that this one time.

Another time when we were on patrol, we received a bit of a workover. We'd just come out from Midway and we were patrolling around the island called Sophie John. On the American maps, it's called Lot's Wife. You know the story: When Lot and his wife were leaving some situation [Sodom and Gomorrah], they were told not to look back. Only, his wife did and she turned into stone [a pillar of salt], so they call that island Lot's Wife because it is a pinnacle raised up out of the water, way down south of Japan. We were patrolling around that area. In daytime, we ran submerged with our periscope up and I guess we were making a wake. There were some Japanese ships going by. We were trying to get a bearing on them in order to make an approach on them, but our position left us a little bit too far out to fire on them.

Apparently, a plane—*a plane!*—spotted our periscope and the Jap dropped a bomb on us. Of course, we didn't see him at all. But when the bomb dropped, it struck the ship itself. Fortunately, the only damage it did was way up on the bridge. The 'scope was "cheated," it had glass on it about this thick [demonstrates a distance of about two and a half to three inches] and it was a gyro-repeater so we could tell what course we were on when we were surfaced. It could also take bearings for us. The electronics and graphics for that were turned off down below. It was a coincidence that they forgot to turn it off, so when the bomb dropped, it broke the glass and water got in. That shorted it out, and the gyro alarm went off. It didn't harm the gyro, but the alarm went off anyway until someone threw the switch to stop it. We also had some other minor leakage from that bomb. So then, after the bomb, the surface craft closed in and started to depth-charge us, but we managed to sneak off after they worked us over for a while. We got on another gradient and went off on a course they didn't know. Before that, we took quite a pounding from the depth-charges. They shook things up inside a lot.

The last patrol I made on the *Batfish* with Walter Stahl was a successful one. We didn't sink any ships, but we picked up three flyers over off Kiushu, which is the Japanese island where Nagasaki is. Around that time was when they were dropping the A-bombs on Hiroshima and then on Nagasaki. These fellows were on a plane that had to ditch and they had been thrown through the Plexiglas, so they were injured. Two of them appeared in good condition. They were the pilot, co-pilot, and navigator. The rest of the crew went down and then got out. We tried to find them that night, but couldn't. So we signaled for someone else to search for them.

They sent out a rescue plane called "Dumbos." They carried a boat underneath of this big flying boat. After a couple of passes, they located them [the survivors] and dropped this boat. Two fliers got aboard the boat and, early the next morning, they homed us in on them and there they were. We took them off the small boat and tried to destroy it. We fired at it with the twenty-millimeter and we couldn't even sink this thing. We finally had to give it up because we were out there in a kind of vulnerable position. As it happened, we had these fliers on board when an American plane came over and bombed us. We were on what they called lifeguard duty. So we operated, had to be, on the surface during daytime. So this guy—an American, no less—comes over and thinks, "Oh, boy, I'm gonna get me a submarine." He circled around and we flashed the recognition signal right up to when he dropped his bomb.

Fortunately, he was a poor aimer and he dropped it quite a ways from us. We dove and got the hell out of there, otherwise we'd have had another sinking of an American submarine by an American. Such things actually did happen several times a year. I think they sank the *Sealion* that way. We took those fliers over to Iwo Jima and left them off because they needed medical attention.

By this time, the fighting was well over and they'd just had a ceremony over on the marine base for the Iwo Jima survivors. I was commissary officer, so I had to go over and find some supplies—we were running low on food—this was before the actual signing of the secession of the war. And I knew they had just boxes and boxes and boxes of chow stacked up out in the open, and beer and turkeys—frozen turkeys, you know—so I drew off some frozen turkeys that had come from Australia and some meat and stuff and we got it back aboard. When I tried to serve the stuff [laughing] everybody was looking at those frozen turkeys—they were so scrawny, we couldn't help but laugh. It wasn't too long after that we headed back and they sent us down to Guam. Then I went back to Pearl Harbor and that was it. I just had to get in that last patrol.

I served on three submarines after the war. My first one turned out to be the *Greenfish* [SS 351], which I went aboard just shortly after she was commissioned. She was still in New London, Connecticut, and we went out on the shakedown cruise. That took us way down to South America, where we put into Barranquilla, Colombia, where there was the port and we had to take a train or a car to a larger city; I think it was Santa Marta. We stayed there overnight and had a little R and R. I'll always remember that cruise. As we were going north toward the city, there were all of these children out in the dump scratching through the trash looking for food. It was so sad to see them; they must have been orphans. We had some liaison people who said that yeah, it was too bad.

After that, we went to Panama and while we were there, I got orders. Since I had come up as an enlisted man, I didn't have any advanced schooling, so they wanted us to get schooling now. I was sent to college for five semesters at the University of South Carolina, where I got my officer's training and the other civilian classes. When I finished there, I went to Newport, Rhode Island, where I went through an entire year of general line school, which is extra training you have to take as an officer. After that I was supposed to go to a submarine on the East Coast, only I really wanted to go to the West Coast. As it happened, a fellow who had a child that needed special medical attention at the hospital in Bethesda, Maryland, had checked in with a request, so they asked me would I swap with him and I told them I would be happy to.

That's how I managed to go to the West Coast and get on the *Segundo*. I spent three years on her as engineering officer. I held that position during the snorkel conversion, then from there I went to the *Bluegill* as the exec. They were getting ready to put the *Bluegill* out of commission, so I only spent about six months aboard her and had to go through decommission. After that, I spent the rest of my time in the navy aboard a destroyer.

At one time, I served at the fleet sonar school in San Diego. I was operations officer there. Something that I skipped over earlier happened when I was aboard the *Catfish*. I was then an officer and the qualifications were a little more severe than for the enlisted, so I had to go through qualification again before I could get my gold dolphins.

Nowadays you see all this Hollywood stuff about the war and everyone has gold or silver dolphins. We didn't have silver ones in World War II. We had this little cloth patch on our sleeves that had a dolphin. It was later on that they changed over to the pin. Anyway, I passed my qualifications requirement, got my gold dolphin, and returned to the *Catfish*.

One thing: Whenever we went to Australia [from Pearl Harbor or another northern port] we crossed the equator. We had the usual ceremony, only rather abbreviated because we couldn't stay on the surface and do all that the surface ships could do. Anyway, all the Pollywogs received their indoctrination into all honors of the Shellback Society. One of the guys going through got his head shaved—he was very egotistical about his hairdo and it was very upsetting to him. I was on the other side of it. Later in my career, I got aboard a destroyer and we went down to Australia during peacetime. We had the whole ceremony then. Actually, I crossed the equator four times. As to how many times I crossed the 180th parallel, I can't begin to tell you, it was so many times.

After the *Catfish*'s sixth patrol, we went back to the shipyard near San Francisco at Hunter's Point. Walter Snow relieved him [Price]. Jake went back and was going to get a new boat on the East Coast. Then I made one more patrol; it was relatively small; it wasn't the most popular trip that I've ever served this country. I don't know, maybe he [Walter Snow] just set everybody wrong, 'cause Jake was so popular. Around WesPac, he was one of the least popular guys. Perhaps he was a bit too regimental [sic]. At any rate, we made the last patrol with the *Batfish*. When the war was over, they sent us back.

En route, we stopped off at Guam and Pearl Harbor, finally tying up at Pearl Harbor for a while. We finally ended up at San Francisco and after many, many months—it took at least six months—I took the *Batfish* out of commission. In one way, that was a sad thing. That boat had been home for so many of us, for so long, it was hard to let go.

On one cruise, we visited up in Acaba, Jordan, which is at the northeast tip of the Red Sea. When we went up there, I got the command band on the *Peaque*. There may have been another submarine that went there since then, but we were the only one to visit there at the time. We made a port visit there and conducted bilateral training missions with the SEALs and our forces along with the armed forces of our allies in the Persian Gulf.

Unfortunately, at the time of the Gulf War, I was on shore duty in Yokuska [sic] Japan and the closest involvement I had was that I was able to be—I just *happened* to be in the Short Targeting Terminal when we sent out the first order to launch a Tomahawk. After sending the message, I went back to my station at Command Administration, which was maybe a hundred yards away and, by the time I got back there, the chief of naval operations already had word that the Tomahawk had already made a strike and wiped out the target. It's incredible the speed at which these things move. I just missed Iraqi Freedom.

I left Command Admin in September 2001, so I was back again on shore duty for that. That makes me either the luckiest guy or the most *un*lucky guy in the submarine service. I think we did them [the Tomahawks] much wiser in Iraqi Freedom than we did in Desert Storm, the first Persian Gulf War. In that war, we didn't appreciate the accuracy or the survivability of the Tomahawks, and we expended many more than we had to on a single target. In Iraqi Freedom, we got a lot more bang for our buck.

Now, changing the subject, when it comes to the modern navy,

Tomahawk land attack missile (T-LAM) rises into the air after being launched from the USS *Florida* (SSGN 728), Ohio Class.

Courtesy of United States Navy

I don't know anything too much about the surface Navy, but from what I can see we're doing a great job. I know that the submarine people are doing a *fantastic* job. I made my first trip on a nuclear boat on the *Nautilus* right after she was commissioned, when Anderson had command of it, way back in 1957. I don't recall if I was on shore duty or another sub at the time. We only went out for a day and came back. They wanted all the officers to get some experience, to get to know what was—what the future—was about. However, I never served on one of them. Still, I think the current nuclear navy is very capable. Since I retire next month [April 2005], I feel confident that they can fulfill their assigned missions very capably.

The future, I'm not so confident about. Because of the current shipbuilding trends, I'm not so sure we will be able to maintain a capable force in the [far] future. Technology is all getting more expensive. Our lack of buying power—we're not going to be able to buy submarines in mass—the industrial production base is collapsing and I see things gyrating and getting out of control.

Tomahawk land attack missile in tube on the USS *Charlotte* (SSN 766).
Courtesy of United States Navy

One thing I have always wished they would go to—one thing they might do is go back to building diesel boats. Then we'd be having a larger fleet of diesel-electric or alternative energy submarines, which might be less of an investment than nuclear-powered submarines.

As far as my various duties are concerned, I served at the fleet sonar school in San Diego. I was operations officer there, setting up operations for the students to go out on submarines and some on destroyers. Then they'd set up and the destroyers would try to find the sub and the sub would make approaches on the destroyers, so they [the students] got it both ways. We also had planes engaged in these.

One of the significant things that happened there at the fleet sonar school, I had a cousin who was in the navy, stationed at an Antisubmarine warfare squadron at San Diego. He went out with his planes in these same exercises. I always knew when he would be going out because I set up the exercises his squadron was participating in. One night, one of these planes had to ditch because it had engine trouble. I came to find out that my cousin was on it. He and the pilot got out of the plane and into the water with life jackets on. They spent the night—all night—together. At least they tried to stay together, but eventually they became separated.

The next morning when they sent a destroyer out to try to find them, they found the pilot but they found only my cousin's body. My uncle lived in Texas, so I had to arrange for the service. He [the uncle] used to come up to visit me when I was in San Diego.

I mentioned the University of South Carolina General Line School. I also served on a destroyer, the *Taussig* (DD 746) and in between [my teaching assignment and the destroyer] I went to the naval ordnance school at Key West. I've had the honor and privilege of earning shellback and blue devil on the same cruise. We never had any problem setting up a proper King Neptune's Court. We'd set up the mess deck and we had the bilges—particularly appropriate places to have people crawl through. In addition, of course, the access beams gave us plenty of places to set up the gags and lines of people.

We'd take everybody to see the Royal Barber and the Royal Baby, and we'd have Davy Jones and all the cast of characters the tradition requires.

Now, when it comes to making future generations aware of life in the submarine service, I think anyone who is curious about submarines during my time, I'd suggest they watch the movie *Das Boot* [*The Boat*]. It's a very good representation of the spirit among a submarine crew and how they go to extraordinary efforts to maintain their ship in operational condition, and still get back and have fun. Several years ago, when the [Soviet] *Kurst* accident occurred, there was a great outpouring of sympathy from American submariners. They definitely felt bad for the Russian sailors who died aboard that submarine. I hope some day that we will be a bunch of submariners who understand that we don't all have to agree on everything, but we can get along. Of course, that's probably Utopian [laughs heartily].

Well, looking to the future: I have my retirement ceremony on April 8, and then I'm going back to the mainland for a month to goof off, but then I'm going to come back here and look for a job. Sure, I miss the *good old days*, and the navy still seems like a home, but I'm looking forward to some fun times.

11

HARRY JACOB JEFFERSON
BT-3, LATER, CHIEF FIRE CONTROLMAN, USN (RET.)

Events began with a rush on January 9, 1965, as the U.S. Joint Congressional Committee on Atomic Energy made public its investigation of the loss of the USS *Thresher* (SSN 593). The politicians pinned much of the blame on the U.S. Navy, claiming that they allowed the submarine to go to sea with the full knowledge that certain flaws in her design and workmanship were evident. However, the truth of these accusations was yet to be proven.

Later in the month, on January 11, the navy stated that all twenty of the recommendations resulting from the congressional study on the loss of the *Thresher* had already been carried out, were being carried out, or were scheduled to be carried out. At the time, it sounded like CYA. Four days later, Vice Admiral H. G. Rickover, USN, received the Fermi Award for his outstanding work on the development of marine reactors. He was the first nonscientist to be a recipient of this award, America's highest in atomic science. Three days after, President Johnson, in his annual message on defense, announced plans to develop the advanced Polaris B-3, which they later deployed as the Poseidon C-3.

Former Chief of the Soviet General Staff Marshal Vasiliy D. Sokolovskii claimed on February 17 that the Soviet Union had achieved "virtual parity" with the United States in nuclear-propelled submarines. In the same public announcement, the retired marshal also claimed that, for the first time, the Soviet Union had fewer men in uniform than the United States, comparing Soviet-claimed strength of 2,423,000 to the U.S. strength of 2,690,000 in military uniform.

Submarine activity lagged somewhat until June 7, when U.S. submarines were involved in conducting "stop, board, and search" missions along the coast of South Vietnam. This was part of the joint navy effort to stop the infiltration of arms for the Viet Cong. The next day, Operation Pole Star, a NATO convoy and antisubmarine warfare exercise began in the western Atlantic. This exercise involved ships of the U.S., Canadian, British, and Dutch navies. It included six submarines, fifteen surface ships, and three aircraft squadrons.

Creating a new escape depth record, a team of Royal Navy divers made a successful experimental escape from a submerged submarine on July 16. This new escape record, achieved from a depth of five hundred feet, astounded even those who conducted the test.

Secretary of the Navy Nimitz ordered a four-month involuntary extension of active duty on August 14. This covered all navy and marine enlisted personnel, beginning August 20 for the marine corps, September 15 for the navy. A most unpleasant announcement arrived on August 27. Ominous news came four days later when Vice Admiral Charles Martell, USN, director of antisubmarine warfare programs in the office of the CNO, announced that Soviet submarines were moving from their rigid operational procedure formerly dictated by politically acceptable doctrine. They had changed their traditional defensive posture to engage in operations in the Mediterranean, Norwegian, and Philippine Seas. Martell declared that the Soviets were moving about freely in these areas and that, in recent operations in the Norwegian Sea, had utilized more submarines than were available in the entire U.S. Atlantic Fleet. He also advised that, to date, no Soviet submarine activities had been detected in the South China Sea.

A tragedy in the making occurred on September 5 when, after a lengthy study, President Johnson's radical leftist Committee on the Economic Impact of Defense Disarmament erroneously reported that neither reduction in defense expenditures nor a complete disarmament would present major problems for the U.S. economy. What the committee's findings failed to reveal was that total disarmament would result in a loss of income for the economy from over 2,500,000 jobs—and that was only active duty military, not counting defense industry and private sector job losses.

The next day, more bad news came as the Indian government announced that the Soviet government had agreed to provide India with an undisclosed number of submarines. Prior to this time, India had not operated submarines. One can only speculate on the difficulty of transcribing the Russian Cyrillic labels on the instruments into Hindu script. The sort of dangers that might be encountered due to a mistake in translation are beyond counting (more on India's submarine adventures later on).

On October 6, the U.S. Department of Defense authorized a Vietnam Service Medal. The award was made retroactive to July 3, 1965. Submariners serving off the coast of Vietnam were also eligible for this medal. On October 13, more bad news descended on submariners when the nuclear submarines *Sargo* (SSN 583) and *Barb* (SSN 596) collided while submerged. The accident occurred during a training exercise fifteen nautical miles west of Oahu, Hawaii. There were no injuries reported and both subs returned to port under their own power. In the days that followed, a hearing into the collision incident was scheduled.

Smoother sailing came the next day as the Polaris A-1 missile was retired when the ballistic missile submarine *Abraham Lincoln* (SSBN 602) arrived

Two crewmen with a Mark 46 antisubmarine warfare Torpedo. *Courtesy of United States Navy*

in the United States to undergo an overhaul and modifications to launch the Polaris A-3 missile. The conversion resulted in enabling the fleet ballistic missile submarines to convert to the longer-ranged, more powerful weapon. On October 28, the U.S. Navy took delivery of its first Mark 46 lightweight antisubmarine torpedo. The weapons were scheduled for construction by Honeywell Corporation. The MK-46 would be fired from MK-32 tubes and ASROC launchers on surface ships, dropped by ASW aircraft and would be launched by an Encapsulated Torpedo (CAPTOR) mine. A versatile weapon, it would remain in use even after the advent of the MK-48.

Nothing of particular note, outside of routine surveillance patrols, intelligence-gathering patrols, and coastal survey patrols, occurred for submariners through the summer and fall. Then, on December 8, when an amphibious and antisubmarine warfare exercise involving fifty ships and twelve thousand men of the U.S. Atlantic Fleet began with assault landings on

Vieques Island, Puerto Rico (currently the center of controversy between Puerto Rican nationalists and the U.S. government). Admirals and other ranking officers in the submarine service paid close attention to the results of the antisubmarine operations. The exercise was quite successful, but raised the ire of certain anti-American elements on the island of Puerto Rico.

The next year, on February 2, the nuclear-powered submarine *George Washington* (SSBN 598) again slid down the ways after an eighteen-month overhaul. Along with the standard overhaul construction, the first Polaris submarine received modifications to launch the Polaris A-3 missile. At that time, all of the first ten Polaris submarines began the process of refitting to accommodate the A-3 missile system. By February 15, intelligence-gathering Cold War patrols intensified around the borders of the USSR.

Good news came for navy personnel when Secretary of the Navy Paul H. Nitze announced to the public that involuntary active-duty extensions of enlisted personnel would be phased out gradually. This process, he further stated, "will be completed by September 30, 1966."

On May 30, the professional agitators were at it again as they rallied an estimated turnout of twelve thousand Japanese to stage a protest demonstration when the nuclear attack submarine *Snook* (SSN 592) arrived at Yokosuka, Japan. Although the *Snook* was the first nuclear submarine to make a port call at Yokosuka, other such ships had repeatedly called at the U.S. base at Sasebo, Japan, without serious incident.

Our British allies celebrated on July 18, when the Royal Navy commissioned and launched the HMS *Valiant*, the first "all-British" nuclear-powered submarine. It was a fine line of distinction, since their earlier (and first) nuke sub, the *Dreadnaught*, had an American-designed propulsion system.

The leftist agitators were at it again on September 7, when they led an unruly mob of some eight hundred alleged "students" into a rock-throwing imbroglio with two thousand riot police in Yokosuka, Japan, during a violent antiAmerican demonstration against the nuclear submarine USS *Seadragon* (SSN 584) when it visited the Japanese port. On September 16, a questionable agreement drawn up in Washington, D.C., between Secretary of State Dean Rusk and Philippine Foreign Secretary Narcisco Ramos resulted in a reduction in the remaining duration of U.S. rights to four bases in the Philippines. The original treaty gave the United States ninety-nine years, beginning in 1951. To be renegotiated or closed were Clark Field and Camp John Hay at Baguio, the navy bases at Subic Bay (submarine base), and Sangley Point. Later, during the Reagan administration, this was recognized for what it was: a disastrous betrayal of U.S. interests in the Pacific.

The French attempted to catch up on October 17, when the submarine *Gymnote* reached completion. Outfitted with diesel-electric propulsion, the *Gymnote* was fitted with four launch tubes for ballistic missiles. It served as a launch platform for the French Navy's *Le Redoubtable* class of strategic missile submarines. Their effort fell short of desired results.

Accidents will happen, but a collision on November 10 resulted in considerable embarrassment as well as expense. The U.S. Navy's nuclear-powered attack submarine *Nautilus* (SSN 571) had an underwater collision with the ASW carrier *Essex* (CVS 9) during an exercise conducted 360 nautical miles east of Morehead City, North Carolina. Although the Essex sustained a gash in her port bow, the *Nautilus* received severe damage to her conning tower. It was rumored that the skipper of the *Nautilus* made an effort to explain to the captain of the *Essex* that the incident had not been an act of revenge by a submariner against an antisubmarine vessel. Both ships returned to their home ports under their own power and without incident. The only casualty that resulted from the incident was a minor injury to one man in the *Nautilus*.

While President Johnson presented the Congressional Medal of Honor

The USS *Sturgeon* (SS 637) was the first in its class. *Courtesy of United States Navy*

to SGT Robert Emmet O'Malley on December 6, the USS *Queenfish* (SSN 651) went into commission. It represented the first of thirty-seven submarines of the *Sturgeon* (SSN 637) class to join the fleet. This particular class was an enlarged version of the *Permit* (SSN 594) class design, featuring a taller sail, which provided more space for masts, greatly improved electronics, and an under-ice capability superior to that of the *Nautilus*-class subs. Her first skipper was CDR Jackson B. Richard, USN.

Other than what had become routine patrols, surveillance of Soviet seaborne operations, communications monitoring patrols, intelligence-gathering patrols (including landing some special operations personnel at undisclosed locales), and nuclear deterrent patrols, nothing much happened for submariners the opening month of 1967. As though that wasn't enough.

Then, on February 10, the British placed in service the HMS *Resolution*, their first nuclear-propelled ballistic missile submarine (SSBN). Armed with sixteen Polaris A-3 missiles, each fitted with British-constructed warheads, she represented a formidable addition to the British fleet.

Not intended as an April Fool's Day joke, the USS *Will Rogers* (SSBN 659) was commissioned on April 1 with CPT R. Y. (Yogi) Kaufman, USN, as CO of Blue crew and CDR W. J. Cowhill commanding Gold crew. This was the forty-first, and last, Polaris submarine. The advent of the Tomahawk was only just over the horizon.

The U.S. strategic missile submarine USS *Abraham Lincoln* (SSBN 602), which was the last of five submarines that carried the Polaris A-1 missile, completed her conversion to the A-3 on June 2, 1967. The *Lincoln* deployed on her first A-3 deterrent patrol on October 26, 1967.

Now, to continue our chronicles of submariners, we come across an exceptional situation. Unlike many of our previous submariners, here is a man who came from a seagoing family. His father was in the merchant marines, and later the U.S. Navy. His uncle became a three-star [rear] admiral. To the surprise of his contemporaries, Harry Jefferson joined the naval reserves at seventeen, while still in high school. This represented a commitment to which he remained loyal. He headed toward a career in the navy by entering Navy ROTC in college. Then along came the Korean War and he enlisted. Unlike many who have shared their experiences, Harry served in the Atlantic fleet and did several long patrols in the Mediterranean Sea.

I come from a navy family, so to speak. My father had started in the merchant marines, and then changed to regular navy during WWII. My uncle Charles joined as a seaman recruit right about the time of the First World War. They called them strikers in those days— and ended up shoveling coal in a battleship. He soon decided that wasn't for him. At the same time, they were starting navy aviation. Determined to escape the "black gang," Uncle Charles went into naval air. Through hard work, he learned all the navy requirements and specifications of fliers: pilot and copilot, navigator, bombardier, gunner. Next, he went to Pennsylvania and got his commission. After receiving his commission and wings, he flew combat missions all through WWII and ended up as a three-star admiral.

I entered service in the naval reserve in high school and continued in the NROTC at the University of California at Los Angeles [UCLA]. I then went on to join the regular navy during the Korean War. I took a battery of tests upon joining and they said, "Now you get the choice of anything you want." With that in mind, I took additional tests for intelligence and submarines. I passed those and decided on submarines. I wasn't married while I was in the submarines, being only in my freshman year of college when we were activated during the Korean War.

My submarine training was at New London. Even though we were at war, they maintained the highest standards at the school. I was very impressed with the quality of education [especially] the math classes. The instructors were generally first class or chiefs. They were very disciplined, very, very knowledgeable in their field, well-qualified, and they taught fine classes. New London consisted of two sections: the upper base, which contained the barracks and schools for officers and enlisted; down below was the maintenance department, submarine school and hands-on training, and the sub pens. This was in addition to actually operating the boats at sea.

Once you graduated and were in the upper 10 [percent] of your class, you had your choice, as close as possible, of your duty station. In addition, you could possibly pick your boat. After school, I drew a posting aboard the USS *Sablefish* (SS 303). Once you're aboard, either officer or enlisted, regulations allow you one year to qualify. If you do not qualify—and we're talking about modified WWII boats—in the nine compartments, you have to leave. The only exception to that is if your boat is out of commission during that time. Let's take a little tour through a typical World War II boat, say starting at the bow.

Compartments aboard one of those boats began with the forward torpedo room, followed by the forward battery. Then you come to the control room. Above that you have the conning tower—which is basically the attack center. Following them, you have the after battery, forward engine room, after engine room, maneuvering room (which is actually the electrical control systems for these electric boats), and the after compartment, which is the after torpedo room. Oh, and the mess deck was usually in the after engine room. Cleaning all of that is a hard and daily job, and then there was scraping and painting—usually done while on the surface and rarely on patrol. Cleaning the battery compartments and bilges were nasty jobs.

One of the good things about submarine duty was the food—and I'm sure it still is. It was the best food anywhere in the military. We had excellent cooks. Not only had they been trained in the navy school, we had a couple who had actually been chefs. Two of them were also bakers; they baked everything you can think of, and cooked as well.

Now, the crew on every submarine I served on, when they sat down to eat, their manners were fantastic. They ate with knife, fork, and spoon, even kept their elbows in. I know that sounds funny, but I tend to take things on the light side.

I think one of the things on a submarine that is impressive is that the typical responsibility that is given to you may well be something beyond your grade or rate, plus additional duties, depending on what the officers thought you could take. It was—there was less regimentation also, than what might have been in larger ships, or maybe the army or the marine corps. They expected you to hold up, and relied on you not only to do your job, but you were also expected to know how to do the next guy's job, too.

After I got on the boats, I think the greatest skipper I ever served under was LCDR Merrill. He was skipper of the *Sablefish* and an okay guy. He was a man of few words, but when he spoke, everybody listened. A very, very intelligent man about submarines, and not only our subs, but also the Russian Navy's. Mostly, he was intelligent in that he used to seek out, and recognize, the qualities of the personnel he had, and treated them accordingly. He was a very high-level guy. Patrols with him were always easy.

I went directly from submarine school to a New London boat. They said to me, "Since you graduated in the top ten of your class, do you want to go to Pearl?"

I said, "No."

The brass asked, "Why not?"

So I said, "Well, I was born and raised in Hawaii. I want to see the rest of the world."

That's how I picked a boat out of New London. I figured it would do a lot more traveling. However, we operated primarily—only—in the Atlantic, up and down the Atlantic coast. Then we did a long tour of duty in the Mediterranean. That was great, really great.

By then I had transferred to the *Sablefish*. The *Sablefish* was a draft three, which meant it was built near the end of the Second World War. It naturally had three settings to become a snorkel. They put on the minisail and stuff like that, and all the electronics. Basically, though, it was a modified WWII boat. Our maximum depth was a lot greater than the 160 feet of the pre-war 1930s. It is still classified, but I know of boats that went far below five hundred feet. We would ordinarily operate at three or four hundred feet. In a lot of it—the ocean—you couldn't because, on the East Coast, you're over the continental shelf, which is wide and pretty shallow. Therefore, you have to get out in the Atlantic before you can go deep. Let's get back to the Mediterranean.

We came in through the Straits of Gibraltar traveling under sealed orders. So obviously, we knew where we were going, but we didn't know when we were going back. We tied up at Gibraltar. The first thing we did when we got liberty was to go to the nearest bar and have a beer.

In one, the barkeep said, "Gee, sorry, we know you Yanks like your beer cold, and I forgot to get the ice this morning. But don't you worry. When you come back in December it's going to be cold."

We looked at each other and wondered how this guy knew we were coming back in December. He knew more than we did.

Going to the ports in the Mediterranean was a lot of fun. Number one at the time was Naples. At that time, submarines and the surface fleet could not go into port at the same time. Either they came in after we left, or we came in after they left. The surface fleet was the enemy [hearty laugh] and they thought of us the same way. Well, we got sub pay, you know, and any time you went—ah, they had some fairly nice bars in Naples. Because, when you came in and you had dolphins on, the girls would always leave whomever they were sitting with and come to your table. That got the feud going with the surface fleet.

Only, one time, we got in a real mix-up with a *real* enemy: the Russians. Let me digress for a minute. Something that has always been an important subject is the different personalities. The old salts had been there before, mainly because they'd been there for years. Most of them were World War II vets. Actually, we did have a lot of reserves aboard that were World War II vets who were recalled during the Korean War. We younger guys took every tour you could think of. We'd take tours to see the Greek ruins or Roman ruins. They were very, very reasonably priced. As a result, you got a good education. That [the tours] was pretty eye-opening. We went into Crete when it was still a touchy situation.

Actually, what happened was we were part of the naval exercises during one of our tours in the Mediterranean, which was going to be in the Eastern Mediterranean, and all of the forces were supposed to be there. That's when the Turks and the Greeks were fighting battles. So they decided—in fact they were shooting at each other in the country—and they decided about that time that they were not going to fight this engagement during the NATO exercises. The Turks dropped out [of the NATO exercises] and the Greeks dropped out, and somebody else dropped out because the Turks had dropped out [laughing now], and somebody else dropped out because the Greeks had.

Therefore, we Americans became the first and largest participant. The British participated somewhat and the Italians. Nevertheless because of the Greeks and Turks fighting, their little war kinda screwed up the exercises. The overenthusiasm of the combatants did not result in any of our forces taking any rounds. As far as any actual combatants are concerned, once we had gotten through there and on station where we were doing the NATO exercises, we were going to be in there for a matter of months. Our particular boat, the *Sailfish*, carried a full complement of mines for the purpose of mining the Dardanelles in case the Russians decided to seize the Mediterranean. We were going to mine it [the Dardanelles] so they couldn't get out. So let's go back to the incident with the Russians.

The only time we saw a Russian ship was a World War II Liberty ship that we had lend-leased to Russia, which they never returned—of course, they never returned anything—and this tub could make probably eight knots. We spotted it through the number one Kollmorgen periscope—but they had a legitimate reason to be there; they were a regular commercial Russian ship. There were no hostilities in anyone's mind.

However, our skipper says, "Well, let's give these guys something to think about."

We surfaced about a couple of miles from them. [This said through gleeful laughter] They turned . . . they turned 180 degrees. You could see the black smoke just billowing out of the stacks of this old stolen Liberty ship. It was obvious they were seriously in need of a great, *major* overhaul. Anyway, they kept on steaming way over the horizon and we were all laughing.

After a while, someone said, "Well, it will take them at least a day to come about and recover the territory. Whatever port they're going to, they're going to be a day or two late."

As I recall it was one of those Kaiser jobs out of Oakland, a regular rust bucket. It had been built to last no more than three years and it was still around going places. That was our only encounter with the Russians and not a shot was fired.

Now [changing the subject] our patrols in the Mediterranean lasted about three to four months on the diesel-electric boats. Then you'd go out to provision primarily for your fruits and vegetables. Crew essentials consisted of anything perishable, because we just didn't have the refrigeration to stay for the duration. I mean that if you're down for three months, you're not going to have a lot of fresh fruits and vegetables. We also did reprovision often in [local] ports for the perishables.

Of all of our patrols, I'd say the most boring was probably the one we had a lot of anticipation for, but ended up being boring because out of everybody who was invited to the NATO exercises, nobody showed up but us [U.S. Navy, Marines, and Air Force]. We ended up doing some exercises with the Canadians, which we [held] down off the coast of Canada and New England. Of course, those were also somewhat boring.

Going into port for liberty was always somewhat exciting [laughs]. We always had a good, much better than average, basketball team aboard. They would always radio out to us and read a list of whatever opportunities would be available to us when we came into port—whatever port it was going to be. One time, we got a message saying that the Greek Olympic team had challenged us to a basketball game. Bad thing; our personnel hadn't seen a basketball court for several months. Anyway, we played the Greek Olympic team. We played by international Olympic rules, which none of us knew. Yet, we ended up beating them.

Back to the most exciting patrol that I experienced. Thankfully, no one was injured. It happened on the *Sablefish* when, one time, we snorkeled at one hundred feet. We had been snorkeling out in the Atlantic and, as you probably know, snorkel induction is [through] an eighteen-inch pipe. The normal induction is a thirty-six-inch pipe. At that time, snorkel induction was only half that size. On the new boats, I don't know the size. However, they have to be large enough to draw sufficient air to run two of the four engines. What would happen when you were in heavy seas . . . there was an electrode below the head valve and, if it got hit by a shot of water, it would send a signal and the head valve would automatically shut before the water got to it so you wouldn't take any amount of water into the engine room. Then what you'd do is you would cease snorkeling and go on batteries and go down to one hundred feet, trim the boat, get everything back into good posture, then do a reverse checklist, just go backward through the functions on that list. Then we'd go back to fifty-four feet, open the snorkel induction and restart the engines and be back up snorkeling again. Well, we did everything except for one important thing. The duty officer forgot to take us back up to fifty-four feet. He told the chief of the watch to open the snorkel induction while we were still at a hundred feet.

The chief said, "Sir, I think you should reconsider that order."

Well, the guy [duty officer] wasn't thinking and he went over and opened the snorkel induction manually. Immediately we took a huge shower of water into the engine room, which got to the deck plates in about three seconds. So now we're going down backward, the bow planes are now the stern planes and the stern planes are now the bow planes and we're going down fast, at a pretty good angle, stern first. As far as the fire control section goes, we soon discovered that we had trapped ourselves. We were in depths beyond our safe operating maximum, according to the depth gauge. The skipper, LCDR Merrill, came in, relieved the diving officer, and took control of the boat. This is the most important thing. We had never done this exercise before, and we shouldn't have even done it the one time. There was *absolutely* no power. There should have been total panic. But hear this: seven guys in the control room and *every one just hung in and did their job*. And, contrary to what you see in the movies where people in the control room are yelling and screaming orders—that doesn't happen, didn't happen then. There was nothing, nothing more than a normal voice. That skipper [LCDR Merrill] came in, took control, and everybody just sat and did their thing. The result: we got out of a jam. Through it all, *everybody* remained very, very disciplined. No panic, nothing. [The whole crew's attitude was] we're gonna get ourselves out of this—and we did. It was all training, discipline, and cool heads. It was just as though we had been running exercises on the situation all along.

We had plenty of exercises in which we did go deep in a controlled dive. Many of these were certain special exercises where we'd go way down, looking for thermal layers, especially during antisubmarine—we did a lot of that—with destroyers and planes, we'd look for thermals to get the destroyers to lose you when they pinged, because the sonar would bounce off the thermal layers.

A high percentage of our work involved training destroyers and antisubmarine planes. Being the guinea pig, so to speak. In fact, we had one exercise where we were off Greece and Turkey, in the Eastern Mediterranean. We had the old navy Neptune that flew out from a base in Italy for a course in antisubmarine warfare. They would operate with us all night long, say ten to twelve hours and then they'd fly back—those things couldn't stay in the air forever—and we would be listening to them, to their communications between the planes. They had to be able to communicate with us so they could tell us what they wanted us to do, you know, run on the surface, submerge, etc. They'd do runs at us while we were on the surface. Of course, we had no lights on and we'd not turn any electronics on so they could not zero in on us. They had to pick us up with their searchlights—usually their radar or searchlights. One of the guys came right over us with a searchlight that didn't work.

So he's using navy terminology I guess, when he went back up and says, "Blue Leader, Blue Leader, this is Red Follower. I just had a malfunction of my searchlight."

Right away, their skipper comes back and says, "Red Follower, Red Follower, you did not have a malfunction of your searchlight, you have a 'bent candle,' repeat, 'bent candle.'"

Our crew was just great. The OD piped that through the boat and we all howled with laughter. We had some humorous people aboard, but that squadron leader took the cake.

One of my favorite funny guys was a black first class engineman by the name of Sam. Sam was the coolest guy in the world.

We'd say when he first got out of the hospital, "Sam how do you want your coffee?"

He would reply, "Black and bitter, like my women."

There's a navy tradition, I don't know whether they still do this or not, if you're going to sea and your wife is expecting, you go prepared with a box of cigars, or a couple of boxes, whatever it takes, and you pass them out among the crew. What happens when your wife has the kid is the base communications sends out a message that describes the event in nautical terms. For example, if it's a boy, they'd say it was a snorkel type and if it's a girl they'd say it was called a standard fleet type. That way, you know exactly what is going on. If it was a boy you passed out the cigars, and if it was a girl you went to the cook and said, "Bake me up a couple of dozen doughnuts."

Anyway, Sam was going to have a baby and they radioed out that Sam's [wife] had had a baby girl. So Sam, having a girl, went to the pastry cook and says, "Harry, make me some chocolate-covered doughnuts." Now there was a guy with a sense of humor.

Another thing, you never lacked for communications. Everyone always talked to everybody. On a big ship—you know, five thousand people on an aircraft carrier—most of the officers don't even know each other. Yet, on a submarine, everyone talks to everyone else. Obviously if you're talking to an officer, you call him "Sir," but still there are always open lines of communication. I mean you can tell jokes; you can do whatever back and forth. There's a lot of mutual respect. The "You can't talk to him because he is the Commander" on a sub, that doesn't make sense.

There's no opportunity to be a wise-ass on a sub. It's quite close quarters, so you have to have dialogue. We had a lot of mutual respect and self-control. Like I said before, we still had a large number of guys during the Korean War who had served in the Second World War, and to *us* they were heroes. These men were the guys who really went through it. Even so, they were normal guys. I never saw anybody lose it. I think if there was ever a time to "go South," it was when we snorkeled at a hundred feet. Instead, everybody remained absolutely calm. I couldn't—you know—to this day, I am so amazed. The enginemen who were shut in that compartment . . . [a long pause] fortunately there was nobody hurt, none of the equipment hurt, everybody just stood real tough.

We had quite a few bachelors, then the married guys . . . they came from all over the country. We even had a couple of guys from Tennessee who had never seen the ocean before.

Did you know there's a place in Kansas called Ocean View? I was listening to one of those call-in programs and they said, "What's your name?"

He says, "Joe." Then the guy on the show asks where he's from and he said, "Ocean View, Kansas."

The guy can't believe it and says, "You've gotta be kidding. You have to go about a thousand miles from Kansas to see ocean."* Anyway, for all the fun we had together, liberty remained our best outlet from tension.

My favorite liberty port was Tripoli, Lebanon. Actually, though, the three that were my favorites were Naples, because you wanted to get out of there as fast as possible. Greece . . . they put us into the port of Piraeus, which was not too good, and in Lebanon. At that time—this was before the Lebanese Civil War—and it was a beautiful

---

*Someone was pulling Jefferson's leg. There is a *Prairie View*, Kansas, but neither the author—who is a native Kansan nor the husband of his copyeditor—also from Kansas—have ever heard of it, nor could they locate an Ocean View on the map of Kansas.

city [Beirut]. It was really, *really* unique. They used to call Beirut the "Paris of the Mediterranean." It was a wonderful, wonderful city. Nice people, great food, I mean you could get anything there. It was interesting, too, to see how harmoniously all of the various religions lived alongside one another. There was probably more ethnic and religious diversity in Lebanon than in any other country in Europe. Sundays the Christians closed their stores, Saturday the Jewish stores closed, Friday another group [the Muslims]. You know, if you could get three days out of a week when all of the stores were open the *same day*, it would be interesting, because there were so many different religions. The food was great; the people were great. It was beautiful country. You could get out into the Axis Mountains with nice tours. When we were there, we'd go into port for three to five days, something like that.

Greece was great, too—not the city of Athens so much—but, like I said, you could go on these tours that were very reasonable. You'd get off at seven in the morning and get back at seven in the night. You'd see a lot of, just a lot of antiquities. Lebanon had a lot of them, too.

The other [good] one, of course, was Italy. Naples itself was not red-hot. The harbor was oil-slicked, covered with scummy foam. A lot of the piers had still not been repaired from the damage in the Second World War. From those that remained, nearly naked kids dived for coins into that filthy water.

It was interesting to see how precise the bombing had been. The bombers—the B-17s and B-24s in particular—would take down sections of the town, like the harbor. They'd go like maybe three blocks in and everything was rubble. On the other side of that everything was standing. Our precision bombing was amazing. Still, they [the Italians] hadn't cleaned up their act in the harbor. This was now 1955, and the war had been over for ten years and there was still a lot of rubble lying around. What we did was take off for Rome, spend maybe three or four days up there. We got an unbelievably inexpensive hotel, which was clean, bug-free, and welcoming. We ordered up a horse-drawn carriage to take us all around Rome, a one-day tour. The guy arrived and spent *all day* with us. We had lunch—we got back for cocktail time at six-thirty that night—but we spent at least ten hours with this guy.

When we started to pay him in cash and he said, "Naw-naw-naw. Do you have cigarettes?"

We said, "Yeah."

He asks, "Do you have Lucky Strikes?" We said yes and he said, "One carton, Lucky Strikes."

To us that was nothing, like today where they're two dollars a pack. This guy spent all day with us for a carton of cigarettes that cost us fifty cents at the ship's store. He was happy with it. [Begins laughing] He thought we'd paid five dollars a pack for them, as they had to do. Another time [still laughing], we were in the catacombs of Rome, where the bars and restaurants were located. I guess they were an original part of Rome, and then these developers came in and made these nice restaurants and bars and stuff like that. We were sitting in one of these bars—Americans start drinking a little earlier than Europeans do, at both lunch and dinner. One of my buddies, Don Hansen, a j.g., was in there having a cocktail and these two gals come in. One was about his age and one was a bit older, about my age. They sat down at the far end of the bar. I had better than 20/20 vision. One of the girls I had gone to school with in Hawaii had attended a girl's prep school on the East Coast called Miss Porter's School. They used to wear rings that read MPS on them. The going joke was that they had broken the girls into three groups. They'd call them Minks, Possums, and Squirrels.

I look down the bar, maybe twenty or thirty feet away, and I saw this gal's ring and I said, "Minks, Possums, and Squirrels."

Just like that, the four of us got together. It turned out to be that the younger girl I was with was one of the Firestone girls. She, and this other lady, who had just gotten over being a very young widow, decided that they should go to Europe to get over their problems.

We ended up great and the one who was with me said, "Let's go and do the town."

Her father had arranged to have a driver named Giovanni with them at all times. Giovanni had this small limousine and he would take us all over Rome at night. That was great. I remember coming home in the morning and I had this feeling of something sticking under my foot. I reached down and picked it up and it was a brown paper bag. However, it was kinda cute, so I opened it up, and it contained *hundreds of lira.*

I said, "Ann, what's this doing on the floor?"

And she says, "Oh, that's where it is. We thought we had lost it. Daddy gave us some spending money."

It must have been the equivalent of five thousand U.S. dollars. That's the great part about just traveling with the socialite class. When that liberty ended we returned to the sub for a new patrol.

We never knew where we were going until after we left port. This was true also even when we were practicing with torpedoes. In fact, we got an additional designation, since we were technically an SSM, signifying that we were a certified submarine mine layer, yet we had no idea why we were doing that, except that we were just becoming proficient in laying mines. We had *absolutely no idea* where we were taking these mines, outside of the fact we knew we were on rotation for the Mediterranean, and that's all we knew. When we got there, the mines we laid in the Dardanelles were real mines. Only thing is, we never got a signal to lay a mine. Our entire mine-laying so far had been with practice mines. We could come back and retrieve them, so now what we had aboard was a full complement of mines with active warheads. At that time, we didn't have authorization to lay a single mine unless we got a signal from Washington saying, "Lay those mines."

We knew exactly where we were going to lay them. We had the patterns and the maps; we knew all of that. We could only if Eisenhower said to do it. When he would say, "Take care of this," it would cost the taxpayers "X" number of dollars.

[Then the interviewer asked about anything that would round out a Sub*mar*iner's life.] Submar*in*er [Henry corrected], was the only way you said it. When anyone said "Sub*mar*iners," we knew he was a fake, or a Limey. The British did say Sub*mar*iner and we'd say *we knew why* [laughs chidingly]. No, they did call themselves Sub*mar*iners, but the Americans were very particular about being called Submar*in*ers.

Anyway, back to the question. It truly is the silent service. That was a slogan invented back during the Second World War to keep lips from slipping and things like that. But it's a very, very appropriate monocle [sic—moniker]—you don't really hear that much about submarines and what they do, even though there are more books coming out now than there ever were before and people are starting to understand. Yet it is basically, "Out of sight, out of mind," you know?

They go out for six months and are underwater for six months, and then they come back and tie up at the pier and nobody ever sees them. They show a few submarine sailors as part—a percentage—of the fleet as a whole. But they're not obvious, they're not *publicity nuts*, and I don't mean this negatively, but the marine corps has *Semper Fi* and they're always in the news, which is great for *esprit de corps*. Submariners are laid-back types, and think, *cool it*. Beyond that, I can truly say that I think the modern nuclear submarine navy is wonderful. I think we should have more nuclear power. It's too bad we have such a great number of uneducated people who don't know anything about it. You know, when you think of the way things are now defined, my understanding is that, obviously, metallurgy technology has a lot to do with submarines. Now, if I take a look into a pressure hull to learn what types of iron—well, types of steel, chrome and nickel and all these good things that go into them—I see it differently than when I was young. I ask myself, How long will it last? The more you dive, you have to figure a certain fatigue factor into this thing. My understanding now is that they have married the capability of a nuclear reactor with the hull life of a submarine.

The hull life of a submarine is now thirty-five years, after which you take it apart, melt it down and start over, or whatever they do with it. The same applies to a reactor. From what I understand, they don't recharge them for thirty-five years. You put them in [the reactor rods] and they go for thirty-five years, then at the end of thirty-five years you take them out and scrap the whole thing. It's wonderful! Think of all the billions of gallons of diesel fuel you just saved. Non-nuclear aircraft carriers use hundreds of billions of gallons of fuel. Opposed to our "bigger is better" admirals' ideas, other nations have fleets of smaller diesel boats. The drawback to that is, the smaller you are and the closer you have to run to the surface, the more vulnerable you are to enemy depth-charges, while the deeper and more silent you are, the more protection you have.

Even so, they are *making* them [the boats] bigger. They're now about the size of a World War II cruiser. I'm just guessing, but I imagine that they will have some smaller boats for special missions. Unfortunately, I don't know positively about what the developments are, other than what you read or the navy releases to us as veterans. However, I don't think you will see a great preponderance of them [smaller subs]. I think we'll see them built for specific coastal missions, like was said about putting people ashore. I know that they have tremendous electronics capabilities as far as listening to the Russians.

Are any of you familiar with the story of plugging into the Russian telephone cable? Well, this happened fairly recently, within the last twenty years or so. Naval intelligence came up with the idea of tapping into the Russian military telephone cables. Moreover, they [Navy G-2] were wondering how to do this.

One of the skippers came up to them and said, "Easy. Every country in the world has buoys with signs reading, 'Do Not Anchor Here—Telephone Cable Crossing,' right? In short, does Russia use a cable?"

As a result, they [ONI]—Office of Naval Intelligence—took their listening devices and spliced into the cable on the ocean floor and, from then on, they monitored the entire of the Russian Navy's communications. It seems that GT and N provided them with special equipment so that they could just put it on the cable tap and leave it there for a couple of months, then come back and unload it of all the information that was on it. It worked perfectly for a number of years.

I know one thing, if I was the same age now that I was when I went into the submarine service, I'd want to be on one of the nuke boats, I think a fast attack boat. There's no more room in one of them now than in one from the Second World War; they've just found more equipment to put in them. I mean, they're a lot bigger, but what makes life interesting is that on a submarine the maximum height is supposed to be six feet. I'm six-three. For a little while, I was the fifth-tallest guy on board that sub. After a few days, you could walk the length of a boat both directions and automatically do this [illustrates ducking and turning partly sideways] or you have too many scars on your head. We learned fast [laughing]. However, I would definitely—I would *definitely*—go back in, if I were . . . I would say that I would like to have been an officer, but as to my being in the reserves and being called up, that's the way life is. But you could voluntarily join the service—good people, very stable, very intelligent, pretty low-key, all together very nice people to work with.

I think one of the most interesting things, it used to be one out of a hundred who applied ever got to go on a submarine—egotistically, or mentally, or even if they had acne [they were weeded out]. One of the more interesting things was that they really wanted to be sure that you had the smarts to do any given assignment, they also wanted to be sure that you were physically capable of doing it, and number three that you weren't claustrophobic and a few other things. One of the tests they give you, it lasts all day. I'm not sure how they do it now, but they used to have like college blue books, with the seal on the side. And we'd all get in a room with a couple of pencils and they'd say, "Open the book. It's eight o'clock in the morning and you've got until noon to finish."

You'd open it up and go one page at a time and on the first page is a picture. And on the following page, there's a picture and you have a narrative: "What are you looking at? What was the causal factor of this? What was the outcome?" If you're lucky, you knew what to write. Anyway, when you got through with that, the book went to a

Navy psychiatrist, generally a lieutenant commander or commander, and they read it over and evaluated your responses.

They went through each one of these again. They ask, "What did you have in mind and can you give a little more explanation of this?"

You may have said something in there that wasn't concise . . . or maybe you left something out. Then they'd reexamine you verbally. They wanted to find out what made you tick. They were looking for a couple of obvious things. I don't know if it's politically correct to say this, but we *could* say this sort of thing fifty or sixty years ago. They were looking for people who were claustrophobic; find out if personal tendencies were not in the best interests of the crew. I'll always remember this, the first page of this thing—and you are timed, you've got twenty-four pictures and you have four hours to do it in—that first picture was of a person laying on a gurney in an operating room. There were nurses and doctors around and the operating light is coming down on the person. In the upper-right-hand corner is a picture of a person with a very stern expression and a beard. How do you tie the two together? What would you say? There is no connection whatsoever between the two and you are supposed to rationalize what's going on. [Interviewer: "I would say that it is one of two things. Either the surgical supervisor observing a less experienced surgeon getting ready to perform an operation, or the patient just died and that was God." Hearty laughter followed.] That was good—those are good. I put down that it was a communist propaganda document denouncing the American Bar Association. When I went in, it was the very first one, and I looked at the examiner and he was laughing and he says, "That's one of the best so far."

I asked, "What is it?"

He said, "It isn't anything. That was a freebie. We just wanted to see how people would react to this thing. Some of the answers are totally crazy. But that was a good one."

Only if you'd see a situation that is really obvious, if you avoid it by writing something else, that, they look for. "Get rid of that guy," they react. It exhibits psychological instability. Yeah, it would be interesting to see it happen once. What I went through is, like halfway during the life of a submarine sailor. It's grown [and changed] another fifty years since then.

It would be interesting to see, to hear, how they train, how they eat, all of the new technology that goes into this new breed of sailors. Obviously, as things progress, the teaching gets better, the equipment gets better, more specialized. I would imagine the guys are . . . well, to get your dolphins you still have to know the routine of every single compartment and be able to step in if the guy is unable to work. That's what qualification is all about.

Even when you go from boat to boat, you have to requalify, to be sure that you know what and where everything is. This isn't any Mickey Mouse operation. You're reading manuals on each department, and then you have to go through with the qualifying officer and he asks you questions, and you've got to explain it [the equipment] and operate it, and so forth. You're not expected to be the lead guy on that particular piece of equipment, but if something goes wrong, you had damn well better be able to turn it on or shut it off or do what it's supposed to do. You don't have many backup people on a sub who are supposed to be running that diesel engine. The big crews during World War II were probably seventy-five to eighty guys. For a lot of those, they had . . . they had dozens able to act as gunner's mates.

Now, these days they don't have gunner's mates on the subs, but these we had were converted World War II boats. During the Korean

War, we were still status-three submarines, just modernized. We could operate those boats most efficiently with fifty-seven guys aboard, as opposed to those days when they had up to seventy. In addition, we didn't have the deck guns and the machine guns aboard this kind of boat. That's what made it crowded. When we ran with fifty-seven, there was more room, guys were able to do more things. I don't know, but it seems the military likes to be overstaffed. Sometimes you're not on patrol, just out there for operations, plus operations for training. The only way you can train effectively is to be on one [sub] and go out there. Every time we went in for an overhaul, we'd always take some of the foremen who worked on it along with us on the first dive.

We'd ask, "Are you sure that stuff you worked on really works? All right, take a ride with us, we're gonna go dive today." It makes them think about whether their guys did a good job or not. It's all they have to do. Repairs are supposed to be inspected. If they ride along on a dive, you're damn well sure they're going to inspect it.

Well, we always kept prepared for a mission, we had to know what and how to do it, but we never had to do it, which was great. The guys whom I think are the heroes are those guys who actually did it in World War II. I mean those guys . . . I can't say enough for them.

We used to say, "Well, when a sub goes down and all hands go with it, at least they had a fifty-million-dollar coffin." Of course, we felt sad about it, but we'd kid among ourselves. Those guys [WWII vets] took it seriously. They did a great job, you know? So few did so much. Essentially, the Japanese made their biggest mistake in World War II by declaring war on us and a number one error in not recognizing the capability of our submarines. Our guys could take on anything up to a battleship and then sink the battleship. Another thing, we didn't have to go into China, Manchuria, Malaysia, or the Dutch colonies in the Southern Pacific to get all of this war material. The Japanese did, because they had no domestic supplies.

The only way they could get raw material from Indonesia back to Japan was by freighter. They lacked one of the strategic sources, because we were going to sink every one of the goddamned freighters. That's exactly what happened. That underestimation was so stupid, that was the dumbest thing they ever did, not recognizing our capabilities. Of course, where *we* were smart—it didn't start out that way—but eventually somebody thought it was a good idea that worked, and then it's *everybody's* idea. McArthur claimed credit, Nimitz claimed credit, Marshall claimed credit, even Halsey claimed credit. It was the Eisenhower plan, which says; "We're not going to waste time on these islands, we're going to bypass them. They aren't going to get any supplies from there [the South Pacific ports], we're just going to run up in there, and everybody [the Japanese] is dead. They can only live off the land for so long. They're gonna run out of material and gasoline and food. And we're not going to let any of their ships back in there."

There were only four or five major invasions during the Second World War, because we bypassed everything else. We just said, "Yep, let's leave it up to the submarines. They [the Japanese] will not be able to get anything out or anything in." That's pure crystal logic. Then, I wasn't part of the Second World War so I should leave the telling of that to those who were.

The navy was my home for many years, and submarines my own room, although Korea was not a submarine war, I'm proud to have served in the theater [war zone] and really miss the days we spent avoiding Russians, and those enjoying some fine liberty ports. I'd especially like to take another cruise in the Mediterranean. I sometimes think these nuke sailors don't realize how sweet it was when we made port in Gib [Gibraltar] or Italy or Greece. I'd never trade that for a million dollars.

12

WADE THODE
MACHINIST MATE FIRST CLASS,
USN (RET.)

Our British allies made the news on February 10, 1968, when they success-fully launched a Polaris A-3 from the Royal Navy's first SSBN, their strategic submarine *Resolution*. The crew conducted the launch while operating sub-merged off Cape Kennedy. The missile flew faultlessly down the Atlantic Missile Test Range to the impact area.

Sad news was in the making for submarine service personnel on May 22, when the nuclear-powered attack submarine *Scorpion* (SSN 589) was lost while making transit from its patrol area with the sixth fleet in the Mediter-ranean en route to Norfolk, Virginia. She was listed as overdue on May 27 and declared as presumed lost with all hands—ninety-nine officers and en-listed men—on June 5.

The first SLBM patrol began on June 22. The *Resolution* carried a com-plement of sixteen Polaris A-3. Built in the United States, these missiles were fitted with British warheads. The *Resolution* would patrol off Russia in the far North Atlantic and Baltic Sea.

On July 6, Indian Navy officials accepted delivery at New Delhi of the

Soviet-built *Kalvari*. This Foxtrot-class submarine was the first of a large number of Soviet-built submarines that the Indian Navy operated from then on. On July 9, Operation Sneaky Pete, which was a U.S. antisubmarine and mine warfare exercise, began off the coast of the State of Georgia. The exercise involved fourteen surface ships, five submarines, and twenty-eight aircraft, all from the U.S. Atlantic Fleet. Sneaky Pete later received recognition as a highly successful learning tool. The navy's Special Projects Office (SPO) was redesignated the Strategic Systems Project Office (SSPO) to reflect the additional responsibilities assigned by the chief of naval operations, encompassing strategic offensive and defensive systems. All future operational missions of coastal and long-range patrol submarines became incorporated under this new planning office.

On August, 16, the prototype first model of the Poseidon C-3 missile (navy designation C3X-1), was successfully launched from Cape Kennedy. The next day, America's largest research submarine, the *Dolphin* (AGSS 555) was commissioned. Able to operate at far greater depth than any U.S. operational submarine, her mission was to explore and collect samples from the deepest trenches of the Pacific and South Atlantic. The *Dolphin* was unarmed. Her first CO was LCDR John R. McDonnell, USN.

On October 30, the wreckage of the U.S. nuclear-powered submarine *Scorpion* was located at an extreme depth of ten thousand feet, approximately four hundred nautical miles southwest of the Azores. The U.S. research ship *Mizar* (T-AGOR-11) made the discovery, and investigation dives were conducted. The cause of the *Scorpion*'s loss was determined to be a torpedo that had begun running in its tube. When an effort was made to launch the defective weapon, it commenced a circular run and struck the submarine.

Getting off to an early start in 1969, the U.S. strategic missile submarine *James Madison* (SSBN 627), the first of thirty-one Polaris missile submarines scheduled for conversion to carry the new Poseidon C-3 missile, entered the General Dynamics Electric Boat Yard at Groton, Connecticut, on February 3 for detailed overhaul and conversion. The Poseidon boats would remain our first line of defense—with a retaliatory capacity—until the advent of the Trident missile.

A costly accident occurred at the San Francisco Bay Naval Shipyard on May 15. The U.S. nuclear submarine *Guitarro* (SSN 665), being built in the yard, sank at dockside in thirty-five feet of water. The naval salvage investigating team discovered that the submarine was flooded through a hatch left open by the negligence of workmen. No one was aboard at the time of the sinking. The *Guitarro* was subsequently raised and completed for service. The office of naval intelligence determined that there was no sabotage involved in the sinking.

On June 30, the Royal Air Force V-bomber force was removed from the strategic deterrent alert at 2044 hours. The Royal Navy's three strategic missile submarines replaced them at 0001 on July 1. The RN's fourth SSBN, the *Revenge*, was completed in December 1969, with a fifth planned Polaris SSBN, which was ultimately not built. All of these submarines carried 165 A-3 Polaris missiles.

The next month, on October 4, the Chief of Naval Operations acted to establish the Underwater Long-Range Missile System (ULMS) program. This later became the Trident Missile Program.

The nuclear-powered attack submarine *Narwal* (SSN 671) was commissioned on July 12. It was a one-of-a-kind boat, similar to the Los Angeles class. It had a natural-circulation (S5G) reactor plant intended to reduce pump noises at slow speeds. Her first commanding officer was named as CDR Willis A. Matson III, USN.

Outside of routine deterrent patrols, submarine operations languished through the end of summer. Then on October 27, the newly refitted nuclear-propelled submersible, the NR-1, was put in service. The deep-operating vessel had a submerged displacement of 372 tons. Its overall length is 136 5/16 feet. NR-1 was manned by a crew of seven, and had an astonishing operating depth of three thousand feet. The original purpose for which the NR-1 had been constructed was as a test platform for small submarine nuclear power plants. From that date forward, she functioned as a deep-ocean research and recovery vehicle, under command of LCDR Dwaine C. Griffith, USN.

The year 1970 rolled in with a momentous treaty coming into force on March 5. The Non-Proliferation Treaty (NPT) was signed on July 1, 1968, and not scheduled for enforcement until this date. As suspected by ONI and other U.S. intelligence services, some of the signatories totally ignored the letter and intent of the treaty and continued to spread nuclear weapons technology through their surrogates.

On April 12, tragedy struck for our Soviet enemy when the nuclear submarine *K-8* of the November class, Russian-built submarines, sank in the Atlantic off Cape Finisterre, Spain. She was the first Soviet nuclear-powered submarine to be lost at sea. On the previous day, the *K-8* had suffered an engineering casualty while operating submerged. However, she was able to surface and most of her crew managed to be rescued before the doomed vessel sank.

The *James Madison* (SSBN 627) became the first strategic ballistic missile submarine to complete conversion to carry and fire the Poseidon C-3 on June 28.

On August 3, the first submerged launching of the multiwarhead (MRV) Poseidon C-3 missile occurred when the ballistic missile sub *James Madison* fired a missile off the coast at Cape Kennedy. Unfortunately, the launch was observed by the Soviet intelligence gathering (spy) ship *Khariton Laptev*. The *Laptev* was part of a fleet of spy ships, disguised as fishing trawlers, which kept constant station off the East Coast of the United States.

On September 23, while still new at his job, Chief of Naval Operations (probably the most ineffective and inept CNO our navy has ever had) Admiral Elmo R. Zumwalt Jr., USN, established the CNO Executive Panel to help provide "a clear understanding of the navy's mission." Unfortunately, Admi-

Deep submergence vehicle.
Courtesy of United States Navy

ral Zumwalt appeared to be ignorant of the fact that leadership by committee had never worked, and didn't in this case, either, as time proved.

Starting in a bellicose mode, 1971 brought us a declaration of President
Richard Nixon on January 4, stating that, if the Soviet Union serviced its
nuclear-powered submarines in, or coming from, Cuban ports, it [the Soviet
Union] risked creating an international crisis. U.S. nuclear submarine deter-
rent patterns changed slightly in the Atlantic to provide closer surveillance of
Soviet activity in Cuban waters.

Not until March 31 did another momentous event occur for U.S. submarines, when the strategic missile sub *James Madison* departed from
Charleston, South Carolina. She was the first U.S. submarine to deploy with

Polaris A-3 fleet ballistic missile lifts off from the USS *Robert E. Lee* (SSBN 601).
Courtesy of United States Navy

the MRV'ed Poseidon C-3 missiles. The *Madison*'s patrol lasted until May 10, 1971. On the same day, the Undersea Long-Range Missile System (ULMS)—which later became the Trident missile system—had the office of project manager established under the auspice of the chief of naval material. The Polaris-Poseidon development remained under the direction of the SPO until designated as PM-1.

More saber-rattling came from the Soviet Union on May 22, when a Soviet naval spokesman announced that a submarine and an auxiliary ship would visit Cuban ports later in the month. He further went on to report that the ships would resupply from Cuban sources and the crews would receive liberty.

On August 8, the U.S. Navy accepted its first Deep Submergence Rescue Vehicle (DSRV) from the manufacturer Lockheed Missiles and Space Company. It was the first of two such deep-diving vessels that could rescue survivors

DSRV-1 (Rescue Vehicle). *Courtesy of United States Navy*

to depths of thirty-five hundred feet to be developed in the wake of the *Thresher* disaster in 1963. The original program that produced this vehicle called for twelve such vessels to be produced, each with a capacity of twelve rescuees. Later, the program changed to six craft each with a capacity of twenty-four men. However, as the program progressed, only two vessels, the DSRV-1 *Mystic* and the DSRV-2 *Avalon*, reached completion.

Once again, on September 25, the Soviet Union made submarine history with the inauguration of full endurance trials of the Soviet Papa-type cruise missile submarine *K-162*. The trials for the submarine would last through December 4, 1971, and would include the swift vessel achieving an underwater speed of 44.7 knots—which remains a world record for submarine speed to this date. The one-of-a-kind nuclear submarine, completed in late 1969, was also the first to have a titanium hull. It is fortunate indeed that the Soviets abandoned this line of development.

On November 6, the Soviets exhibited their arrogance and militaristic

A den of polar bears curiously approach the bow section of the U.S. Navy (USN) Los Angeles Class Attack Submarine USS *Honolulu* (SSN 718) after the ship surfaced in the Arctic Circle. *Courtesy of United States Navy*

stance with a cover article in their publication *Soviet Diplomatichesky Slovar* (Diplomatic Lexicon)—whose chief editor was Foreign Minister Andrei Gromyko (!), which demanded that the Baltic Sea be closed to the naval units of all nonBaltic powers. The United States "complied" by the simple means of increasing deterrent patrols in the Arctic Circle and Baltic Sea.

France, the United States' occasional ally, placed into service their first-of-class strategic missile submarines on December 1. *Le Redoubtable* would carry sixteen M-4 ballistic missiles. She was also the first French nuclear-powered submarine to go to sea. In addition, during the month of December, the Soviet Navy completed the first Alpha-class submarine. It was a highly automated, high-speed (forty-three knots), deep-diving nuclear submarine. This prototype experienced extensive technical problems and modifications, and the Soviets scrapped it in 1974. The Alpha prototype was followed by six production model SSNs, completed between 1979 and 1983.

Intensified deterrent patrols began in early 1972, and continued through 1990. Nineteen seventy-two began with a sort of bang, when the U.S. Navy released a statement on January 5 that five hundred gallons of slightly radioactive water were accidentally spilled into the Thames River near New London, Connecticut, during a routine transfer between two ships, which were not named. On the same day, the *New York Times* reported that the United States had entered into an unpublicized agreement with the government of Bahrain to construct and operate a permanent naval station there—including submarine facilities—in a suitable port. The reason for this move revolved around the fact that the island of Bahrain was a strategically located nation in the Persian Gulf. In future years, this would prove a fortuitous decision.

On March 14, Turkish Premier Nihat Erim declared that his government would reopen Turkish ports to U.S. Sixth Fleet ships. The Turks had halted these visits in 1969. This followed the injury of several sailors in anti-American riots.

On May 4, the U.S. Department of Defense announced that a Soviet diesel-electric submarine of the Gulf-class recently entered a port of Cuba's northern coast. The Gulf-class subs carry three ballistic missiles. Accompanying the submarine were a destroyer and a submarine tender. On May 5, the U.S. Navy celebrated the commissioning of the one hundredth nuclear-powered submarine, the *Silversides* (SSN 679), at Groton, Connecticut, with CDR John E. Allen, USN, as her first commanding officer. On May 16, Secretary of Defense Laird signed an approval put forth by the navy to change the name of the ULMS program to the Trident program. On May 26, in Moscow, representatives of the United States and the Soviet Union signed the interim SALT (Treaty), an agreement on Anti-Ballistic Missile (ABM) systems. The SALT agreement established limits on the numbers of land-based and submarine-launched missiles each country may have. We should take note that no such limits were placed on strategic bombers.

Our nuclear-powered submarines continued deterrent patrols uninter-rupted. Rumbles of discontent over these operations came from Moscow, only to be ignored by the U.S. government. A reply of sorts was made by U.S. forces on August 18, when the ballistic missile submarine *Ulysses S. Grant* (SSBN 631) launched four Poseidon C-3 missiles in the first quadruple missile launch by a U.S. submarine. Prior to this, the largest number of SLBM launches in a single day from a U.S. submarine had been two.

On October 17, the first test flight of the U.S. Navy's Harpoon antiship missile occurred. Originally developed to attack Soviet cruise missile sub-marines while on the surface, this successful test of the Harpoon opened the doorway for the weapon to enter service in 1977 and quickly became the most widely used antiship missile in the West. Soviet designs of similar missiles continued to be unsatisfactory.

Doubtless, everyone visualizes machinist mates as represented by Holly-wood, just like torpedomen. They are all wearing faded khaki uniforms or skivvie shirts and dungaree trousers, heavily greasestained, some with frayed cuffs. That might have been the case during an extended sixty-day war patrol during World War II. However, such conditions are never seen aboard a nuclear submarine. This is not only because of the presence of washers and dryers, but because of the need for absolute cleanliness in the engine and reactor rooms. Our next spokesman served on two nuclear-powered submarines, USS *Skate* (SSN 578) and USS *Swordfish* (SSN 579). Of all the ratings held by our submariners, that of Nuclear Power Engineer (NPE) is one of the most often overlooked when considering military prowess. Not so for those who know the intricacies of life and duty aboard a submarine, however. Every member of a crew, as we have heard firsthand, has to know and be able to assume the duties of every other rating aboard. Not quite so much for cooks, but then, recall the comments made about crew members being at liberty to experiment with different favorite dishes, and cook in idle hours, as well. Here is yet another example of the broad underpinnings of cross-training that served to the advantage of various crews.

I entered the navy a year after high school. We had moved from Maine to Hawaii and I had attended Eatonvillie High School in Honolulu, Hawaii, graduating in June 1980. I enlisted on January 12, 1981, and served until May 5, 1991. During that time, I had the honor and privilege to serve in two nuclear-powered submarines, the USS *Skate* (SSN 578) and USS *Swordfish* (SSN 579). After qualifying for submarine duty, I attended nuclear power school in Iowa. It was there that I knew positively that I wanted to serve on a nuclear submarine. People frequently asked me, how can you learn a submarine's power plant in the center of the midwest? The answer is simple: The power plant is stationary in the nuclear power compartment. It is the sub that moves, taking the reactor with it.

Prior to attending power school, I achieved a rating as a machinist mate. Fortunately, I have always done well with both academic and technical/mechanical jobs. My first assignment to a submarine was in Pearl Harbor, not all that far from my childhood home. It was aboard the *Skate*. One of the first exciting things—at least to me—was when the *Skate* participated in an exercise. It was my first and we—the whole squadron—went out into the Pacific, west of Hawaii, for this exercise with a small task force that used a destroyer screen like those the Soviets employed.

We dived just outside Uniform Tango—the last channel marker buoy you pass on the way out of port and the first you come to when entering port—and went deep. At our first sonar contact, we went even deeper, under a thermal layer, which effectively blinded the surface ship's sonar and water-penetrating radar. Anyway, all of the subs began feeling somewhat cocky and, during the exercise, a couple of 637s tried to get under the screen. However, the destroyers caught them because they had the old-style bow planes and those made noise. During that time, all of our early nuclear submarines had bow planes, like the *Nautilus*. Therefore, the 636s and 637s all had bow planes. But by the late seventies and partway through the eighties, they had the sail planes. Those made it easier to keep an even keel, and were a lot quieter.

Unfortunately, the early nukes had a problem with the bow planes, causing them to breach easily. If your diving planes are only in the middle and at the back, you have trouble controlling the front, but with bow and stern planes, you can control your depth. We learned from that.

Now, with bow planes and sail planes you can control your depth with ease. You can't do an underhaul [to work in tandem with another sub or subs] of surface ships unless you can control your depth. What we don't want to be doing is to be lagging down maybe five minutes behind him [the partner sub]. You have to go down and up whenever he does. That's where the twin planes and twin screws come in, which likewise affects the operation of an escape pod. It has to go through the twin hulls in a level attitude and get free of the boat. That's why they all have sail *and* bow planes now.

The sail sets way up high and we need to maintain a constant depth, with twenty feet of water above us . . . above the sail. Therefore, with only sail planes, you don't have that much bite in the water, whereas when you're down deeper, you have more water for the planes to bite into. For all of that, the round, thick nose, the bow planes, and twin screws allowed us to do a lot more around the ice. It was a gas, because we could go close in around the icebergs. When an iceberg came in too close, we could go down, turn, and go away. It was easy—you know, back one-third, ahead one-third, down on the bow planes. We never went to the Pole when I was aboard, but we went under the ice a few times. It was all right. [laughing] It was *cold*, is all I'll say.

We had this fuel line going through there about this big [illustrates with both hands a pipe diameter of about four or five inches] and with that big a [sic] trunk line, we had to keep it cold, so there was no heat in there because of the motors—hot motors and stuff—we could just about freeze out there. We had temperatures of about twenty-eight or thirty degrees outside. But of course, seawater is saltwater and can stay liquid even below normal freezing. When we got up to thirty knots speed we *knew* it was cold. The neat part, though, was for some periods that [seawater] was the only water we had, except for drinking. Some guys found it rough for shaving, but I had a beard . . . clear up until '86, I had a beard. Most of us sent away—you could send away for anything you wanted—so I sent and got hair gel and gunk for my beard. When I had my beard, I used to wear these red high-top tennis shoes all the time. When I was in Korea and in these stores they had what was called Super Bongs, which were a sort of Korean brand of tennis shoes which were a bright red, but they were a size like fourteen, so I bought 'em. I used to wear them, but they were real thin, like the old Converse used to be on the bottoms and were so high that the toes collapsed. Before long, the whole crew began to wear these high-tops, in all sorts of colors. The crew had neon green or blue or darker, wild colors, until it seemed the entire boat was doing that: buying super-sized shoes, walking on top of the main engine until they'd get hot and curl up the toes, and they'd put these stupid laces in so they'd glow in the dark. Some of them started growin' a beard [laughs heartily again]. It all actually became a form of entertainment.

When you don't surface for months at a time, what else can you do? You can only read so many books and watch movies. When we went to WesPac, we had only two movies in the entire patrol out of WesPac—*two movies*. They were *Star Trek: The Wrath of Khan* and *Flash Gordon*. That's *all* we had to watch for a whole six months. The drill was I had to run the projectors every night. I think I can do the whole movie for you if you want. Before that, we had *Strange Duel* and *Comfort Wells* and I can do those for you, too. We had a VCR hookup, but there was only one TV and we only used it to record . . . we used to plug it into the periscope to record what the 'scope was seeing for the benefit of the crew. We had this two-track thing . . . in our racks and we could listen to that because they had something for all tastes—you know, like the Mamas and Papas sort of stuff. Of course, today they have their own headphones and listen to their CD players and whatever.

Anyway, back to the end of my enlistment. At the time, I was on the *Swordfish*. I also had an apartment out there in town [Honolulu]. I had a job lined up, working at a 7-11 store and there was a little community college—Chaminade University of Honolulu, where I later got a master's in business administration—and I was saving up money—I had fifteen grand—for going to school.

The old man came to me and said, "We want to keep you in."

So I said, "Well, I don't want to go to training schools again, or return to cleaning up rigs and fixing them. I've had enough of fixing things. I don't want any of that. Send me to a training command, and give me my bonus. I want to reenlist on the *Bowfin* and I want the flag that's flying on the *Bowfin* when I reenlist and I want four marks to sea. Then, I want the Zucker Training School up in Bangor, 'cause that's close to my childhood home. I'll agree to re-up for that."

"Oh, will you?" he asked.

"Yes. Give me that and I'll reenlist."

As it happened, three days go by and he came and said, "Come on, let's go. We're going to the *Bowfin*."

I asked, "What? What's broken now?"

"Nothing," he said. "We're going to reenlist you, that's why we're going. You said you would reenlist."

I said, "Yeah."

"Then let's go."

We went over to the *Bowfin*, I got reenlisted, took the flag, got orders to Bremerton. There I went to the training school and spent about three years there, teaching PGLs, evaporators, distillers, ignitions, and stuff. Even better, I was able to *park* my tools.

I finally got back to the boats, particularly the *Sam Houston*, an old boomer, which we decommissioned in Bremerton. I went to the *Sam Houston* for six days. What happened was kind of a sad thing. Bryan, who was an instructor with me, used to ride his motorcycle, wrecked it, and broke both of his legs, his hips and back, everything, and ended up in Tripler [Army Medical Center]. Three days later, this guy named Barney, who taught Pumping Valve Operator (PVO) up there, got in a wreck and got killed. We saw their bikes—their motorcycles—up there at Campbell and they were just [sic] in parts.

Someone asked, "Who's going to teach the PVO?" because everyone who operates a nuclear valve on a nuclear ship has to have that course.

So they said for me to go back to Bremerton because we have to transfer in new instructors. So I went back to NACPAC for eight more months.

When I came back over they said, "Oh, well, they replaced you on the *Sam Houston.*" They had gotten someone who was qualified so that the *Sam Houston* could go into the shipyard in Bremerton. They wanted me to manage the decommissioning there. They had someone to replace me so that the *Houston* goes on in.

I said, "Well, if you've got someone to replace me, and they're already up in Bremerton, the full management of the decommissioning crew was already there."

Only, they said, "We want someone really qualified to handle this."

To which I said, "I don't . . . Well, my wife is due and she . . ."

He interrupted and said, "Your wife is going to have babies by herself."

But putting out to sea for eight or nine months of a year wasn't my wife's idea of having a good time. Whereas if I got a boomer, she'd accept that—as far as two months out, four months in port— she could live with that.

They said, "Well, it's too late now. We know that it's going to be hard, but you guys are living here and you'll have to take a boat out of here."

I said, "I want to have kids." Therefore, I got out. I mean, you know, I looked at it as a job. If you [the navy] offered something more than I could get on the outside, I'd stay in. However, if you can't . . . which isn't really, bad, I'd leave. I'd thought that even before I got off the base and said [to myself], "Make plans to get out." When I found out, I asked them "What can you offer me that's as good as or better than on the outside?"

That's all it took. Now, I know, it's a lot more complicated. I got out, and went to work and school and never looked back. Well, that's not quite true. I surely did miss my days in the boats, the friendships we made, and the things we did. Even the Russians didn't piss me off enough to spoil my good memories. I miss the schools, too. Even though teaching some of them—as I've said—was a pain. Being in the subs was a good life.

13

HENRY G. SPENCELEY
YEOMAN SECOND,
(YM-2), USN (RET.)

Although the Cold War years remained quiet years, the expansion of the submarine service continued. On February 16, 1973, the navy announced they had let contracts for construction of a $550 million base for Trident submarines at Keyport, Washington, on Puget Sound. The base near Bangor, Maine, was designated to serve submarines operating in the Northern Atlantic and Artcic Oceans.

On April 28, the U.S. submarine rescue ship *Pigeon* (ARS 21) was placed in commission. The *Pigeon* and her sister ship, the *Ortolan* (ARS 22), were constructed as catamaran (twin-hull) vessels. It was a design that permitted them to support DSRVs and deep-diving operations, which were part of the navy's rescue-and-salvage operations. This program had developed after the 1963 loss of the *Thresher* (SSN 593). In the original plan, the navy called for six such ships for deep-submergence operations.

On August 10, a momentous occasion occurred: The Polaris missile was phased out of U.S. Navy service in the Atlantic-Mediterranean theater, when the submarine *Robert E. Lee* (SSBN 601) transferred to the Pacific Fleet. In her place, four British SSBNs continued to operate in the Atlantic with Polaris A-3 missiles, using British warheads. Seven days later the bad news was released by Secretary of Defense James R. Schlesinger: the Soviet Union had successfully test-flown a Multiple Independently Targeted Reentry Vehicle (MIRV) warhead. Many of our naval missile experts believed that their system was comparable to those of the United States.

Deterrent patrols by our SSBN subs continued throughout the year. The nuclear saber-rattling by the Soviets did not interfere with the navy's declaration on November 19 that the U.S. Sixth Fleet had been taken off alert status and returned to the status of stand-by "normal training condition."

On January 10, 1974, U.S. Secretary of Defense, James R. Schlesinger, stated that he planned to improve the accuracy of U.S. long-range missiles, with an accompanying disclosure of his intention of having some of those missiles retargeted to strike Soviet military targets, in addition to the currently targeted population and industrial center. The expected Soviet response came swiftly, with more ominous threats, arrogant demands, and a whine and snivel to the U.N. about American imperialism. Our government ignored it all.

On February 6, the U.S. strategic missile submarine *George Washington* (SSBN 598) successfully launched five Polaris A-3T missiles on the sixth. This was the first quintuple missile launch by a U.S. submarine. Prior to this, the largest launch consisted of four SLBMs in a single day. It clearly represented an "in your face," to the Soviet effort to intimidate the United States.

In a typical—for him—announcement, Chief of Naval Operations Admiral Elmo R. Zumwalt Jr., USN, declared in an interview published by the *New York Times* on May 13 that he was convinced that the United States had lost control of the sea lanes to the Soviet Union.

On the anniversary of D-Day, June 6, the U.S. strategic missile submarine *John Marshal* (SSBN 611), completed her final Polaris A-2 deterrent patrol. That placed all eight submarines that carried the Polaris A-2 undergoing conversion. In the future, they would carry the Polaris A-3 or Poseidon C-3 missiles, and the A-2 would be completely phased out. On June 27, the navy took three steps back by signing an agreement with the Soviet Union to further limit quantities of ballistic missile systems. At the same conference, the United States and the Soviet Union began to bargain over the problem of permanent limits on offensive strategic weapons. This soon proved a big mistake because the Soviet Union *never, ever* kept its word given in treaties.

On July 21, Soviet General Secretary Leonid Brezhnev, in remarks to the major European news agencies and the Associated Press, proposed mutual withdrawal from the Mediterranean Sea of all Soviet and U.S. ships carrying nuclear missiles. As an aside, the laughter that followed echoed through the Pentagon for days.

A great Christmas present was handed the American people on December 23 when the first flight of the Rockwell International B-1A supersonic strategic bomber occurred. Only four prototype models were built before the aircraft was cancelled by President James E. Carter Jr. in 1977, acting in concert with the agenda of his political party, promising further, deeper cuts in military research and development projects including submarine R&D. (Odd, since Carter was a former submarine skipper.) Also picked for destruction by Carter were the B-1 bomber project (which the Reagan administration later resurrected, along with improvements in submarine-launched missiles) and further submarine design and development.

True to their pro-Soviet leanings, the *New York Times* reported on May 24, 1975, that U.S. submarines had been conducting electronic surveillance operations near the Soviet Union. The article went on to expose the fact that, frequently, some of these forays were within the three-mile limit. The *Times* revealed that the surveillance had been conducted for close to fifteen years, in a top secret, need-to-know operation called Holystone. Neither the *Times* nor whoever leaked the highly classified information to the newspaper ever received punishment for their treasonous acts.

On July 2, Secretary of Defense Schlesinger released a statement that read that, under some war conditions, the United States might make first use (preemptive strikes) of strategic weapons against carefully selected Soviet targets. The initial thrust of this strategy would be our SSBNs. The effect of this decision electrified submarine commanders in both the Atlantic and Pacific Fleets.

Bad decisions and bad news haunted the U.S. Navy, and the submarine service in particular, through January 1976, culminating on January 24, when a five-year treaty of friendship was signed with Spain, in which the United States agreed to remove its Poseidon submarines from the base at Rota beginning in 1979.

An eleven-day exercise under the auspices of the United States Third Fleet began on March 2 off the coast of southern California. Participating in the exercise were ships from Australia, Canada, Great Britain, and the Netherlands, in addition to the U.S. contribution. At the conclusion, the convening authority declared the exercise a rousing success.

Scandal appeared once again when on June 25, 1976, the *Washington Post* reported that thirty-seven sailors from the crew of the ballistic submarine *Thomas Jefferson* (SSBN 618) were removed from the submarine after she arrived at Bangor, Washington. The Office of Naval Criminal Investigation (later NCIS) accused them of being a part of a marijuana investigation.

On August 15, the United States submarine *Snook* (SSN 592) arrived at Perth, Australia. It was the first nuclear-powered submarine to visit the country. Australian maritime union (communist) demonstrators held a protest rally against the visit, although three U.S. nuclear-propelled surface warships had previously visited Australia.

A Soviet guided-missile submarine of the Echo II class collided with the

United States frigate *Voge* (FF 1047) in the Ionian Sea on August 28. The *Voge* incurred damage to her propeller that required her to be towed to Suda Bay, Crete. The Soviet submarine received minor damage. Later, on March 11, 1977, a U.S. Navy report of the accident stated that the Soviet submarine was at fault in the collision.

Great news and a dignified, restrained celebration accompanied the commissioning of the first boat of the *Los Angeles* (SSN 688)–class nuclear submarines, under command of CDR John Christiansen Jr., USN, on November 11. The ship had been built at the Newport News Shipbuilding and Dry Dock Company in Newport News, Virginia. With an underwater operational speed of around thirty-three knots, the *Los Angeles* was the fastest United States nuclear submarine to enter service since the *Skipjack* (SSN 585) class, completed from 1959 to 1961. This class was later configured to fire the Tomahawk cruise missiles.

The year 1977 opened with a gloomy outlook for the future. On January 2, the *Washington Post* reported that a new disclosure released in late December 1976 by the National Intelligence Estimate (NIE) of Soviet military intentions, developed by the United States intelligence community, indicated that the goal of the Soviet Union was to strive for military *superiority* over the United States rather than maintaining military parity. This was with a view toward invasion and conquest of the United States. A committee consisting of civilian and retired military experts, including former Secretary of the Navy Paul H. Nitze, assisted in compiling the NIE of Soviet intentions. Later the same month, on January 21, President Carter (the *only* President to have served as skipper of an American submarine) further created a climate of shameful doom by issuing a Proclamation of Pardon for violators of the Military Selective Service Act during the Vietnam era (from August 4, 1964, to March 28, 1973). The only bright spot was that the pardon did not cover deserters; their cases would be reviewed on an individual basis. On January 22, a navy spokesman acknowledged that nine sailors from the strategic missile submarine *Casimir Pulaski* (SSBN 633) were removed from the submarine at Holy Loch, Scotland, and charged with drug offenses.

Attacks on the military in general, and the navy in particular, continued to come from the Carter White House all through March and April, and into May. On May 3, a spokesman for the United States Navy acknowledged that thirty-three enlisted men—about one-quarter of the crew—of the nuclear-powered attack submarine *Los Angeles* (SSN 688) were transferred from the submarine following an investigation into alleged drug use. The navy cited no trials, nor were any discharges acknowledged. Submarine activities continued to figure largely in May, and on May 27, Reuters News Service reported that the USS *Bluefish* (SSN 675) had made port in Haifa, Israel, marking the first visit by a nuclear-powered submarine to Israel. On the same day, President and Mrs. Carter embarked on a cruise off Cape Canaveral, Florida, on the attack submarine *Los Angeles*. This marked the first time President Carter had been in a nuclear-powered undersea craft. He had earlier served in diesel-electric submarines, achieving the rank of Lieutenant Commander and skippering a boat.

On June 28, celebration was the order of the day, as Queen Elizabeth II reviewed 150 British and foreign naval ships during the Silver Jubilee Naval Review off Portsmouth, England. Present, among others, representing the United States were the cruiser *California* (CGN 36) and the submarine *Billfish* (SSN 676). This was the first such celebration in which a U.S. nuclear submarine participated.

USS *Bluefish* (SS 222) in 1943.

Courtesy of United States Navy

Nuclear attack submarine USS *Los Angeles* (SS 688).

Courtesy of United States Navy

Starboard bow view of the U.S. Navy attack submarine, USS *Los Angeles* (SSN 688).

Courtesy of United States Navy

The *Los Angeles*–class nuclear attack submarines, such as the *Albany* shown here were first launched in the 1960s, formed a large and key part of the U.S. submarine force.

Courtesy of United States Navy

Los Angeles–class nuclear-powered attack submarine USS *Buffalo* (SSN 715) under way.

Courtesy of United States Navy

Right side of the torpedo room onboard the *Los Angeles*–class nuclear-powered fast attack submarine USS *Hartford* (SSN 768).

Courtesy of United States Navy

The galley of the USS *Dallas*.

Courtesy of United States Navy

Launcher board, USS *Tucson*.

Courtesy of United States Navy

September 20 saw a near-tragedy averted when the U.S. nuclear-powered submarine *Ray* (SSN 653) struck bottom in the Mediterranean Sea, south of the island of Sardinia. Three crewmen incurred minor injuries, which the sub's corpsman treated. After the accident, the *Ray* surfaced and continued to Sardinia on her own power.

On October 27, the *Washington Post* gloatingly reported that the U.S. Navy had acknowledged the highest enlisted desertion rate in its history during the fiscal year 1977. The *Post* took delight in announcing a rate of 31.7 desertions per one thousand enlisted naval personnel (this amounted to 14,539 out of a total enlisted force of 459,857). This represented six times the previous desertion rate of 5.5 per one thousand during World War II, nearly quadruple the Korean War rate of 8.7, and more than double the Vietnam War-high of 13.6 in fiscal year 1971. The report went on to declare that more than 72 percent of deserters were between the ages of eighteen and twenty. The article claimed that 92 percent were on their first tour of duty, 79 percent had assignments on ships, and 66 percent were in the lower mental categories (IQ).

One success allowed for some hope among submariners. The *Post* conveniently neglected to report that desertions from the submarine service were insignificant.

A report from the Associated Press on October 21 indicated that the Egyptian government refused the British nuclear-powered submarine *Dreadnaught* transit through the Suez Canal. The AP quoted an Egyptian representative as stating that the reason for Egypt's refusal was due to the government's objection to nuclear ships using the canal.

Delays and cost overruns plagued the Trident strategic missile submarine program in November. The navy made a statement, which was not elaborated on, that the *Ohio* was one year behind schedule and that the cost of the submarine would be some 50 percent higher than the original estimate of

$800 million, thus bringing the total to $1.2 billion to complete the vessel. The announced target date for completion was spring of 1980.

Early progress was noted at the start of 1978 when, on January 26, Secretary of the Navy W. Graham Claytor Jr. announced the navy's choice of Kings Bay, Georgia, for the site of a new submarine support base for FBM submarine support. The base would open in May 1979.

The navy recorded more success on February 1, when the USS *Barb* (SSN 596) successfully launched the first Tomahawk cruise missile while operating off the coast of California. This was a memorable first launch of the Tomahawk from a submerged submarine. Following that, the Tomahawk enjoyed enormous success in accuracy and ease of guidance in the Gulf War and Operation Iraqi Freedom. Undersecretary of the Defense for Research and Engineering William J. Perry stated in his annual report to Congress that the first five Trident Submarines of the *Ohio* (SSBN 726) class would, unfortunately, be delayed because of (in his words) "inefficiencies and lower-than-expected productivity" at the Electric Boat Yard in Groton, Connecticut. He estimated that the Trident program might be delayed but that, through hard work, it could be back on schedule in fiscal year 1983, and ready for delivery of the first six Tridents (at that time).

On February 19, the *Boston Globe* released a questionable report based on an "unofficial" study that the newspaper called an "alarming rate of cancer deaths" supposedly among Portsmouth, New Hampshire, naval shipyard workers. The claim put forward was that the workers' jobs brought them into the area of nuclear submarine reactors. It was implied—although not directly stated—that if dockyard workers were thus affected, then what about the men who served in those boats or any who got near them? This alleged death rate was more than twice the national average and nearly 80 percent higher than the rate for other shipyard workers, whose jobs did not take them near the nuclear reactors. Although no formal investigation followed

USS *Ohio* (SSBN 726). *Courtesy of United States Navy*

USS *Ohio*-class carried the Trident missile. *Courtesy of United States Navy*

this spurious allegation, it was later determined to be a total fiction, invented by a staff writer for the *Globe* in an effort to generate fear among the general populace of nuclear-powered vessels of all types.

On March 11, the USS *Abraham Lincoln* (SSBN 602) became the first U.S. strategic missile submarine to complete fifty deterrent patrols. The *Lincoln* had achieved an astonishing record of endurance during its seventeen years of service. One-half of her operating time was spent submerged, which constituted 74,571 hours. Further, the *Lincoln* had traveled 420,666 *nautical miles*, which represented the equivalent of circumnavigating the earth nearly seventeen times.

A navy study on radiation hazards in shipyards and on nuclear-powered ships was revealed by the Associated Press on April 22. The navy concluded that radiation exposure to shipyard workers resulted in less than *1 death* in 100,000 people, compared to the industrial accident rate at naval shipyards of

Trident T submarine-launched ballistic missile is launched from the nuclear-powered strategic missile submarine USS *Nevada* (SSBN 733).
Courtesy of United States Navy

7 per 100,000. Coincidentally, the annual death rate attributed to *smoking* was 150 per 100,000. The navy report harshly criticized the *Boston Globe*–sponsored study that falsely alleged that Portsmouth, New Hampshire, shipyard workers who were involved in the nuclear areas of submarines suffered *twice the normal cancer rates.*

On 7 September, President Jimmy Carter suffered a severe setback in his plans to reduce the effectiveness and strength of our armed forces, when the House of Representatives voted 206 to 191 to override his veto of the fiscal year 1979 budget. This was surprisingly *not* along party lines, since the Democrats had control of the House at the time. But the good news did not last.

Early news programs on October 5 covered a startling announcement from the FBI, which disclosed the destruction of a plot to steal the nuclear-powered attack submarine *Trepang* (SSN 674) and sell it to an undisclosed purchaser. Three men were arrested in the investigation, which had gone on for several months, according to a spokesman for the FBI. Later on, one

Nuclear ballistic submarine
USS *Maine* (SSBN 741),
Ohio-class submarine.
Courtesy of United States Navy

of the would-be boatjackers turned prosecution's witness. The other two went to trial for fraud in U.S. District Court in St. Louis, Missouri. On the day of the apprehension, the navy also announced settlement of nearly all of a $2.7 billion settlement in ship construction contract claims with Newport News Shipbuilding and Dry Dock Company in Virginia. The settlement related to the construction of nuclear-powered surface ships and attack submarines.

Throughout the narrative of these submarine sailors, there has been mention of submarine tenders. They served a vital link with the fleet submarines and the huge stores of munitions in Pearl Harbor, Midway, and in Australia. During World War II, they were absolutely vital. The vast reaches of the Pacific Ocean and the South China Sea defied the range of our submarines—given that they desired some time on patrol, not just transiting to and from Hawaii, the West Coast of the United States, or Brisbane, Australia. Regardless of their rate, the men who served in the tenders were a breed apart, yet always considered themselves to be close cousins to the submariners whom they supported.

I started out with the intention of becoming a submariner. I served in the U.S. Navy from my enlistment on January 10, 1942, until the conclusion of the war [WWII]. I left boot camp on February 14, 1942, and arrived at submarine school in New London, Connecticut. I had originally planned to attend submarine school, but that did not materialize. After the sorting-out process, I received an assignment to the USS *Griffin* (AS-13). By February 28, we were well on our way to Australia, by way of the Panama Canal. When we reached Panama, before passing through the canal, we went into dry dock. All hands—just the enlisted men, that is—went under the side and scraped paint on the bottom.

After transiting the canal, we were traveling at sea and, all of a sudden, we were ordered to look for submarines. However, none appeared until finally we saw a conning tower. CDR S. D. Jupp, our skipper, was on the bridge at the time and he later said he wondered when his spotters, or lookouts, would locate these subs. We picked up the six submarines of Submarine Squadron Five, which we were to tend, and toured on down to Brisbane, which was a major submarine base in Australia. We later learned that the subs of Squadron Five struck hard, devastating blows at Japanese shipping in the area between Australia, through the islands of Indonesia, and up around the Philippines. We spent *many* days traveling at nine knots—all the way down. With nothing more than routine watches to stand, it quickly grew boring, although, the very real threat of Japanese submarines kept many of us on edge. When we arrived in Brisbane, we broke out all the gear stored aboard.

On the *Griffin*, we had all of the repair shops necessary to service every department [of a submarine]. We had carpentry, metal shop, paint, telescope parallax repair, electrical motor repair, torpedo repair, radar, and radio services. In addition to this, it was our continuing responsibility to provide food and ammunition, torpedoes and fuel. We also repaired a number of merchant ships, this being a time of great need among our merchant fleet.

At times, we had as many as six or seven submarines alongside, all going through various stages and types of repair. We serviced them wherever they and we happened to be—in Brisbane Harbor, at Midway, Pearl Harbor, or Anacortes, Washington.

Back to my own navy career. When I enlisted, of course, I was an apprentice seaman, and I climbed up to Seaman First. Finally, I went to yeoman school in Pearl Harbor and ended up a yeoman second class at the end of the war. While serving on the *Griffin,* I naturally came to know the ship fairly well, although we carried a complement of approximately 750 men in three deck divisions, and crew [technicians] to fill all the various departments. We had a free-diving crew aboard. The ship also carried a decompression chamber for any use that might have been required of it, but to my knowledge, I don't believe it was ever used. However, being a "b'lowdecks" sailor most of the time, I was not cognizant about everything that went on aboard, on the surface or on the boats alongside. When I was first in deck force, I was in Division Three. There, I sat deck watches for Commander Jupp and Captain Christie, who served as the squadron commander at that time.

After the *Griffin*'s stay in Brisbane, we had assignments to many locales to perform tending duties for the submarines in the Pacific. We departed Brisbane for the Fiji Islands on November 11 and on December 1 we sailed to Bora Bora to escort Submarine Division 53 to the Canal Zone. We arrived at Balboa, Panama, on January 7, 1941. From this western mouth of the canal, we continued on north to Oakland, California, arriving on January 20. First, though, WesPac ordered a recall that sent us to Mare Island, California, for refit and alterations. We received heavy-duty cranes to lift damaged parts from a sub onto deck and below for work. Also, improved communications equipment went into the *Griffin*. They replaced our radar with a much more powerful model, which provided greater range on the surface. Japanese aircraft were still active and, even from the relatively low silhouette of a submarine tender, the early warning from radar gave us an edge. After we completed the refitting, we headed for Pearl Harbor.

En route, we received some minor damages and diverted to San Diego for repairs. After they made us shipshape in San Diego, we departed for the Pacific, sailing on April 27, 1943. We arrived in Pearl [Harbor] on May 4 and took up the vital support duties that tenders had been created to provide. We remained there until January 3, 1944.

From Pearl, we serviced submarines for nearly six months. We repaired several that had received serious damage due to enemy action. One sub had suffered from a ramming that had cut a deep gouge in its conning tower and control room. Another had run aground during a training exercise there in the islands. Although we on the tender did not encounter enemy action, we deeply sympathized with the guys from the subs that had taken serious hits. During that time, the *Griffin* performed refits, battle repairs, and general upkeep on submarines before we went back to California for another refit, sailing to Mare Island to arrive on January 10, 1944. With completion of the refit, we received orders for Fremantle, Australia. *Griffin* returned to Pearl Harbor on March 17, 1944. We departed again on April 8 for the great submarine base at Fremantle, Australia. We remained there for an extended period. The subs operating in the South China Sea and up around the Philippines took quite a pounding and our services were frequently called upon.

Following Fremantle, we operated at Mios Woendi, New Guinea. By that time, the effective force of the Japanese had been reduced to such an extent that our duties consisted primarily of resupply operations. One thing I noted was the reduction in the requests for a full complement of torpedoes. With so little enemy shipping and warships to shoot at, they frequently came in with several fish [torpedoes] remaining. Lack of food and other items forced an end to their patrols.

While in harbor at Mios Woendi, we reestablished the submarine base there and sailed for Subic Bay, via Leyte. We arrived on February 10, 1944 and the *Griffin* set up one of the first submarine repair facilities in the Philippines since the Japanese occupation in 1942. At one point, she also helped in the salvage of the damaged destroyer *LaValette*. While anchored out one time with four submarines on our port side and the heavily damaged destroyer *LaValette* to port, along with the USS *457*—I'm not sure why the *457* had tied up with us. We sent down our divers on the *LaValette*, and to the best I can recall, this is the report made by Hugh Loveall, who was one of the divers, all of whom received the navy and Marine Corps medal for their courageous action.

"We went into the ship through the hole blown in the side . . . Because of watertight integrity, we could not open any of the hatches. I went in first and brought the first three bodies out. They had been in the water long enough that the first ones I found were floating against the top of the compartment. We would tie a line around them and the crew on top would pull them out. After the bodies were recovered, we then put a plate over the hole in the side, using high-velocity tools. We shot bolts into it and into the sides of the *LaValette*. We worked sixteen hours straight so the water pumps could keep enough water out that it could get under way back to Pearl Harbor. The *LaValette* hit a mine while on patrol off Corregedor."

On March 22, 1945, we returned to Pearl Harbor via Leyte. We arrived in the Hawaiian Islands on April 10, where we received orders to transit to the Philippines to assist in rebuilding a submarine base at Manila Bay. *Griffin* departed on May 10 for Midway.

That turned out to be an interesting assignment. While the sub base had been in Japanese hands, what we had not bombed to ruin, the Japanese had destroyed on their departure. A lot of the replacement equipment came in on large cargo ships, such as cranes, floating dry docks, and other large items. We applied our expertise to creating repair shops and outfitting them properly. In addition, we serviced the subs that came in off patrol until the base reached a condition where they could take over that duty.

When we were relieved at Manila Bay, we went on to Midway Island to reestablish a similar base there for the subs. This proved an even more difficult task, since the Japanese had more time to conduct demolitions to render the existing base useless. We worked hard and for long hours to establish a suitable place for the subs to come in for refitting. While we were there, the word came that the Japanese had surrendered. Our stay there was quite pleasant and I considered it a lovely place to end the war. We remained at Midway until September 10, when we sailed to Pearl Harbor and then on to San Francisco. We entered the bay on September 24, 1945. Our *Griffin* was decommissioned at Mare Island on October 12 (ironically on Columbus Day) and placed in reserve. Later she received a transfer to the Stockton group, Pacific Reserve Fleet, where she remained in service, tending reserve submarines through 1967.

After all of this, I had only one regret: Throughout the war, we were never involved in direct combat. In addition, the *Griffin* never received an attack by air or surface ships. Scuttlebutt had it that the Japanese had tailed us into Brisbane, but no proof came forth. For all of that, I loved every minute of my service. I am proud of the part we played in the destruction of the Japanese military fleet and shipping, which helped bring an end to the war.

CONCLUSION

Submarine activity worldwide accelerated in 1979 when, on March 30, the *Baltimore Sun* reported that a submarine base was under construction at Cienfuegos, on the southern coast of Cuba. Lacking anything resembling a navy, the base was obviously not for Castro, but rather for Soviet submarines. A formal protest was filed with the Soviets by our state department, which the Soviets chose to ignore.

The next month, on April 10, the USS *Francis Scott Key* (SSBN 657) carried out the first submerged launch of a Trident C-4 missile. The firing took place off the coast of Florida, near Cape Canaveral. The missile traveled successfully down the Atlantic Missile Range to the target area. On the next day, the USS *Patrick Henry* (SSBN 599) launched three Polaris A-3TA [Tactical Attack] missiles off the Florida coast. These became the last Polaris missiles launched from a U.S. submarine. The first Polaris A-1 launch from a submarine came from the USS *George Washington* (SSBN 598) on July 20, 1960. Thus, the *Patrick Henry* launch marked the end of an era.

USS *Francis Scott Key*
(SSBN 657).
Courtesy of United States Navy

On June 10, 1960, the United States took a step backward when the U.S. submarine tender *Canopus* (AS 34) departed Rota, Spain, with Commander, Submarine Squadron 16 aboard. Her sailing marked the complete withdrawal of U.S. Polaris-Poseidon support facilities from Rota, Spain.

The U.S. strategic missile submarine *James Monroe* (SSBN 622) arrived at Kings Bay, Georgia, on July 6 to undergo the first SSBN refit at that base. The *James Monroe* had previously departed from the former tender site at Rota, Spain, on patrol and, on completion received orders to make port at Kings Bay. The facility there had been completed on July 2, which was only one day after the required closing of the base at Rota. It would receive formal designation as a submarine base on April 1, 1982.

On September 30, a momentous occasion occurred that would adversely affect our submarine force in the future. The U.S. government turned over control of the Panama Canal zone to the Panamanian government, thus ending three-quarters of a century of American control of the strategic passageway—twenty-four years *before the treaty required it*. Not three years passed before the Panamanian government appealed, not to the United States, but to the communist Chinese to provide skilled canal managers and lock workers. From this point forward, due to the Marxist leanings of the dictator of Panama, Manuel Trujillo, the canal was virtually closed to U.S. military vessels.

A report in the *Wall Street Journal* indicated that the U.S. Navy would require some officers to involuntarily enter nuclear-power school training. This was in order to help overcome the severe shortage of officers for nuclear submarines. Only 42 percent of nuclear-trained officers remained after their initial tour of duty in 1978. This loss of personnel occurred despite a generous bonus pay program. As though to emphasize this situation, the next day, the strategic missile submarine *Francis Scott Key* began her first U.S. deterrent patrol, departing from Charleston, South Carolina and carrying the C-4 Trident missiles.

A jolting revelation was made on December 1 by a U.S. Department of Energy (DOE) official, who disclosed that about three-quarters of the warheads of Polaris A-1 SLBMs probably would not have functioned during the mid-1960s because of a mechanical defect. This announcement came as part of the ongoing debate over the comprehensive nuclear test ban. The problem, as described by the unnamed official, revolved around the aging of materials used in a missile safety device. First detected in 1965 during a routine examination of Polaris missiles, a broader testing of Polaris A-1s in November 1966 revealed that "three were bad to one good," according to the DOE official. This was extremely bad news for SSBNs.

Ending the year on this sour note, more bad news follows on February 25, 1980, when the Navy announced plans to retire twenty ships during fiscal year 1981. Among the active ships to get the axe were the ballistic missile submarines *Theodore Roosevelt* (SSBN 600) and *Abraham Lincoln* (SSBN 602). These were the first such submarines to be decommissioned. The reason for this was that, under the SALT One agreement with the Soviet Union, the completion of the Trident missile submarine *Ohio* (SSBN 726) in 1981 depended on the retirement of the older SSBNs.

On March 3, the nuclear-powered submarine *Nautilus* (SSN 571) was decommissioned. (After modification, tugs towed her to Groton, Connecticut, in 1985, and turned her into a museum.) On April 12, the U.S. Navy announced that the eight Polaris-armed missile submarines based at Guam were to be withdrawn between July 1980 and September 1981. These were the only remaining submarines armed with the Polaris A-3 missile.

Just in passing, on April 24, President Jimmy Carter implemented his grandiose scheme to rescue the United States hostages held by the Iranians in Tehran in the U.S. embassy. The highly complex operation involved the U.S. Air Force *and* the Navy. The plan was to invade Tehran via helicopter and extract the hostages. After two of the helicopters were forced to land short of the initial point by a sandstorm and the third one developed mechanical problems, the mission, "Carter's Folly," was cancelled. A midair collision far out in the desert, involving a C-130 and a RH-53D helicopter during a refueling at the remote desert jumping-off point called "Desert One," added insult to injury.

The Poseidon-armed U.S. submarine *Ulysses S. Grant* (SSBN 631) arrived at La Spezia, Italy, on May 6. She stayed there for a four-day visit, marking the first occasion on which an SSBN visited an Italian port.

On July 15, the British government announced that Great Britain intended to procure the Trident missile system for their submarine fleet, replacing the Polaris A-3 missile as their nation's nuclear deterrent force. This represented a step forward in the ability of the British to provide for their own defense.

CONCLUSION

A *Seawolf*-class christening for the USS *Jimmy Carter* (SSN 23). *Courtesy of United States Navy*

Bad news came for American submariners on September 10, when Secretary of the Navy Hidalgo revealed that delays were expected in the delivery of seven nuclear-powered submarines currently under construction at the Electric Boat Yard in Groton, Connecticut. Among the problems was a five-month delay in the delivery of the first *Trident* submarine, the *Ohio*. Further delays for six *Los Angeles* (SSN 688)–class attack submarines were indicated to last from three to fourteen months.

The *Washington Post*—never a reliable source of information—reported on October 5 that the Three Mile Island nuclear accident had accelerated a "crisis" in the navy's nuclear submarine force. The *Post* accused private utilities of hiring away experienced navy nuclear-qualified specialists. Vice Chief of Naval Operations, Admiral James

267

D. Watkins, added some confirmation of this in a statement in which he said, "I consider it [the loss of navy nuclear-power specialists] to be the most serious personnel readiness situation that I have seen in thirty-one years in the navy." Adding credence to this, the U.S. Undersecretary of the Navy, Robert J. Murray, testified before Congress on October 12, claiming that the shortage of submarine officers had become particularly serious. Of the seven hundred new submarine officers needed in the current year, the navy predicted a one-hundred-officer shortfall. While the navy needed to retain 60 percent of its submarine officers following their five-year obligation, Murray remarked that, in 1979, only 42 percent were retained. The secretary also stated that they [the navy] anticipated a 34 percent drop in the 1980 officer retention rate. Another issue revolved around enlisted submarine retention. Also perceived as being critical, this situation revealed an established goal of keeping 60 percent of the second- and third-term submariners, yet so far only 45 percent were reenlisting.

Former President Richard Nixon boarded the nuclear fast attack submarine *Cincinnati* (SSN 693) on November 14 to enjoy a brief cruise. Later, on November 25, the *New York Times* published an article claiming that the U.S. Navy's Trident submarine program suffered from technical and managerial problems. It further stated that the anticipated completion of the first Trident submarine, the *Ohio*, might be delayed until 1982. To counter this report, the Department of Defense stated that the *Ohio* was "on track for a June 29, 1981, delivery."

On December 2, the Department of Defense reversed an earlier statement and declared that there had been several slippages in work on the Trident submarine *Ohio*, which caused her delivery date to be uncertain. She was months late.

A surprise Christmas present came from President Carter on December 23, when he signed into law the Military Pay and Allowances Benefit Act of 1980, which substantially increased sea and submarine special pay, making the submarine special pay a career incentive similar to aviation career pay.

On January 7, Admiral Harry D. Train II, USN, the commander in chief of U.S. Atlantic Fleet, reported that fleet retention had increased in the wake of Carter signing the Military Pay and Allowances Benefit Act. Atlantic Fleet reenlistments had increased by 25 percent, with career (including submarine officers and enlisted men) reenlistments increasing by 14 percent.

The greatest event came on January 20, when Ronald Wilson Reagan was sworn in as the fortieth president of the United States (with the author present to witness it). Simultaneous with Reagan taking office, the radical imams of Iran freed the fifty-two hostages taken at the American Embassy on November 4, 1979. Included in the released hostages, after 444 days of captivity, were nine marines and three navy personnel. All of those freed arrived in the United States on January 25 and were formally welcomed home by the president.

The U.S. Polaris missile submarines *Theodore Roosevelt* (SSBN 600) and *Abraham Lincoln* (SSBN 602) were decommissioned and stricken on February 28. They constituted the first Polaris submarines to leave the fleet, which marked the first time since 1967 that there had been less than forty-one strategic missile submarines commissioned in active service in the navy.

On March 12, Vice Admiral Earl B. Fowler, USN, commander of the Naval Sea Systems Command, testified before the House Armed Services Seapower Subcommittee. The substance of his testimony revealed that problems continued at the Electric Boat Yard in Groton,

Connecticut. Fowler said that the quality assurance problems had significantly delayed construction of both the *Ohio* and the *Los Angeles* (SSN 688). Feathers begin to fly on March 25 when P. Takis Veliotis, general manager of the Electric Boat Division of General Dynamics Corporation, defended his corporation's situation before the House Armed Services Seapower Subcommittee. In a prepared statement, he claimed that the navy had unfairly criticized the yard for submarine delays. According to Veliotis, much of the blame for delays rightly belonged to the navy for the navy-provided equipment and frequent design changes.

Situations affecting submarines and submariners continued on April 1, when the navy announced that the option with the Electric Boat Division of General Dynamics Corporation to construct the ninth Trident submarine (SSBN 734), authorized in fiscal year 1981, would not be exercised. The fact that the option expired on March 31, 1981, coupled with the continued delay in a contract award, exhibited the navy's concern over slippages in the construction schedules for the eight *Ohio*-class submarines already under construction at Electric Boat. Eight days later, on April 9, the U.S. strategic missile submarine *George Washington* (SSBN 598) collided with the 2,350-ton Japanese merchant ship *Nissho Maru* some 110 nautical miles southwest of Sasebo, Japan. Two Japanese died in the collision. Only minor damage was incurred and no injuries on the *George Washington*. On April 20, Secretary of the Navy Lehman announced that the U.S. Navy accepted full liability for the collision. In the interim, better news came, when on April 10 the United States Department of Defense announced that the Extremely Low Frequency (ELF) communications project near Clam Lake, Wisconsin, would be activated, with a planned initial operational capability in the fall of 1981. ELF constituted a shore-to-submerged submarine communications system.

It permitted signal reception while the submarine was at operational depths and speeds.

On May 5, Admiral H. G. Rickover, USN (Ret.) testified before Congress. As head of the navy's nuclear-propulsion program, he pointed out alleged inefficiencies in private shipyards building navy ships. He stated in particular that the navy should start building submarines and perhaps acquire private facilities—such as the Electric Boat Division of General Dynamics Corporation—to accomplish this. He further added that it would be possible for the navy to hire civilian managers to operate such facilities. Near the end of that month, on May 26, the USS *John Marshal* (SSBN 611) began the final offloading of Polaris A-3 missiles from a U.S. submarine. Completed on June 20, 1981, the offload allowed the *Marshall* to receive a change in classification to fast-attack submarine (SSN) status.

The U.S. strategic missile submarine *James K. Polk* (SSBN 645), with a complement of sixteen Poseidon missiles, returned to Charleston, South Carolina, on June 27. It marked the completion of the two thousandth SSBN deterrent patrol since November 1960. This verified the efficiency of such actions in the Cold War era.

On July 1, the navy activated the U.S. submarine base at Bangor, Washington, to support *Ohio*-class Trident missile submarines. This represented another positive step forward in the navy's effort to protect the United States from Soviet aggression.

Not until September 26, did the navy and the Electric Boat Division of General Dynamics announce that an agreement had been reached on the delivery dates for the first eight Trident submarines of the *Ohio*-class, the first of which was now scheduled for delivery to the navy on October 1, 1981.

Also on October 1, the U.S. strategic missile submarine *Robert E. Lee* (SSBN 601) completed the last U.S. Polaris deterrent patrol.

However, the Polaris A-3TK variant of our missile stayed in active service in four British submarines. On October 2, President Ronald Reagan announced his plan to revitalize United States deterrent forces. To do so, he proposed to: (1) improve communications and control systems, (2) modernize strategic bombers, to include production of one-hundred B-1 bombers with continued research and development of "stealth" bomber aircraft, and (3) continue construction on Trident submarines while developing the D-5 missile, giving a delivery date for deployment of 1989. And further, to develop and deploy the Tomahawk land-attack missiles, to be equipped with nuclear warheads. Two other items were on his "to-do" list, deployment of one hundred MX land-based missiles in hardened silos and upgrades of strategic defenses. On October 8, the Department of Defense announced that President Reagan had approved a plan to proceed with an expansion of an improved Extremely Low Frequency (ELF) shore-to-submarine communications system with transmitter sites in Michigan and Wisconsin. On October 27, a threat reared its ugly head when the Soviet submarine *U-137* of the Whiskey class ran aground near the Swedish naval base of Kariskrona, three hundred miles south of Stockholm. The Soviet sub constituted a deadly threat, as later discovered. The grounding occurred in Swedish territorial waters and within a restricted military area. Later, a Swedish salvage team refloated the submarine and released her on November 6, 1981. The salvagers discovered that the submarine had two nuclear torpedoes aboard. The Swedish government considered this a severe threat and an open attempt at an intimidating confrontation.

Captain A. K. Thompson, USN, became commanding officer of Blue crew and Captain A. F. Campbell, USN, was CO of Gold crew as the USS *Ohio* was finally placed into commission at Groton, Connecticut, on November 11.

CONCLUSION

On December 1, the Trident missile submarine *Ohio* departed Bangor, Washington, to begin her first deterrent patrol. The *Ohio*'s principal armament consisted of twenty-four C-4 missiles. After a routine cruise, she returned to port on December 10, 1982.

The year 1983 opened with another recordmaker. On January 11, two nuclear-powered attack submarines, the *Aspro* (SSN 648) and *Tautog* (SSN 639) surfaced together at the North Pole. It was the first two-submarine surfacing since July 31, 1962. The two subs remained surfaced at the top of the world for sixteen hours. On February 23, the French put in service their first nuclear-powered attack submarine, the *Rubis*. The *Rubis* was a considerably smaller sub, being only slightly larger than the USS *Tullibee* (SSN 597), our smallest nuclear sub.

Tragedy struck for the Soviet Union on June 23, when the submarine *K-429* of the Charlie II class sank off Petropavlovsk on the Kamchatka Peninsula, resulting in the loss of sixteen crewmen. The nuclear submarine was salvaged and repaired, only to sink again at dockside. It became an immobilized training submarine. In October, the navy's SSPO undertook the full-scale engineering project development of the Trident II/D-5 strategic missile. They were destined to be placed aboard our submarines.

In 1984, a collision occurred between a Soviet nuclear-powered Victor-class submarine and the U.S. aircraft carrier *Kitty Hawk* (CV-63) in the Sea of Japan. It happened about 150 nautical miles east of South Korea. The incident report from the captain of the *Kitty Hawk* indicated that the Victor SSN had surfaced ahead of the carrier, which then struck it. Both vessels were damaged. Following the disentanglement of the ships, the damaged Soviet submarine steamed to the port of Vladivostok, escorted by a Soviet cruiser. There were no reported injuries to personnel, but U.S. intelligence experts suspected that some of the Soviet sailors had been seriously injured or perhaps killed.

The Soviets were losers again on September 18 when a Soviet Victor-class nuclear-powered attack submarine collided with the *Soviet* merchant ship *Bratstvo* in the Straits of Gibraltar. The submarine was making a night transit, leaving the Mediterranean Sea. The submarine received extensive damage. It was compelled to limp into Hamamet, Tunisia, to effect repairs conducted by a Soviet support ship.

Submarine sailors watched with sinking feelings when the strategic missile submarine, *Sam Rayburn* (SSBN 635), began to offload her complement of Poseidon C-3 missiles in preparation for decommissioning and dismantling on August 21, 1985. She was the first missile submarine to be retired in compliance with the SALT One. The dismantling of the *Rayburn* began on September 16, 1985.

While deterrent patrols continued uneventfully in the beginning of 1986, March 22 brought yet another collision with a submarine. This time the U.S. Navy tug *Secota* (YTM 415) lost power after completing a personnel transfer and struck the stern planes of the USS *Georgia* (SSBN 729). It received considerable damage and sank. All but two of the contract hire crew of the tug were rescued. The *Georgia* was unharmed.

The submarine service made history again on May 6 when three nuclear-powered attack submarines, the *Archerfish* (SSN 678), *Hawkbill* (SSN 666) and *Ray* (SSN 653) surfaced together at the North Pole. The operation—named Icex 1-86—was the first time in history that three submarines were at the North Pole at the same time.

In October, a U.S. submarine collided with a Soviet vessel again, this time in the North Atlantic. Our intelligence services knew that the Soviet Navy's Delta-class strategic missile sub was known to have at least one companion in the area at the time. Our attack submarine the *Augusta* (SSN 710) managed to make it to port, after incurring $2.7 million in damage. The Soviet submarine was reported to have received only minor damage.

It was payback time on October 6 when the Yankee-class ballistic missile submarine *K-219* sank itself some six hundred nautical miles east of Bermuda. Their naval collision survey commission attributed the cause of the sinking to an accident three days earlier, when seawater entered one missile tube of the submerged submarine. At that time, the *K-219* was on patrol with six SS-N-6 missiles with nuclear warheads. After the damage had been done, there followed an explosion of missile propellant and the escape of toxic gases and a series of fires. The *K-219* managed to surface but, in spite of frantic damage control efforts and an attempt to tow the submarine, she sank forty hours after the explosion. The total loss of life was four—two from the explosions, and two others who died later from their injuries. Soviet investigators later determined that one of the launch tubes was not in use due to an earlier accident.

Submarine service officers and men continued to hone their expertise in the following years. Fewer collisions occurred, deterrent patrols went off safely and satisfactorily, professional studies made submarine commanders even more competent than at any time in history. Then, on April 24, 1988, tragedy again struck when explosions and fires broke out aboard the USS *Bonefish* (SS 582), one of the last few diesel-electric submarines on active duty. The *Bonefish* was conducting exercises off Cape Canaveral, Florida, at the time. Three of her crew of ninety-two were killed and several more were injured. The submarine was subsequently towed to Charleston, South Carolina, where she was decommissioned.

More bad news came on June 30, when the General Dynamics

Electric Boat Yard shut down due to a strike by union workers. The strike continued until October 12, which further delayed the completion of strategic missile submarines in the Ohio-class. Good news came on August 6, when the nuclear-propelled submarine *San Juan* (SSN 751) went into commission with CDR Charles B. Young, USN, commanding. She was the first submarine of the improved Los Angeles–class SSNs to be fitted with twelve vertical launch tubes for Tomahawk missiles, and improved underwater detection systems and GPS/satellite guidance capabilities.

Progress of this type continued through 1989 and beyond. Most notable were improvements in technical equipment and knowledgeable sailors to operate it. Situations occurred in other parts of the world that brought the United States to a condition of war. Saddam Hussein, once an ally of the United States, grew belligerent and planned an invasion of neighboring Kuwait. Although sanctioned by the United Nations, Saddam continued his reckless course. Unmindful of everything against him, Saddam occupied Kuwait, claiming it as the sixteenth province of Iraq.

Momentous events occurred in 1991 when, on January 17, Operation Desert Storm began. During this period, U.S. Navy warships and submarines fired 288 land-attack variants of the Tomahawk missiles. Of these, 106 were fired during the first twenty-four hours of the Gulf War. On January 19, the U.S. submarine *Louisville* (SSN 724), operating submerged in the Red Sea, launched the first of eight Tomahawk missiles she fired against targets in Iraq. This constituted the first combat missile launch in history by a submarine. Following this, the submarine *Pittsburgh* (SSN 720) fired four Tomahawks from a position in the eastern Mediterranean. Later evaluations—based on results obtained in Operation Iraqi Freedom—indicated that this massive launch constituted overkill, with a deplorable lack of accuracy or success.

Undisputed by anyone at the time, Saddam Hussein's possession of weapons of mass destruction and his efforts to obtain suitable yellow cake uranium from Niger to complete his nuclear weapons program, prompted yet another attack on Iraq in 2002. Coupled with the knowledge of the brutal murder of thousands of innocent people, and the protection and training of al-Qaeda terrorists by the Hussein government, the United States and its allies felt they had no other course open.

Once again, U.S. submarines became involved in the initial phase of Operation Iraqi Freedom, which culminated in the most extensive and accurate test "under fire" of the Tomahawk system when the USS *Cheyenne* (SSN 773) fired the first Tomahawk missiles into Baghdad on March 19, 2002, at the outset of Operation Iraqi Freedom. Accompanied by the *Los Angeles* (SSN 688) and the remainder of the squadron, their missiles struck at strategic military targets and at the Darah Farms palace of Saddam Hussein. Hostile Iraqi forces incurred great damage, which rendered three military airfields useless and closed Saddam International Airport.

Air strikes and missile launches from submarines resulted in killing and injuring a number of ranking officers at a meeting at Darah Farms, which also resulted in wounding Saddam Hussein. Intensive use of submarine and cruiser-launched Tomahawk missiles, and highly accurate bombing by navy aircraft from the *Abraham Lincoln* (CVN 72) quickly reduced the aggressive capability of the Iraqi forces to reliance exclusively on ground troops of the Republican

Submarine Service dolphins.
Courtesy of United States Navy

Guard. Many of the Iraqi regular army personnel deserted after only token resistance, although these desertions did not come in the numbers anticipated.

As the war dragged on, one of the best pieces of news was that the increased accuracy in aiming and guiding the missiles and guided bombs resulted in nearly a 300 percent increase in efficiency of the total engagements.

A ROSTER OF SUBMARINES
SERVED IN BY THE INTERVIEW SUBJECTS

Boats are named in the order they appear in narratives.

BOAT NAME	HULL NUMBER	
USS *Searaven*	SS 196	
USS *Pickerel*	SS 177	
USS *Sealion*	SS 195	Second Generation (SS 315)
USS *Seawolf*	SS 197	Second Generation (SSN 575)
USS *Sailfish*	SS 192	Second Generation (SSN 572)
USS *Skipjack*	SS 184	
USS *Seahorse*	SS 304	
USS *Skate*	SS 305	
USS *Pompon*	SS 267	
USS *Segundo*	SS 398	
USS *Greenfish*	SS 351	
USS *Buffalo*	SSN 681	
USS *Medregal*	SS 480	
USS *Drum*	SS 228	
USS *Wahoo*	SS 238	
USS *Burrfish*	SS 312	
USS *Char*	SS 328	
USS *Tunny*	SSG 282	
USS *Sculpin*	SS 191	
USS *Bluegill*	SS 242	
USS *Blower*	SS 325	

BOAT NAME	HULL NUMBER	
USS *Catfish*	SS 339	
USS *Aspro*	SS 309	Second Generation SSBN 648
USS *Pomodon*	SS 486	
USS *Tench*	SS 417	
USS *Spikefish*	SS 404	
USS *Picuda*	SS 382	
USS *Balao*	SS 285	
USS *Bugara*	SS 331	
USS *Sea Leopard*	SS 483	
USS *Patrick Henry*	SSBN 599	
USS *Guardfish*	SS 217	Third Generation SSN 612
USS *Barb*	SSN 596	
USS *Flasher*	SS 249	Second Generation SSN 613
USS *Bass*	SS 551	
USS *Tiro*	SS 426	
SSK 1	Mini-sub	
SSK 2	Mini-sub	
USS *Carbonero*	SS 337	
USS *Cusk*	SS 348	
USS *Puffer*	SSN 652	
USS *Scamp*	SS 588	
USS *Rasher*	SS 269	
USS *Halibut*	SS 232	Second Generation SSGN 587
USS *Tiru*	SS 426	
USS *Pomfret* (DA)	SS 391	
USS *John C. Calhoun*	SSBN 630	
USS *Batfish*	SS 310	Second Generation SSN 681
USS *Sablefish*	SS 303	

GLOSSARY OF NAVAL AND MILITARY TERMS

Airdale Navy term for an aircraft crewman, e.g., crew chief, A&P mechanic, armorer, etc.

AO Area of Operation—patrol area for submarines.

Boomer Fleet Long Ranger Ballistic Missile Submarine (SSBN).

BOQ Bachelor Officers' Quarters—common to all services.

CDR Commander, Navy equivalent of army, air force, marine lt. col (0–5).

CNO Chief of Naval Operations. Usually at least a vice admiral.

COB Chief of the Boat. The most ranking enlisted man on a submarine (usually E-7).

ComSubPac Submarine Command, Pacific, headquartered at Pearl Harbor, Hawaii.

DivCom Division Commander (Submarine Service).

DNCO Duty Noncommissioned Officer.

FBM Fast Boat, Missile (SSN).

HMS His/Her Majesty's Ship (British).

Kollmorgen Periscope manufacturer's name for most U.S. submarine periscopes.

LCDR Lieutenant Commander, Navy equivalent of army, air force, marine major (O-4).

LT Lieutenant. Navy equivalent of army, air force, marine captain (O-3).

LT, j.g. or LTJG Lieutenants Junior Grade. Navy equivalent of army, air force, marine first lieutenant.

Momson Lung A self-contained breathing device for use *outside* a sub for escape.

MRV or MIRV Multi-(Independent) Reentry Vehicle. A multiple warhead for a missile.

OCS Officer's Candidate School. Added to navy program during WWII.

ONI Officer of Naval Intelligence (G-2).

OOD Officer of the Deck. His hat "changes" with each duty section.

S5G An experimental type of reactor plant cooling system for nuclear-powered subs.

SS Designation for hull number of a diesel-electric submarine.

SSBN A boomer, long-range missile submarine.

SSN Fast-attack nuclear submarine.

TDC Torpedo Data Computer. A large, self-contained vacuum tube–powered computer that provides information to aim a torpedo. Obsolete since the advent of nuclear subs.

WesPac Western Pacific patrol area, headquartered on Midway Island.

XO or Exec Executive Officer. Second in command on a submarine; can be a LT or LTCDR.

Other Navy and Military terms are defined in the text, often in brackets [ ].

INDEX

Page numbers in *italic* indicate photographs or illustrations.

INDEX

INDEX